D1611772

THE SCARY MASON-DIXON LINE

SOUTHERN LITERARY STUDIES

Fred Hobson, Series Editor

THE SCARY MASON-DIXON LINE

AFRICAN AMERICAN WRITERS AND THE SOUTH

Trudier Harris

Louisiana State University Press
Baton Rouge

Published by Louisiana State University Press
Copyright © 2009 by Trudier Harris
All rights reserved
Manufactured in the United States of America
First printing

Designer: Michelle A. Neustrom
Typefaces: News Gothic BT, Arno Pro
Printer and binder: Thomson-Shore, Inc.

Library of Congress Cataloging-in-Publication Data

Harris, Trudier.
    The scary Mason-Dixon Line : African American writers and the South / Trudier Harris.
      p. cm.
    Includes bibliographical references (p.) and index.
    ISBN 978-0-8071-3395-8 (alk. paper)
    1. American literature—African American authors—History and criticism. 2. Southern States—In literature. 3. African Americans in literature. 4. Fear in literature. 5. Slavery—Psychological aspects. 6. Racism—Psychological aspects. 7. African Americans—Race identity. 8. African Americans—Psychology. 9. Literature and history—United States—History—20th century. I. Title.
    PS153.N5H293 2009
    810.9'896073—dc22

2008031341

The paper in this book meets the guidelines for permanence and durability of the Committee on Production Guidelines for Book Longevity of the Council on Library Resources. ∞

For my former students everywhere . . . May your lives be healthy and prosperous and your careers productive and rewarding.

Contents

Acknowledgments

This book has had a long conception, and many individuals and institutions have contributed to its final shaping. I offer my thanks to the following: Pete Banner-Haley, who invited me to present the W. E. B. and Shirley Graham Du Bois Lecture at Colgate University in 2003; John Lowe of Louisiana State University, where I lectured in 2003; Carol Marsh-Lockett of Georgia State University, where I also lectured on the topic in 2003; Gary Taylor and Celia Daileader, now of Florida State University, who invited me to participate in a conference held at the University of Alabama in 2005; Crystal Clark and Michelle Mouton of Cornell College in Iowa, where I made a presentation in 2005; Lovalerie King, who invited me to participate in the novel conference held at Pennsylvania State University in 2005; Joseph T. Skerrett Jr. and Anne Herrington of the University of Massachusetts at Amherst, where I presented a portion of this work as the Sidney Kaplan Lecture in 2005; and Kameelah Martin Samuel, formerly of Florida State University, who invited me to participate in a conference she hosted in 2005.

I also thank J. Lee Greene, professor emeritus of the University of North Carolina at Chapel Hill, who organized the Gathering Conference at which I lectured in 2005; Maryemma Graham of the University of Kansas, who invited me to spend two weeks during the summer of 2005 exploring this topic with graduate students there; Gloria A. Kelley of Winthrop University, who invited me to present the keynote address at the Dorothy Perry Thompson Colloquium in 2006; Jim Watkins and other organizers of the Southern Women Writers Conference at Berry College in 2006; Bruce Dick of Appalachian State University, who invited me to discuss my work in 2006; Kathy James of Barton College, who invited me to present the Elizabeth Hereford Jordan Endowed Lecture in 2006; Emily Wright, who organizes the Southern Writers Symposium at Methodist College and who gave me the opportunity to speak on Raymond Andrews; Valerie Lee, chair of the English Department at The Ohio State University, who invited me to inaugurate the Distinguished Alumni Lecture Series with a presentation on Yusef Komunyakaa; and Elizabeth Brown-Guillory of the University of Houston, who invited me to present several lectures in 2007.

My thanks go as well to Bert Hitchcock of Auburn University, who invited me to present a portion of the work as the 2007 Carl Benson Memorial Lecture; Seodial Deena and Bruce Southard of East Carolina University, where I presented a lecture in 2007; Carol Boggess and Rob Neufeld, who invited me to present a portion of the work for the Big Read Program in Asheville, North Carolina, in 2007; Kenneth C. Randall and Al Brophy, formerly of the University of Alabama School of Law, who invited me to present my work in 2007; the Carol Woods Retirement Community, where I discussed the work with a reading group in 2007; the Carolina Speakers Series sponsored by the University of North Carolina at Chapel Hill, through which I made presentations on the topic in 2007 and 2008; Marc Conner of Washington and Lee University, where I lectured on the topic for the Shannon-Clark Lecture in 2007; Tara Powell of the University of South Carolina, who invited me to discuss the work in 2007; the Wayne County chapter of the University of North Carolina General Alumni Association, to which I made a presentation in 2008; and Horace A. Porter of the University of Iowa, who invited me to inaugurate the F. Wendell Miller Lecture in 2008.

I thank students in my African American literature classes, especially those in 2006 and 2007, who joined me in exploring various interpretive possibilities with the texts I cover in this volume.

I thank Maria Frias for inviting me to the University at La Coruna in Spain to discuss this work at a conference she sponsored in October of 2003.

I thank the University of North Carolina at Chapel Hill for supporting me with a Research and Study Leave during the spring semester of 2005.

As usual, I am indebted to my Wintergreen sister writers, who are invariably supportive. In this instance, I thank Daryl Cumber Dance of the University of Richmond and Joanne V. Gabbin of James Madison University for reading and commenting on chapters in this manuscript.

I am indebted to Sandra Y. Govan of the University of North Carolina at Charlotte and Wanda Macon Morgan of Jackson State University for their constant encouragement.

I thank Candis LaPrade for the instrumental role she played in this book's finding a home with the Louisiana State University Press, and I thank Fred Hobson for his support throughout the process. None of this would have happened without all the editors, staff, and production personnel at the Louisiana State University Press; I am grateful to all of you for the care with which you have handled my work. Thanks as well to Cynthia Landeen, the perfect indexer, who worked her usual magic. In addition, thanks to Margaretta Yarborough for her careful proofreading.

And, as always, I thank my family, especially my sister Anna Harris McCarthy, who is unfailing in her support of whatever I do.

THE SCARY MASON-DIXON LINE

Introduction

SOUTHERN BLACK WRITERS NO MATTER WHERE THEY ARE BORN

How does geography shape literary imagination? That is the central question for this study. How, more specifically, has the southern territory of the United States shaped the imaginations of African American writers, whether or not they were born in the states traditionally identified as southern? A look at the works of a host of African American writers reveals that, at some point in their creative histories, they elected to write about the South. Why that is the case and how they conceive that territory to which they are drawn helps us to understand creativity operating under the influence of history as well as under the influence of race. Given history and culture, it is perhaps not surprising that a large number of African American writers align a crucial portion of their identities with the site on American territory, that is, the American South, that most defined how people of African descent were perceived historically and how they are perceived even into the twenty-first century.

In this study, I focus on several twentieth-century African American writers and their mostly troubled relationships to the American South. No matter where an African American writer is born in the United States, whether it is Boston or New York, or Idaho or California, or Texas or Georgia, or Alabama or Mississippi, he or she feels *compelled* to confront the American South and all its bloody history in his or her writings. "In the Deep South," writes New York–born James Baldwin, "Florida, Georgia, Alabama, Mississippi, for example—there is the great, vast, brooding, welcoming and bloodstained land, beautiful enough to astonish and break the heart," a paradoxical attraction to which Baldwin returns again and again in his works.[1] Whether it is to celebrate the triumph of black southern heritage over repression or to castigate the South for its horrible treatment of black folks, African American writers cannot escape the call of the South upon them. The American South, therefore, becomes a rite of passage for African American writers. Not one of them considers himself or herself truly an African American writer without having confronted the South in some way.

Like Baldwin, other African American writers also exhibit both an attraction and a repulsion to the South. Consider Richard Wright's perspective as he leaves Jackson, Mississippi, and Memphis, Tennessee, for Chicago:

> I was leaving the South to fling myself into the unknown, to meet other situations that would perhaps elicit from me other responses. . . . Yet, deep down, I knew that I could never really leave the South, for my feelings had already been formed by the South, for there had been slowly instilled into my personality and consciousness, black though I was, the culture of the South. So, in leaving, I was taking a part of the South to transplant in alien soil, to see if it could grow differently, if it could drink of new and cool rains, bend in strange winds, respond to the warmth of other suns, and, perhaps, to bloom. . . . And if that miracle ever happened, then I would know that there was yet hope in that southern swamp of despair and violence, that light could emerge even out of the blackest of the southern night. I would know that the South too could overcome its fear, its hate, its cowardice, its heritage of guilt and blood, its burden of anxiety and compulsive cruelty.[2]

Prominent black northern and southern writers, therefore, join in expressing an appeal as well as an abiding caution about the South. It is noteworthy in Wright's comment that he qualifies his relationship to the South with "black though I was." That ambivalence—being a part of the South and not quite embracing it, being both insider and outsider—informs all of his efforts to claim nativity in a society that always calls that status into question. Wright's titling of his first novel *Native Son* (1940) similarly reflects that ambivalence.

More often than not, in depicting this duality of attraction and repulsion, African American writers place their characters in situations where there is a pronounced fear of the South—the physical landscape, the legacy of injustice/ Jim Crow, mob violence, mental and physical restrictions, a general fear of southern white people. In treading through dreaded territory that could result in death just as easily as it could result in safe passage, black writers show, to borrow a phrase from Claude McKay, that the South is a "cultured hell," with more emphasis on the second word in the phrase.[3] Navigating the territory of the South is a visceral experience that begins, for travelers from the North who entered the territory during the days of segregation and up to the era of integration, with trains that converted carriages to Jim Crow cars as they crossed into southern territory, which is roughly equivalent with the drawing of the Mason-Dixon Line. Charles W. Chesnutt's Dr. William Miller experiences the transformation in *The Marrow of Tradition* (1905) just as forcefully as Helene Wright experiences it in Toni Morrison's *Sula* (1974). The pattern so pervasive in history and literature is also reflected in the African American folk tradition. As one tale goes, a black man who has migrated from the South to the North is invited to return to Mississippi and "help the others." He responds that he is "going to talk to the Lord about it." When those who have invited him follow up on their query, he comments: "I told the Lord my friends in Mississippi needed my help and asked Him if He would go back South with me, and the Lord told me, 'I'll go as far as Memphis.'"[4] If God fears the South, then obviously there is little hope for mere black mortals.

Another folktale emphasizes an innate, primal, generic fear of the South. A pregnant woman from the North goes south to be with her mother during the birth of her first child. The father, back in Harlem, waits and waits for news of the baby's delivery. The ninth month passes, then the tenth—still no baby. Finally, the father insists that his wife go to the hospital in spite of the fact that there are no immediate signs of a forthcoming delivery. The doctor is shocked and proceeds to examine the woman by pressing his stethoscope to her abdomen to listen for sounds of the baby. Here's the remainder of the tale:

Quite clearly and distinctly inside the body of the mother, was a voice singing the blues:

I won't be born down here! No sir!
I won't be born down here!
If you want to know what it's all about—
As long as South is South, I *won't* come out!
No, I won't be born down here.

He wasn't. She had to come back to New York to have her baby and Harlem-ites swear that that child had plenty of sense.[5]

Innate, ingrained, preternatural fear, even under the guise of laughter, is clear from the tale's overall emphasis.

The legal control of black bodies had its psychological counterparts in the explicable fear that many writers, historically and literarily, recount as being characteristic of knowledge of entering into or having to operate habitually on southern soil. Consider the images that landing at the airport to begin civil rights work in Atlanta in the mid-twentieth century conjures up for James Baldwin: "My mind was filled with the image of a black man, younger than I, perhaps, or my own age, hanging from a tree, while white men watched him and cut his sex from him with a knife."[6] Consider Alice Walker's Grange Copeland being paralyzed into immobility in the presence of the white land-owner for whom he sharecrops in the 1930s. We see the situation from the perspective of Brownfield, Grange's young son: "Brownfield was afraid of his father's silence, and his fear reached its peak when the truck came. For when the truck came his father's face froze into an unnaturally bland mask, curi-ous and unsettling to see. . . . But after watching the loading of the truck for several weeks he realized it was the man who drove the truck who caused his father to don a mask that was more impenetrable than his usual silence." Brownfield in turn becomes frightened of "the man who froze his father."[7] As with Grange, mental shackles control black bodies as aggressively as did legal sanctions in the South. In history and literature, therefore, the physical space of the South combines with the psychological implications of being on southern territory to provide historical figures and literary characters with experiences that are often more hellish than welcoming.

For black male writers, discomfort with the South manifests itself at the personal level of their very bodies, which they in turn project onto their char-acters. As Baldwin imagined himself being physically threatened, so too does he allow his characters to experience what it means to have black flesh and blood come into contact with southern mores and justice. Baldwin there-fore centers several of his works, such as "Going to Meet the Man" (1965), on lynching and castration, as well as on the stripping of the black male psyche that results from the keen knowledge of confinement and restriction on southern territory, as is apparent in his treatment of Richard Henry in his play *Blues for Mister Charlie* (1964), to which I give a chapter in this study.

W. E. B. Du Bois in "The Coming of John" (*The Souls of Black Folk*, 1903), Jean Toomer in "Blood-Burning Moon" (*Cane,* 1923), James Weldon Johnson in *The Autobiography of an Ex-Colored Man* (1912), Langston Hughes in "Home" (*The Ways of White Folks,* 1934), Richard Wright in "Big Boy Leaves Home" (*Uncle Tom's Children,* 1938) and *The Long Dream* (1958), William Melvin Kelley in *A Different Drummer* (1962), Robert Hayden in "Night, Death, Mississippi" (*Collected Poems,* 1985), Daniel Black in *The Sacred Place* (2007), and many other black male writers similarly portray what the South means in terms of detriment to the black male body.

In an earlier study, *Exorcising Blackness: Historical and Literary Lynching and Burning Rituals* (1984), I enumerate the ways in which the black male body throughout southern history was used to undertake ritualistic and violent revenge any time a black man was remotely accused of acting inappropriately with whites, whether that inappropriateness was as "criminal" as not stepping off a sidewalk quickly enough or a definable crime such as actually having committed murder.[8] African American literary works from the mid-nineteenth century to the mid-twentieth century depict mutilated, castrated, shot, burned, and hanged black male bodies—with an occasional female sharing that dreadful fate. It could easily be surmised, therefore, how southern territory came to be identified with torture and death for black males or with such a violation of the mind that it took years to overcome—if such violation could be overcome.

The black male psyche dominated by southernness is nowhere more apparent than in Yusef Komunyakaa's personae in *Dien Cai Dau* (1988) and in Ernest Gaines's "Three Men" (*Bloodline,* 1968), both of which I treat in this study. Komunyakaa's personae carry the South in their heads from America to Vietnam. All the mental and physical restrictions they have experienced in the American South get played out on Vietnamese soil as these soldiers engage in various competitions with their fellow white soldiers; nowhere is that competition manifested more explicitly than in the realm of the sexual. Gaines's characters present their bodies as tablets upon which white racists write their notions of black subservience and inhumanity. Jefferson, in Gaines's *A Lesson Before Dying,* is literally labeled a "hog," but Procter Lewis in "Three Men" introduces himself as a puppet seen through the eyes of the white law officers to whom he presents himself for having been in a fight with another black man. The fascinating thing about Procter is his ability to analyze the role into which he has been cast and which he readily plays for fear of bodily harm. The violence involved in fighting another black man is nothing to him compared to what whites can do to his body if he does not act out the minutiae of living Jim Crow.

Still other black male writers, in their rite of passage through the South, use it as a point of reference for less violent but still unpleasant references. Some of them, such as Idaho-born Wallace Thurman in *The Blacker the Berry* (1929), simply create characters and represent them as being from this most backward part of the United States, as is a woman who attends college with Thurman's Emma Lou. William Melvin Kelley, in *A Different Drummer*, seems to be so awed by the territory from his New York and Boston perspectives that he can only create a mythical southern state in which to depict the consequences of historical repression upon twentieth-century black male bodies. A heritage of servitude ends only when a diminutive black man claims the freedom that has been denied to his family for five generations.[9] For Robert Beck (Iceberg Slim), the South is anathema because he cannot identify with southern blacks and the "foreign" language they speak.[10]

For Randall Kenan, whom I treat as well, the South is scary because of its warped responses to alternative sexuality. When the sixteen-year-old Horace Cross in *A Visitation of Spirits* (1989) realizes that he is gay, he judges himself through the eyes of the small-town southern black community, Tims Creek, that Kenan has created. For black males as well as for white males, to be homosexual is considered vile and evil. The only way Horace can deal with his "abnormality" is to take drastic and tragic action. The implication is that, in a different environment than the horribly religious and restrictive South, Horace might have been able to declare his homosexuality and still live. In this instance, black *and* white communities come together in the South to deem it a fearful, destructive place.

While black women writers might echo the themes of their black male counterparts about the South, they do so with a difference. Their characters step into hell and lower the temperature of the fire instead of trying to avoid it altogether. Consider the issue of southern white assault upon black bodies. Black women writers are drawn to historical, iconic murders just as black male writers are. The murder of Emmett Till, for example, finds its way into Bebe Moore Campbell's *Your Blues Ain't Like Mine* (1992), Toni Morrison's *Song of Solomon* (1977), and Nagueyalti Warren's and Marilyn Nelson's poetry. However, in none of these instances does the writer dwell overly long on the gruesomeness of the physical destruction of the black male body. In *Blues,* the focus is more on a black woman trying to survive through selling home-cooked meals in the repressive southern environment where the Till character dies. Morrison uses the Till case as the impetus, in part, to the founding of the Seven Days, a black vigilante group bent on retaliating against whites for violence against blacks. Warren muses upon the implications of the murder as a seasonal aberration, not upon the graphicness of it. Most fascinating, Nelson creates a book for young readers that treats the Emmett Till murder in "a heroic crown of sonnets." By audience alone, if for no other reason, her poetry cannot reflect the historical graphicness of the violence with which Till was executed. Nelson notes that the form she used in the poems served as a containment against her own potential emotional disintegration: "The strict form became a kind of insulation, a way of protecting myself from the intense pain of the subject matter."[11]

While black women may have been raped, as Nanny and her daughter—Janie's mother—are in *Their Eyes Were Watching God* (1937), they did not have to contemplate the actual physical loss of a body part, as black men did in contemplating castration. I do not want to get into fruitless discussions about who suffered more—physically and psychologically traumatized black men or physically and psychologically traumatized black women—but I do want to suggest that black women and black female characters, even after rape, move on with their lives. Nanny nurtures Janie after her daughter, Janie's mother, disappears, and though her advice to Janie can be questioned at times, her basic healthy survival cannot. Nanny does not contemplate removing herself from hell. She stays on the soil and forges a life for herself.

Gloria Naylor also deals with the issue of rape on southern soil. The daughter of a sharecropper, a young woman with a twisted foot from birth, inadvertently attracts the attention of the landowner. Her parents, Elvira and Ben, agree to her working in the home of Mr. Clyde, since her injury prevents her from working in the fields. When the girl confides that Mr. Clyde is using her sexually, Elvira refuses to believe her. Ben, sensing that his daughter is telling the truth, is too weak to confront Mr. Clyde or to stand up to his wife, who openly taunts his lack of manhood in not giving her more children to help work their land. The daughter finally leaves, but not for the big cities of the North. "The girl disappeared one day, leaving behind a note saying that she loved them very much, but . . . if she had to earn her keep that way, she might as well go to Memphis where the money was better."[12] From her more profitable employment, the daughter sends money home to help her parents, which only increases Ben's opportunities to drink himself into oblivion. When Elvira leaves Ben "for a man who farmed near the levee," Ben heads north and to Brewster Place, carrying more psychological than physical wounds. The daughter, we are left to presume, continues to thrive in her less-than-acceptable profession. Again, Naylor does not deny that rape is traumatic; how that trauma is manifested, however, shifts the focus away from the female body to the black male psyche. There is no graphic description of the daughter's violation, no haunting story about what happens to her following her repeated rapes at the hand of the white landowner.

Alice Walker joins James Baldwin in focusing on lynching in a short story entitled "The Flowers," as does Margaret Walker in *Jubilee* (1966). In "The Flowers," a young girl skipping through the woods outside a southern city has her life changed forever when she comes upon a skeleton and a rope that lynchers have been used to kill a black man. ". . . [S]he stepped smack into his eyes. Her heel became lodged in the broken ridge between brow and nose, and she reached down quickly, unafraid, to free herself. It was only when she saw his naked grin that she gave a little yelp of surprise."[13] She drops the flowers she has been collecting, a sign that the witnessing of a former lynch scene has effectively ended her childhood. However, the drop does not occur before she examines the scene carefully and notes the man's height. She is "unafraid" enough to register all the horror, but that horror does not lead young Myop, the child in the story, to a resolution to depart from the land that has spawned her. She simply recognizes that innocence is a state that she cannot retain upon southern soil. Again, the descent into hell becomes another way of living, not a reason to reject—at least not completely—the hellish conditions under which one must live.

As one of the few women writers who focus on lynching in their works, Margaret Walker gives the actual event even less attention than Alice Walker does. For Margaret Walker, the story of a couple of enslaved black women being hanged for allegedly poisoning their master becomes an object lesson on the difficulties of slavery. While the masters might think that the lynchings serve to deter future episodes of poisoning, to the enslaved persons witnessing them they operate as lessons on survival. If one dares to be so bold as to tamper with the food of one's master, then one had better be adept at hiding the evidence. Of course, slavery was a system under which no amount of preknowledge could get one exonerated if a master was intent upon seeing guilt in a black person's actions. Nonetheless, for Walker, the lynching itself is not the life-stopping event for black witnesses that it obviously is for the victim. By contrast, Baldwin and his characters *always* seem traumatized by the mere prospect of lynching.[14]

Legacies of slavery obviously provide their share in conceptualizing the cultured hell of the South, whether those legacies are realized in racial repression, white supremacy, or violence against blacks. Legacies of slavery can be personal or institutionalized. Personal legacies dominate the literary landscapes in Octavia E. Butler's *Kindred* (1979), Sherley Anne Williams's *Dessa Rose* (1986), Phyllis Alesia Perry's *Stigmata* (1998), and Edward P. Jones's *The Known World* (2003), all of which I treat in this study. Attempted escape from the South is more a theme when one confronts the *institutionalized* legacy of slavery, as Grange Copeland does in Alice Walker's first novel, *The Third Life of Grange Copeland.* For Grange, who finds himself deeply in debt to white landowners in Georgia, life can be lived only in the animalistic cycle of going to work in heat-laden cotton fields, coming home exhausted and falling into bed, and getting drunk on weekends to try to escape from the pattern. The sharecropping system that controls Grange's life is the compromise that white Southerners made with their former black workers following slavery. Grange still finds himself caught in it well into the twentieth century. Life is hell for him, and he in turn makes life hell for his wife and son. He believes that he can escape only by migrating to New York.

Walker does not deny the circumstances in which Grange is caught up, nor the one in which his son Brownfield will be caught up following Grange's departure to the North, but Walker does make clear that there is a point where blaming others for one's situation leaves off and one must take responsibility for one's own existence. Later, in his third life, Grange realizes this and can say to his son Brownfield that, as far as white people are concerned, "*you got to hold tight a place in you where they can't come*" (265–66). In his first life in Georgia, however, Grange has not yet arrived at that state of wisdom, and he acts like an animal toward his family as a result of pressures he feels as a sharecropper. Still, his fear of southern white men does not force him to fight with his wife; he makes that choice. Similarly, Brownfield's acquiescence to the sharecropping system is as much his responsibility as it is the will of the white men on whose land he works. Even though a repressive institution is in place, Walker nonetheless makes her characters responsible for their own humanity within that evil system. To do otherwise would make them animals.

On some occasions, the writers themselves experience the hellish culture or other fears of the South. With Zora Neale Hurston, the South became scary when she traveled collecting folklore in Florida and Louisiana as well as when she wrote about poor whites in Florida. Certainly traipsing around the South alone in the 1920s and 1930s could have been scary for a black woman, especially going into sawmill camps and juke joints far out in rural areas. But writing also put Hurston in a precarious situation. For those judging the actions of writers, Hurston crossed a line drawn in history and blood when she dared to deviate from writing about black people; it was scary, therefore, to deal with different subject matter. Yet Hurston could not resist the call of the South in its many guises, and so she wrote *Seraph on the Suwanee* (1948), about poor whites in Florida. And she suffered the consequences of having dared to believe that she could portray a southern white experience as unopposed as when she portrayed southern black experiences.

Nonetheless, with all the fears that black women writers and their characters encounter in the South, there is nothing comparable to the "loss of manhood" theme that pervades the writings of black male authors. What would it mean for a black woman to experience a loss of womanhood in the South? Or is that lack so obvious that it does not need to be stated? Is the loss of womanhood inherent in the usual general disregard for black women on southern soil? These questions have no immediately obvious answers; however, it is clear that black women do not hold any appreciably better position on southern territory than black men do.

So what, finally, is scary about the Mason-Dixon Line, and what does it mean for African American literary creativity? The scariness means, first of all, as James Baldwin points out, that the very southern landscape and the white people in it become enemies of black people. Think of the instances in which trees have been used to lynch black men. Consider Billie Holiday's song, "Strange Fruit," in which she sings of that phenomenon. Black male bodies, hanging like leaves or flowers from various trees, cause the trees to have "blood on the leaves and blood on the root." One of Marilyn Nelson's "heroic crown of sonnets" for Emmett Till complements Holiday's song.

> . . . I remember, like a haunted tree
> set off from other trees in the wildwood
> by one bare bough. If trees could speak, it could
> describe, in words beyond words, make us see
> the strange fruit that still ghosts its reverie,

misty companion of its solitude.
Dendrochronology could give its age
in centuries, by counting annual rings:
seasons of drought and rain. But one night, blood,
spilled at its roots, blighted its foliage.
Pith outward, it has been slowly dying,
pierced by the screams of a shortened childhood. (*Wreath*, n.p.)

Baldwin contemplates black bodies on trees as he is about to embark upon civil rights activity in Atlanta: "It was on the outskirts of Atlanta that I first felt how the Southern landscape—the trees, the silence, the liquid heat, and the fact that one always seems to be traveling great distances—seems designed for violence, seems, almost, to demand it. What passions cannot be unleashed on a dark road in a Southern night!" (*Nobody*, 108). Of white men raping black women historically and figuratively stealing power and freedom from black men, Baldwin offers: "How many times has the Southern day come up to find that black man, sexless, hanging from a tree!" (*Nobody*, 109). Indeed, for Baldwin, the essence of fear of the South can be summed up in the image of trees: "Which of us has overcome his past? And the past of a Negro is blood dripping down through leaves, gouged-out eyeballs, the sex torn from its socket and severed with a knife" (*Nobody*, 213).

Literarily, writers join Holiday and Baldwin in painting the paradoxical nature of the southern landscape—as a source of death and a source of beauty. Even Paul Laurence Dunbar, who is usually considered a mild-mannered black writer, nonetheless wrote a poem entitled "The Haunted Oak."[15] The tree is personified to relate the tale of how a black man was hanged on its branches. Toni Morrison's Sethe in *Beloved* (1987) harbors troubling horrible/beautiful memories of the landscape at Sweet Home plantation:

> . . . [T]here was Sweet Home, rolling, rolling, rolling out before her eyes, and although there was not a leaf on that farm that did not make her want to scream, it rolled itself out before her in shameless beauty. It never looked as terrible as it was and it made her wonder if hell was a pretty place too. Fire and brimstone all right, but hidden in lacy groves. Boys hanging from the most beautiful sycamores in the world. It shamed her—remembering the wonderful soughing trees rather than the boys. Try as she might to make it otherwise, the sycamores beat out the children every time and she could not forgive her memory for that.[16]

From Dunbar and Jean Toomer, therefore, to Richard Wright, to Margaret Walker and Alice Walker, to Morrison, to Daniel Black and Natasha Trethewey, and a host of others, African American writers have documented the fear of the South in terms of how the landscape can be used against black people. But of course it is people who are manipulating the landscape, so the major tales of fear have to do with white human beings.

Numerous are the stories of black people traveling through some town, large or small, in the South and being threatened in some way. Blyden Jackson, who was one of my colleagues in English at the University of North Carolina at Chapel Hill, used to recount how he made his first trip to Louisiana to join the faculty at Southern University. At a gas station not too far from his destination, the gas station owner pulled a shotgun and threatened him—just because he was black. What made the story so striking is that Blyden Jackson, who became a well-known scholar of African American literature, was barely taller than four feet. If this strikingly tiny black man, an intellectual, one of the "safe" Negroes, inspired a southern white man to pull a gun on him, then imagine how much more threatened white Southerners feel when they encounter large black men. Whites have stereotyped these large black men as *always* being "big" and "burly," with connotations of animalism. In attempting to turn black males into animals, white Southerners could justifiably lynch them with impunity. So in almost every account of an accusation for rape in the South, and for which lynching was the result, the accusers said the black man was "big and burly."

The documentation of human threat and thus human-inspired fear of the South by black people is constant throughout history and literature. Complementing the human threat is the fear of particular spaces in the South. In the macro-arena, the fear of the Mason-Dixon Line is located specifically in the courthouses of the South. Nowhere have sanctions against black people been kept in place more than in the legal system. The fear of the absence of justice thus finds its way into the folklore as well as the literature that African Americans produce. This is no more vividly represented than in the folktale relating the experiences of black people in southern courts when they go looking for justice. That's what they find, so the tale goes, "just us"—all black people at the fickle mercy of whites. Or, as another tale goes, the situation is comparable to a goose who brings a case against a fox, in which she fights for equal right to sail on a lake when the fox challenges her. She arrives in court to discover that "de sheriff, he wus er fox, en de judge, he wus er fox, and der tourneys, dey wus fox, en all de jurymen, dey was foxes, too." As the lone, lonely defendant, her goose is literally cooked. The tale ends with a moral: "Now, my chilluns, listen to me, when all de folks in de cotehouse is foxes, and you is des' er common goose, der ain't gwine to be much jestice for you pore cullud folks."[17]

On the microcosmic level, the fearful space is specifically the homes of white people in the South. I am thinking of black women who went to work after emancipation and throughout the twentieth century in the homes of white women and ran the risk of being sexually violated by the sons and husbands of the women for whom they worked.[18] That fear has manifested itself in the literature as well. Consider Jean Toomer's "Blood-Burning Moon," in which the white Bob Stone considers it his "right" to seduce the black woman, Louisa, who works for his family. If she does not consent to seduction, then rape will follow. The same dynamic holds sway in Raymond Andrews' *Appalachee Red* (1978), in which the white family patriarch considers it his "right" to have sex with the young black woman who works for his family. He continues that relationship in spite of the fact that she is married and that her husband is tremendously humiliated by this violation. That humiliation is strikingly vivid with Stamp Paid, who, in Toni Morrison's *Beloved*, actually escorts his pretty young wife to the white plantation owner rapist; the price he pays in powerlessness and shame leads to his adoption of his nickname. For economic reasons, however, black women historically *had* to go into those spaces, no matter how fearful they might have been of them, and they had to make the adjustments necessary in order to work in those white homes. If children resulted from those forced and embarrassing unions, the women brought the "red" babies home to their families and moved on with their lives.[19]

Fear of southern territory, therefore, whether manifested in lynching or rape, had a direct impact upon black bodies. It also had an impact in terms of the codes by which black people were expected to live and operate in the South. There is no better literary representation of these codes than Richard Wright's essay "The Ethics of Living Jim Crow" (1938). Wright documents the psychological and physical tightrope walking that black people had to effect in order to be relatively safe in the South. Any minute deviation from the norm could lead to injury, rape, or death. The scary Mason-Dixon Line, therefore, became an almost tangible entity that black people carried around in their heads. "You can do this." "You can't do that." "If you take this course of action, you will run the risk of punishment in these ways." "You cannot walk here." "You better stay over there." Black people and black characters had to become diviners, fortune tellers who must always read any situation correctly or suffer the consequences of not having done so.

A couple of decades after Wright articulated the ethics of living Jim Crow, Baldwin recorded an experience he had in Montgomery, Alabama, that echoes well what Wright had in mind. Baldwin is aware of unwritten rules to which he must adhere if he is to be safe, but he is at a disadvantage in not knowing all the rules. He remarks:

> I felt that I was walking on this rug, this wall-to-wall carpet. Beneath it is a com-
> plex system of wires, and one of those wires, if you step on it, will blow up the
> whole house. . . . And everybody in the South knows where that wire is except
> me. I've got to cross this rug, too. But I don't know how I'm going to get across
> it, because every step I take is loaded with danger. Every time I open my mouth
> I'm wrong. The way I look at people is wrong. The way I sound is wrong. I am
> obviously not only a stranger in town, I'm an enemy. . . . I'm also endangering
> everybody else, which gives you another fear. Then you really get scared.[20]

Baldwin's musings on the South and his depictions of it in his fiction put him at the forefront of black writers who paint the territory in ugly ways.

African American writers have thus played a large role in creating a nega-tive mythology of the South, in contributing to its image as an unhealthy place for people of African descent. Certainly, this is not without justification. On the other hand, what are the implications of this wholesale indictment of part of the United States? While many writers, such as Richard Wright, were born and raised in the South, others, such as Baldwin, indict it from afar, the last occasion being his book of essays, *The Evidence of Things Not Seen* (1985), about the Atlanta child murders that occurred between 1979 and 1981, when over thirty black adolescents in Atlanta disappeared; while many of their bod-ies were found and properly buried, others have never been found. Northern-born Toni Cade Bambara wrote *Those Bones Are Not My Child* (posthumous; 1999), also about the Atlanta child murders. Yet Bambara lived in Atlanta for many years and was a community activist there before she returned to Phila-delphia, and it is important to note that she was raising her own child—a daughter—in Atlanta at the time of the murders. It is instructive to consider Baldwin's and Bambara's essayistic and literary treatments of the cases with that of Tayari Jones, a young Atlanta-born contemporary African American woman novelist. In *Leaving Atlanta* (2002), which I discuss in this volume, Jones domesticates fear, so to speak, and moves it from the realm of unrelenting horror that defines northern treatment of the same subject matter.[21]

Again and again, therefore, this combination of approach/avoidance, love/hate, damning the South but not being able to get away from it comes up in African American lives and literature. I would venture to say, however, that black writers born out of the South tend to indict it more; lack of intimacy creates a larger monster. It is left to the Margaret Walkers, Alice Walkers, Tina McElroy Ansas, and Natasha Tretheweys, all true Southerners, to balance the love with the hatred. These women, and writers who share their stances, are able to contain their fear sufficiently to show the beauty and the ugliness of southern American territory.[22] And while their efforts might be comparable to whistling while walking past a cemetery—to control fear—they nonetheless succeed in showing that fear may have controlled—or may control—the lives of black people in the southern United States but did not and ultimately does not conquer them. A strikingly vivid example of that position is Raymond Andrews's novel *Baby Sweet's* (1983), with which I end this study.

In terms of the cultured hell, then, perhaps it comes down to a situation that Toni Morrison describes in *Beloved*. Remember that Sethe Suggs has had her back cut to pieces by schoolteacher and his nephews before she runs away from Sweet Home. Recall that she encounters Amy Denver, the indentured white girl who has also run away and is heading to Boston to find lace. Cultured hell, then, comes down to lace and lashings. Morrison surrounds the ugliness of Sethe's beating with the beauty of lace. Amy in turn labels the pattern she notices on Sethe's badly lashed back a tree, an image that seems inconsistent with the ugliness displayed there.

For black women writers, the possibility for survival, for survival *whole,* as Alice Walker asserts, takes precedence over the violence, the white supremacy, the institutionalized racism, and the legacies of slavery. Wherever one finds one's self on southern soil, these women writers posit, the possibility exists for transcendence without permanent damage to the psyche. That is the lesson that Baby Suggs teaches in her sermons in the Clearing in Morrison's *Beloved;* there is an untouchable core in black humanity, she argues—as does Alice Walker in *The Third Life of Grange Copeland*—that allows it to hover above the muck and mire of the swampy lands of slavery, violence, and degradation. It is that tendency for transcendence that separates black women writers and their southern imaginations so conspicuously from their male counterparts.

THE MOUNTAIN OF THE SOUTH AND THE BLACK WRITER'S IDENTITY

In 1926 Langston Hughes published "The Negro Artist and the Racial Mountain" in the special issue of *Survey Graphic* that focused on black writing. Race, Hughes suggested, was the mountain that stood between aspiring black writers and the successes that should have come to them simply as writers. Young black writers should not feel constrained by the implications of race, Hughes asserted; instead, they should claim individuality to write whatever they pleased. He proudly claimed at the end of the essay: "We younger Negro artists who create now intend to express our individual dark-skinned selves without fear or shame. If white people are pleased we are glad. If they are not, it doesn't matter. . . . If colored people are pleased we are glad. If they are not, their displeasure doesn't matter either. We build our temples for tomorrow, strong as we know how, and we stand on top of the mountain, free within ourselves."[23]

That high lookout of a perch, which sought to deny the claims of race upon black people, ignored—or perhaps simply disregarded—the solidity of the mountain on which it stood. In this study, that mountain for black writers is the South. They cannot stand on its top, for that offers nothing to which they can hold. They must, instead, tunnel through the mountain. Tunneling through the mountain of the South enables them to arrive at the other side with a heightened sense of who they are as writers. Complete identity as an African American writer seems to come only after a confrontation with black history and American history as represented by and in the South. That history of repression, violence, and lack calls out to each generation of African American writers, and each generation responds in its own way. The main thing is that *every* generation responds.

In addition to providing validation and authentication, tunneling through the mountain of the South for African American writers also establishes kinship and unity with the masses of black people. Unlike some black people not born in the South who assert that they have no relatives who were enslaved and who try to distance themselves from the history and legacy of slavery, black writers embrace the entire geographical span of African American history and identity. They achieve thereby a certain right to represent black experience. Consider the mantra issued to black writers of Frederick Douglass's generation. Even though they hightailed it out of the South, they nonetheless remembered where they had come from and used their writings to assist in the process of acquiring freedom for all black people. That refusal to turn their backs on the South and the plight of blacks still enslaved there has its twentieth- and twenty-first century manifestations in those writers who willingly embrace all the ugliness of southern and African American history in modern efforts to represent African Americans accurately and well—if possible—no matter where the writers live in the United States.

Perhaps, too, there is an element of empathy achieved through imagining the plight of southern blacks that layers the creative output of nonsouthern black writers. A writer such as Toni Morrison, for example, has ancestral roots in the South, but she herself lived there only briefly. Yet, by tunneling through the history of slavery, she is able to provide in *Beloved* an empathetic representation of slavery in all its horrors as well as a representation of the southern territory on which events during slavery played out. Through historical research and imagination, she is able to imbue her characters with a clarity of cultural saturation that echoes what Pennsylvanian David Bradley allows John Washington to achieve in *The Chaneysville Incident* (1981). Neither Bradley nor Morrison is native to the South, yet they gain authentic African American southern credibility, so to speak, by immersing themselves in all the muck and yuck they experienced while tunneling through that mountain of the South. Just as whites contemporary with publishers of freedom narratives authenticated the production of those narratives, so African American writers appear to be engaged in their own, almost subconscious, form of authentication by showcasing an ability to write about the most problematic part of the country historically for black self-realization and fulfillment.

By collecting their credentials through empathetic portrayals of southern African American experience, nonsouthern black writers attain a representative status in their writings. They join African American writers born into and experienced in southern black culture in an allegiance to history and culture, no matter how painful that allegiance may be. Some of these writers, as I have implied, are obviously more adept at tunneling through the mountain of the South than others. For example, both William Melvin Kelley and James Baldwin have some difficulty imagining—without stereotype—southern landscape and white southern character (sometimes they experience difficulty even limning black southern character). Yet they tunnel toward the attainment of a goal that aligns them historically and creatively with African American writers throughout the United States. It is that tunneling—fearful, painful, and difficult though it may be—that defines all the writers I cover in this study as true African American writers.

SUCH A FRIGHTENING MUSICAL FORM

James Baldwin's *Blues for Mister Charlie*

In 1979, James Baldwin published *Just Above My Head,* his last novel. While the novel is a conglomerate of many things and indeed could have used some severe editing, it is also the story of a singing quartet of young black men who travel from Harlem to various sites in the South. While they are apprehensive about going south, with all its political and social activist undertakings in the middle of the twentieth century, they nonetheless go. And in that pattern peculiar to black folks traveling in the segregated South, instead of staying in hotels, they stay at the homes of black church folks and other black folks during their travels. Before their departure from Harlem, Baldwin's narrator, Hall Montana, observes: "Look at a map, and scare yourself half to death. On the northern edge of Virginia, on the Washington border, catty-corner to Maryland, is Richmond, Virginia. Two-thirds across the map is Birmingham, Alabama, surrounded by Mississippi, Tennessee, and Georgia."[1] To actually travel those states and along the roads observed on the map "can be far more frightening than the frightening map" (400).

By the time Baldwin published *Just Above My Head,* he had had extensive experience working for civil rights in the South, and he had written about those experiences. He therefore infuses the novel with his own memories of having frightful experiences in the South. After his first trip, he could not bring himself to move from a "cold-water flat" for five days. He had suffered, he said, from "a kind of retrospective terror which had paralyzed me so long. While in the South I had suppressed my terror well enough, in any case, to function; but when the pressure came off, a kind of wonder of terror overcame me, making me as useless as a snapped rubber band."[2] One of his experiences combined mental terror with the possibility of bodily harm. He expresses an

> unbelieving shock when I realized that I was being groped by one of the most powerful men in one of the states I visited. He had got himself sweating drunk in order to arrive at this despairing titillation. With his wet eyes staring up at my face, and his wet hands groping for my cock, we were both, abruptly, in history's ass-pocket. It was very frightening—not the gesture itself, but the abjectness of it, and the assumption of a swift and grim complicity: as my identity was defined by his power, so was my humanity to be placed at the service of his fantasies. . . . This man, with a phone call, could prevent or provoke a lynching. (*No Name*, 61, 62)

The articulation of fear of southern territory in *Just Above My Head* and the memory of personal fear are continuations but not yet culminations of Baldwin's love/hate relationship with the American South. While I argue that Baldwin presents the South as an engulfing woman, a chimera out to destroy black men in *Just Above My Head,* there are other ways of looking at this love/hate relationship.[3] Whether by maligning the South for producing Gabriel Grimes in *Go Tell It on the Mountain* (1953) or worrying about missing children in *The Evidence of Things Not Seen* (1985), Baldwin is fixated upon including the South in his writings. Whether he deals with lynching and castration, or the disappearance of black bodies, or the peculiar pressures placed on black manhood in the South, Baldwin joins his fellow writers in tunneling through southern history and violence and considering the South a rite of passage for African American writers, and he joins other writers in various confrontations with the South.

For Baldwin, the primary confrontation almost always involves black men encountering white men and invariably entails a psychosexual dimension. In *Go Tell It on the Mountain,* his first and best-known novel, Gabriel Grimes, the father in the story, goes from slimy sexuality to transplanting his brand of ugly fundamentalist religion from somewhere in the South to Harlem. The dirty, ugly, restrictive practices of Gabriel's church are a direct indictment of the

South. In his short story "Going to Meet the Man" (1965), Baldwin highlights the lynching of a black man; the lynching serves as a transfer of sexual power from the lynched and castrated black man to a white male who witnessed the scene.[4] In *Another Country* (1962), Baldwin asserts that white males in America have difficulty getting erections without imagining violence being done to some black person. And one of Baldwin's characters in *Just Above My Head* remarks,

> . . . [Southern white males could use anything] as an excuse for violence, if not murder, or one of them might, simply, go mad, and release his pent-up orgasm—for their balls were aching. . . . [And then he addresses an imaginary white man] Maybe the difference between us [that is, black men and white men] is that I've never been afraid of the prick you, like all men, carry between their legs and I never arranged picnics so that I could cut it off of you before large, cheering crowds. By the way, what did you do with my prick once you'd cut the black thing off and held it in your hands? You couldn't have bleached it—could you? You couldn't have cut yours off and sewn mine on? Is it standing on your mantelpiece now, in a glass jar, or did you nail it to the wall? Or did you eat it? How did it taste? Was it nourishing? (397, 398)

While Baldwin depicts violence in the South in all of his works in which the South is even remotely mentioned, he uses *Just Above My Head* to highlight the physical violence, both imagined and real, that can be done to black men and the psychological violence that other black males suffer as a result of it. While the quartet from Harlem is singing in a small southern town, one of its members, on a trip to the outhouse behind the church, simply disappears. No amount of searching uncovers his whereabouts. No amount of searching locates his body. He just disappears. It is that fear of disappearance on southern territory that informs the notion of a scary Mason-Dixon Line. The fear of castration is tangible and psychologically destructive enough, but imagine the greater fear of actually having a body lost and never finding it, indeed never learning a single fact about how it disappears or where it might have ended up. In that mental space of the possibility for and the knowledge of disappearance is where James Baldwin and many other nonsouthern black writers reside when they think of the South. Your body can be destroyed. You can disappear. You will be lost and not found.

Fear of the disappearance of the black male body permeates Baldwin's work and is perhaps his greatest fear of the South because the intangible realm of imagination—thinking about disappearing—precedes any actual act of disappearance. Imagination pollutes the very air that Baldwin's narrator breathes in *Just Above My Head*. He extends that fear to the physical territory on which the characters travel and then onto the bodies acting out the drama he has imagined, that is, the innocent black boys from the North and the evil white men in the South.

The fear of disappearance is so aligned with southern territory, according to Baldwin's conception of the South, that it exists independently of evil white men. There is no better example of this in Baldwin's works than *The Evidence of Things Not Seen*, his discussion of the disappearances of more than thirty young black people in Atlanta in the late 1970s and early 1980s. In this historical moment, imagination and reality combined for Baldwin; of course, everything he had ever thought about the South was true, because it was so clearly verified in the evidence of missing bodies. Though unseen, those bodies testified to the poisoned air reflected on the poisoned map and in turn reflected in the poisoned minds of perpetrators who were so blatantly inhumane and so violently committed to their sinister objectives.

Equally fearful to Baldwin as the black body disappearing is the black body hanging on southern territory. There is no more vivid example than his depiction of the lynching in the flashback in "Going to Meet the Man." The lynched black man, accused of the age-old crime of impropriety toward a white woman, is the image that fuels racism and repression. The white sheriff in the story who remembers his father taking him to the lynching, castrating, and burning of a black man, conjures up that image to gather the scattered pieces of his manhood when he is confronted with young black demonstrators in an unnamed southern town. By recalling the lynching and imagining that as the "rightful" place for black men who step out of line, Jesse, the sheriff, can collect his nerves sufficiently to confront the demonstrators and his sexuality sufficiently to make love to his wife "like a nigger."

Lynching black men but desiring the very sexuality that has presumably led to the lynching, Baldwin posits, is the natural position of white men in the South and the natural reason for black men to be fearful of the South. Indeed, it is almost impossible in a Baldwin work to be a black *man* in the South. The two states are irrevocably oppositional. Yet another way that Baldwin exhibits fear of the South in his work is that of the psychological loss of manhood. While this fear might accompany the physical loss of the ability to do the things usually associated with being a man, such as going where one wants, holding a job, or providing for one's family, it is the breaking down of the black male mind, of the ability to think of one's self in a masculine vein, that Baldwin finds most distasteful. This is keenly evident with the characters in *Blues for Mister Charlie,* Baldwin's 1964 play.

Richard Henry, the young black man who has spent a few years out of the South and returned home, is impatient with his preacher father's ways of dealing with white folks. To Richard, his father Meridian is too much the Uncle Tom, the hat-in-hand, "agree 'em to death and destruction" image of black manhood that one of Ralph Ellison's characters recommends in *Invisible Man.* How can his father stand to interact with whites the way he does, Richard wonders, when Meridian Henry joins Richard in suspecting that Meridian's wife—Richard's mother—was probably pushed in the fall down a flight of stairs that led to her death. Richard, loosely based on Emmett Till, refuses to back down when the local white supremacist, Lyle Britten, believes that Richard has behaved inappropriately in front of Lyle's wife. For Richard, it is a question of whether or not a man can be a man no matter where he is. For Lyle, it is a matter of the only good "niggers" being dead, Uncle Toms, or sexually available to him. Richard therefore acts out Baldwin's fear when he tries to meet Lyle on a level of equal manhood. Lyle will have none of it and simply shoots Richard to death. Or, given the dynamics of the South, Richard knowingly commits suicide, for a black male cannot claim manhood on southern territory, from Baldwin's perspective, and live to tell the tale.[5]

In *Blues for Mister Charlie,* then, Baldwin works through in detail the forces that make him most fearful about the South. For both blacks and whites, that fear may well begin with the threat of sexual interaction or sexual pollution. Richard's knowledge of how white men in the South read black men, especially those from the North, leads him to confront this fear head-on by bragging, as it is suggested Emmett Till did, about the white women he has known in New York. He shows photographs of them to a couple of his friends when they visit Papa D.'s joint, which leads Papa D., the local Uncle Tom and friend of Lyle Britten, to exclaim: "Where'd you steal those pictures, boy?" and then, "Put them pictures away. I thought you had good sense."[6] Papa D.'s response illustrates the generational fear induced in African American males by virtue of living in the South, and it echoes the white sentiment for the possibility of sexual pollution. As Richard observes, "Ain't that a bitch. He's scared because I'm carrying around pictures of white girls. That's the trouble with niggers. They all scared of the man" (27).[7] Implicit in Papa D.'s comment is the suggestion that Richard should stick to nice black girls, as any black man with "good sense" would do, instead of venturing into dangerous territory.

Sexual pollution, or the threat of "race-mixing," is constantly on the minds of the white characters as the rationale for keeping blacks repressed. One of Lyle's neighbors addresses Lyle's wife with the following observation: "Mrs. Britten, you're married and all the women in this room are married and I know you've seen your husband without no clothes on—but have you seen a nigger without no clothes on? No, I guess you haven't. Well, he ain't like a white man, Mrs. Britten. . . . Mrs. Britten, if you was to be raped by an orang-outang out of the jungle or a *stallion*, couldn't do you no worse than a nigger. You wouldn't be no more good for nobody. I've *seen* it" (50). Myth keeps the white women in place in the scenario that paints black men as ever eager to pounce upon them sexually, and the personal testimony from a trusted acquaintance bolsters the myth. White women, then, in literature as was historically the case with lynching, serve as the impetus to white men keeping black men in their place. Another neighbor comments that "you might be able to scare a black nigger, but you can't do nothing with a yellow nigger," to which the preacher responds: "That's because he's a mongrel. And a mongrel is the lowest creation in the animal kingdom" (50). Nowhere in these conclusions that white males draw so easily is acknowledgment of how mongrelization occurred in the first place—white men coupling with black women.

While white men such as Lyle want to keep white women from black men, there are no similar restrictions articulated to keep white men from black women. Indeed, the opposite is true. White men are given a certain license to expend their "excess" or "hypersexual" sexual energies with black women, an idea that Baldwin develops here as well as in works such as "Going to Meet the Man." Lyle comments, in response to a hypothetical situation that his friend Parnell proposes, that any son of his can have sex with an "African princess" if he is in school in Switzerland, "long as he leaves her over there" (59). Lyle is unwavering in his assertion that he can have sex with black women but white women can't have sex with black men because "men [meaning white men] is different from women—they ain't as delicate. Man can do a lot of things a woman can't do" (60). Men have to sow their "wild oats," Lyle asserts.

Where white men elect to sow their wild oats leads to another consideration in the fear of sexual pollution. This fear is the one that is visible from the position of black women who could be coerced into relationships with white males or simply raped, as well as the fear that arises when black relatives witness the potential for such encounters. Here Baldwin echoes Jean Toomer and anticipates Raymond Andrews in similar white male violations of black female sexuality. Parnell's rather romantic attraction to Pearl, the daughter of his family's black maid, is overshadowed by the color and power dynamics that inform that attraction. While he and the young woman, as seventeen- and eighteen-year-olds, are fairly innocent, the girl's mother knows the historical and social context in which this seemingly innocent attraction has been forged. She therefore knows that it can ultimately mean no good for her daughter. It is a testament to Parnell's latently developed liberalism that he understands and can articulate how Pearl's mother perceives the situation when she comes upon the two of them kissing:

> She didn't say a word [Parnell tells Jo Britten]. She just looked at me. She just looked at me. I could see what was happening in her mind. She knew that there wasn't any point in complaining to my mother or my father. It would just make her daughter look bad. She didn't dare tell her husband. If he tried to do anything, he'd be killed. There wasn't anything she could do about me. I was just another horny white kid trying to get into a black girl's pants. She looked at me as though she were wishing with all her heart that she could raise her hand and wipe me off the face of the earth. I'll never forget that look. I still see it. She walked over to Pearl and I thought she was going to slap her. But she didn't. She took her by the hand, very sadly, and all she said was, "I'm ready to go now. Come on." And she took Pearl out of the room. (64)

Pearl's mother whisks her out of town, and Parnell never sees her again. The mother's action makes clear her understanding at that precise moment what Parnell only came to understand later: that black women should fear instead of embrace the possibility for sexual interaction across southern racial lines, because all the cards are stacked against the black woman.

Parnell is the character through whom we get additional testimony about the vulnerability of black women. He tells Jo: "A lot of the other kids in school used to drive over to niggertown at night to try and find black women. Sometimes they bought them, sometimes they frightened them, sometimes they raped them. And they were proud of it, they talked about it all the time" (62). Parnell may be different in his feelings about and actions toward Pearl, but he nonetheless gives credence to the reasons black women should fear southern environments.

Juanita, the character to whom Richard, Meridian Henry, Parnell, and Pete (one of the demonstrating students) are all equally attracted—though she reserves her affection for Richard—knows that southern history as well. As a young black student activist during the period in which the play is set, she understands, and is perhaps able to articulate better than Pearl's mother, what white men can do to black women—with or without their consent. When Richard comments that Juanita has "the same loud voice" she had when they were growing up, she observes that "the reason my voice got so loud so early, was that I started screaming for help right quick" (23). Since black males are essentially powerless in any potential protective role for black women in the South, presumably Juanita's screaming would have led more to a white male slinking away in embarrassment if he tried to approach her than it would have worked as a seriously effective response to her possible sexual exploitation. The point is that Juanita understands the vulnerability of black women on southern soil, just as Pearl's mother understood that vulnerability. A sane response to such vulnerability is to fear the potential violator of one's person. Even Parnell, who is more sympathetic to the black woman's plight than any other white character in the play, realizes that Pearl is initially afraid of him: "[S]he was *scared*, scared of me, but much too proud to show it" (63).

Of all the characters who could articulate the reason for that fear, Lyle Britten is the prime candidate. He makes black women vulnerable, and he inspires fear and submission in them. He is able to do so because his white supremacist power is unmatched and unchallenged, a situation that anticipates Rufus Weylin's interaction with Dana Franklin in Octavia E. Butler's *Kindred*. Though Rufus may initially appreciate Dana, he grows into an understanding of how the system under which he lives grants him the power to do with her mostly as he pleases, which is what Lyle does with the black woman he selects to violate. For Baldwin, then, a bit of the dynamics of slavery creeps into the twentieth century, for Lyle's legacy is that of a slaveholder. Almost everyone in the black community knows that Lyle has had an affair with the wife of Old Bill, a local black man. Juanita and Pete attest to Lyle's license as well as his power.

JUANITA: He shot a colored man a few years back, shot him dead, and wasn't nothing never said, much less done, about it.
PETE: Lyle had been carrying on with this man's wife, dig, and, naturally, Old Bill—his name was Bill Walker, everybody called him Old Bill—wanted to put a stop to it. (25)

Old Bill's confrontation with Lyle, much like Joe's with Spunk in Zora Neale Hurston's short story "Spunk," is all in favor of the bully. Lyle simply shoots Old Bill to death when Bill asserts that Lyle has cheated him at his store (Old Bill cannot even confront the sexual issue directly). And, unlike Spunk, there is no comeuppance for Lyle. He does what he wants because he knows he can get away with it. His exploits make him legendary in the black community, but what he has to say about the matter reiterates even more the reasons that black women should be fearful of southern environments.

Lyle admits his attraction to Willa Mae, Old Bill's wife, just as in *Kindred* Rufus admits his attraction to Alice, his black childhood playmate turned woman. We might even argue that Lyle's attraction to the black woman is cast in a mold not far from that Parnell holds for Pearl. Lyle drunkenly comments to Papa D.: "You remember them days when Willa Mae was around? My mind's been going back to them days. You remember? She was a hot little piece, I just had to have some of that, I just *had* to. Half the time she didn't wear no stockings, just had them brown, round legs just moving. I couldn't keep my eyes off her legs when she didn't wear no stockings. . . . [S]he'd just come into a room sometimes and my old pecker would stand up at attention" (115). In this drunken state, Lyle asserts that Willa Mae claimed he made love to her better than any black man. From Lyle's perspective, Willa Mae welcomes his advances, yet a comment he makes to Parnell questions that assessment. He tells Parnell that after Richard returns and trouble begins, "I started thinking about her, about Willa Mae, more and more and more. She was too young for him. Old Bill, he was sixty if he was a day, he wasn't doing her no good. Yet and still, the first time I took Willa Mae, I had to fight her. I swear I did. Maybe she was *frightened*. But I never had to fight her again. No. It was good, boy, let me tell you, and she liked it as much as me" (67–68; my emphasis). Given the nature of black/white relations in the South in the mid-twentieth century, this seems to be a prime example of delusion on Lyle's part. Force the black woman into sex, then don the role of superstud and claim that she has never experienced such good sex before. Rufus urges Dana to assist in getting Alice to yield to him sexually so that he will not have to force her to have sex with him. Implicit in the comments of both white males is the knowledge that they have the power to do as they please with the bodies of these black women. Apparent delusions about how good the sex was for Willa Mae serve Lyle in good stead in his beleaguered position as the reigning white supremacist. Since Willa Mae left town after Old Bill's death, and since we have no witness to her feelings and no direct commentary from her, we can interpret Lyle's comments only in the context of his own personality. He is intent upon making the world as he wants it, and Willa Mae is just a young sapling he bends to his will. She was a captive release for his horniness, a place to deposit the lust and sperm that he sees white women as too pure to receive.

His vision of the places that black women and white women hold in his scheme of things becomes even clearer in another comment Lyle makes to Parnell. He expresses to Parnell his desire to marry Josephine as well as his fear that she may say no; after all, he has had a reputation as a woman chaser. His reason for desiring Jo is simple: "But, I swear, Parnell, she might be the only virgin left in this town. The only *white* virgin. I can vouch for the fact ain't many black ones" (108). To Lyle, black women are made to receive his "wild oats," to serve as temporary outlets for his before-marriage sexuality. They are the realm of promiscuity and forbidden sexuality, unbridled passion and funkiness. White women are the preserve for family, children, and heritage. With this self-condemnation for how he uses black women, therefore, it is even harder to believe Lyle when he asserts that Willa Mae appreciated his attention, rape, and repeated sexual encounters. She may have just resigned herself to the situation by recognizing a pattern in which so many black women in the South were caught. She was obviously there only for Lyle's sexual use. Also, if Lyle has experimented with so many black virgins, there is no reason to assume that he would have made an exception of affection with one of them.

If the actions of Lyle and white men like him render apparent the reasons black women are vulnerable and should be afraid, equally important in this scenario is how black women manage to cope with this vulnerability and fear. Historically, their men could not protect them, the legal system did not consider them, and they themselves had little with which to fight back except their bodies, which could be conquered easily in the battle in which they were engaged. The primary coping mechanism in history and in literature, therefore, became religion and the church. Pearl's mother does the compromised, turn-the-other-cheek thing by refusing to pursue action against Parnell. Willa Mae disappears "up North." Mother Henry, Richard's grandmother and Meridian Henry's mother, tries to get Richard to turn from thoughts of violence to thoughts of God.

RICHARD: You know I don't believe in God, Grandmama.
MOTHER HENRY: You don't know what you talking about. Ain't no way possible for you not to believe in God. It ain't up to you.

RICHARD: Who's it up to, then?

MOTHER HENRY: It's up to the life in you—the life in you. *That* knows where
it comes from, *that* believes in God. You doubt me, you just try holding
your breath long enough to die. (19)

Mother Henry, like Mama Lena Younger in Lorraine Hansberry's *A Raisin
in the Sun* (1959), believes it her duty to raise her children in fear of God. To
adjust to circumstances over which one has little control, such as the repression of black people throughout the South in the first half of the twentieth
century, countless black Southerners learned to cope through Christianity,
through taking their burdens to the Lord and leaving them there. It was an
old, if not consistently effective, strategy.

Through religious practice in *Blues for Mister Charlie*, however, Baldwin
posits another fearful possibility. What if Christianity fails? The fear of the
failure of Christianity saturates the text and raises questions about that safety
valve as a true source of transcendence.[8] The questioning begins with Richard's comments to Mother Henry, but it permeates the text. For Richard, the
problem is what Christianity does not allow. It did not allow his father to
protect his mother or seek vengeance for her death; indeed, revenge is the
antithesis of what Christianity is all about. Richard, however, would have
preferred an alternative option for Meridian Henry. ". . . I just wish, that day
that Mama died, he'd took a pistol and gone through that damn white man's
hotel and shot every son of a bitch in the place" (20). "*My* Mama," he continues, "I never believed she fell. I *always* believed that some white man pushed
her down those steps. And I know that Daddy thought so, too. But he wasn't
there, he didn't know, he couldn't say nothing, he couldn't *do* nothing. I'll
never forget the way he looked—whipped, whipped, whipped, whipped!"
(20). With Christianity as the guiding force in his life, Meridian Henry can
only suffer in silence and get Richard out of the environment that might potentially reduce him to silent suffering.

Even as Meridian struggles to believe in the principles to which he has
committed his life as a minister, there is the looming possibility that the chosen path is inadequate to deal with current realities. At the beginning of the
play, when Juanita and the other young people are getting instructions in
nonviolence from Meridian, the emotional intensity of their role playing in
Meridian's church becomes so powerful at one point in a simulated scuffle
that it boils over into violence as Ken, one of the trainees, "*steps forward and
spits in Arthur's face*" (3). Ken has been unable to step out of the role playing

when Meridian calls a halt to it. If the young people cannot contain themselves under Meridian's Christian guidance at this point, and in a church setting, then even less will they be able to do so when hostile whites confront them directly. If mere imagination leads to violence, then how much more so will the reality of being attacked by whites.

The scene occurs following Richard's death, which gives added impetus to the anger. Lorenzo perhaps articulates what most of the young people are thinking. Chastised for saying "goddammit" in church, Lorenzo comments:

> Well, I wish to God I was in an arsenal. I'm sorry, Meridian, Mother Henry—I don't mean that for you. I don't understand you. I don't understand Meridian here. It was his son, it was your grandson, Mother Henry, that got killed, butchered! Just last week, and yet, here you sit—in this—this—the house of this damn almighty God who don't care what happens to nobody, unless, of course, they're white. Mother Henry, I got a lot of respect for you and all that, and for Meridian, too, but that white man's God is *white*. It's that damn white God that's been lynching us and burning us and castrating us and raping our women and robbing us of everything that makes a man a man for all these hundreds of years. Now, why we sitting around here, in *His* house. If I could get my hands on Him, I'd pull Him out of heaven and drag Him through this town at the end of a rope. (4)

The only response Meridian the preacher can offer is "No, you wouldn't." Beyond that, he does not deal with Lorenzo's outburst.

When the group learns that two white men have been found tinkering with the gas pipes under the home of a black family and begins a calling chain to warn other blacks, Lorenzo is almost sarcastic in his reference to the Bible, one of the primary Christian symbols: "Tell them to fall on their knees and use their Bibles as breast-plates! Because I know that each and every one of them got *Bibles*!" (34). Another student, Pete, recounts an occasion when the students were jailed and how futile it had been to call on God: "And Anna Mae Taylor was on her knees, she was trying to pray. She say 'Oh, Lord, Lord, Lord, come and help us,' and they kept beating on her and beating on her and I saw the blood coming down her neck and they put the prods to her" (90–91). The immediacy of beatings and blood makes calling on "the Lord" comparatively weak for these young students who are not accustomed to or experienced in the trials of faith. The question becomes whether or not it is possible to revitalize a symbol, to graft onto Christianity a true functionality in a world of white supremacy.

The ideas Baldwin explores in *Blues for Mister Charlie* in suggesting that Christianity has run its course are not unlike those he puts forth in *The Fire Next Time* (1963), in which he asserts: "It is not too much to say that whoever wishes to become a truly moral human being (and let us not ask whether or not this is possible; I think we must *believe* that it is possible) must first divorce himself from all the prohibitions, crimes, and hypocrisies of the Christian church. If the concept of God has any validity or any use, it can only be to make us larger, freer, and more loving. If God cannot do this, then it is time we got rid of Him."[9]

In the southern environment that Baldwin creates in *Blues for Mister Charlie,* Christian directives are ultimately ineffective in containing the immediacy of racial violence. Although Meridian is a minister who preaches, prays, and makes a heartfelt attempt to guide others along the Christian path, his questions about the efficacy of believing in a just God to deliver one from racial harm are no less acute than Richard's and Lorenzo's; the only difference is that he is not as vehement in putting them forth. He is also slower to voice his dissatisfaction, which is understandable, for, if one gets rid of Christianity, with what does one replace it? There is a fear of that void. Does one then lead one's people into a suicidal confrontation with the forces of white supremacy? Nonetheless, the cauldron of dissatisfaction smolders with Meridian; the furnace containing black acquiescence—or at least black refusal to retaliate violently—can explode at any given moment.

More important in the Christian scenario, believers can stop believing at any moment, or they can begin questioning why they have chosen the spiritual path that they attempt to follow. Meridian voices that questioning in a conversation with Parnell: "[W]ould I have *been* such a Christian if I hadn't been born black? Maybe I *had* to become a Christian in order to have any dignity at all. Since I wasn't a man in men's eyes, then I could be a man in the eyes of God. But that didn't protect my wife. She's dead, too soon, and we don't really know how. That didn't protect my son—he's dead, we know how too well. That hasn't changed this town—this town, where you couldn't find a white Christian at high noon on Sunday! The eyes of God—maybe those eyes are blind—I never let myself think of that before" (38).

It is noteworthy that Meridian speaks with Parnell about his lessening faith, rather than with his mother, members of his church, or the young people under his guidance. This gives readers and audience members more insight into the decision that Meridian seems to move toward at the end of the play. It also, however, paradoxically keeps his minister/leader role in place with the black characters in the play. Parnell provides an outlet for Meridian to sound off, to hear his tentative changes of belief voiced aloud, and to see them challenged by someone who is less vested in his ultimate decision than the others would be.

Although they profess to be Christian, both Mother Henry and Meridian turn from the ways of the righteous during the course of the play. Mother Henry swears, under oath, that Richard did not have a gun, although he had shown her the sawed-off pistol he had brought from New York. That blatant lie is a long way from the "thou shall not bear false witness" directive that is a cornerstone, or should be, of her professed belief in Christianity. Certainly, we can argue that she is clinging to a sense of racial loyalty by not giving the white lawyer what he wants, or that family matters more to her. After all, what difference does it make in the investigation of her grandson's murder whether or not he owned a gun, especially since he was the one gunned down when he was unarmed? The higher morality, however, demands truthfulness, which Mother Henry is not able to deliver. That inability, even under the sworn oath of testimony, points to the impending failure of Christianity for most of the characters in the play.

Meridian begins to move closer toward embracing the smoldering fire when his hopes in a heavenly intervention through earthly forces finally fail. He had been hopeful that Parnell, the good white liberal, could bring about some productive result in response to Richard's death. He had perhaps even hoped that the legal system might, just might, dispense a bit of justice. When all these hopes come to naught, Meridian's conversion to militancy is perhaps just as powerful as his conversion to Christianity had been. During the trial, Meridian is able to speak publicly about the reservations he has about Christianity. It is the opportunity for him to embrace Richard's rejection of Christianity by expressing his own doubts about professing Christians. When Lyle's attorney asks if Meridian has raised Richard "according to the precepts of the Christian church," he avows: "I tried. But both my son and I had profound reservations concerning the behavior of Christians. He wondered why they treated black people as they do. And I was unable to give him—a satisfactory answer" (101).

Meridian identifies even further with Richard by swearing that Richard never carried a weapon, though Richard has given the pistol to him for safekeeping. When Lyle finally admits, in front of Meridian, Parnell, and several others at the end of the play, that he did indeed shoot Richard, Meridian's comments are quietly reflective: "You know, for us, it all began with the Bible and the gun. Maybe it will end with the Bible and the gun" (120). When Parnell seeks verification that Meridian has the gun, he responds: "Yes. In the pulpit. Under the Bible. Like the pilgrims of old" (120).

As with the scotch and soda that Sonny's older brother offers him in Baldwin's "Sonny's Blues," there has been much speculation about the precise direction of the presumed militancy implied by Meridian's comments, which are his final words in the play. Given the failure of the legal system, however, and given the wavering of Meridian's own beliefs, it is safe to assume that a purely Christian perspective will not guide his actions from this point forward. The extent of that militancy is left to the imaginations of viewers and readers. What is important here is that Christianity with a capital "C" has failed. Meridian is no longer afraid of its failure. He recognizes it, accepts it, and is willing to move forward.

Ultimately, however, the fear that surrounds Baldwin's characters is the fear of the loss or denial of manhood—how it affects the individual man and how the man views it as affecting those around him. This means that, in the final analysis, *Blues for Mister Charlie* is a male text with female window dressing. The narrative is really about the relationships and/or conflicts between Richard and Lyle, Lyle and Meridian Henry, Parnell and Meridian Henry, and Lyle and Parnell—with a few other male/male encounters thrown in for good measure. The social system and all its problems are the backdrop against which these men work through their notions of how to be men in a world that already has that designation laid out for some of them, such as Lyle and Parnell, or that denies that designation to others, such as Meridian Henry, Richard, Papa D., and Old Bill. The lines between black and white are drawn around notions of manhood.

Males in the text measure manhood in terms of relationships (primarily sexual ones) and domination. Lyle determines that Old Bill is not sexually useful to Willa Mae, so he decides to show what a man can do by becoming her lover. Parnell is not man enough to ask Juanita to become romantically— or even sexually—involved with him; neither is Meridian nor the wimpy Pete, the student who obviously loves Juanita. Parnell claims that he "loved" Pearl, but he was not man enough to act on that claim. Lyle cannot back away from Richard's presumed insult to Jo because of his notion of what a man should be and do in the South. Similarly, Richard is too proud to back down from a sense of what he as a black male ought to be able to do anywhere, even in the South.

Richard initially falls into the trap of defining manhood by hypersexuality, but it eventually becomes a conflict with Lyle in which it is important for Richard to break out of the cage of confinement to which the white South consigns him. Home from New York, an interrupted musician and a recovering drug addict, there is very little that Richard can show to his relatives in the South. Unlike the pattern of success that many black migrants to the North seek to present to their so-called backward southern relatives, such as returning south with expensive clothes and driving expensive cars, Richard has only his diminished self. In an effort to gain some status in the black community to which he has returned, he resorts to telling stories about the white women with whom he has had sex in New York and to showing their pictures to his friends in the South.

A disturbed young man, Richard resorts to braggadocio to make up for his lacks—lack of status in his current community, lack of security about his manhood. Even as he brags about white women, he admits to Juanita that having sex with them had progressed from excitement to chore. He got into drugs because he couldn't "stand" the white women he "was making it with" as well as because his managers were giving him a hard time (29). Having accepted his body as the measure of manhood, and then having found that criterion inadequate, Richard becomes a psychological and physical mess. The stereotyped expectation of having sex with white women has backfired as the women readily accept him merely as a sex machine, a walking phallus. Realizing that sexual relationships do not make a man, and neither does art (music) or drugs, Richard is adrift in gender identity when he returns to the South. Hearing about Lyle having shot Old Bill and then meeting Lyle present a challenge for Richard to restore some sense of manhood. If he cannot find it in his body or his art, then perhaps he can find it by measuring himself against the most virulent white supremacist around.

In reading Richard, therefore, it is important not to waste sympathy. I mentioned earlier that Richard commits suicide (or at best he has a death wish). The sequence of events still supports that assertion. When Lyle enters Papa D.'s joint, there is no reason for Richard to engage him there or later. Indeed, Lyle even apologizes for having bumped into Juanita as Richard and Juanita are dancing ("Pardon me" and "I sure hope your stay'll be a pleasant one" when he finds out Richard is new to the area; 31).[10] Richard nonetheless sees Lyle as the site on which he can reclaim his manhood. If he can compete with Lyle, the recognized man with a capital "M," and cause that man to back off, then Richard will have reclaimed whatever it is that he lost in the beds of white women and under the influence of drugs in New York. When he enters the Britten store, he is strikingly rude to Jo. She points out the Coke box to him, and he asks: "Did you put them in this box with your own little dainty dish-pan hands? Sure makes them taste *sweet*" (72). Jo is obviously taken aback, but that does not stop Richard. He makes much of the fact that the Brittens do not have change for twenty dollars; in the process, he ties that lack to sexuality. "Stud ain't got *nothing*—you people been spoofing the public, man" (73). Jo urges Lyle not to fight Richard, to remember their baby, to which Richard offers this amazing sexual insult: "A baby, huh? How many times did you have to try for it, you no-good, ball-less peckerwood? I'm surprised you could even get it up—look at the way you sweating now" (74). It is only logical that a direct confrontation would ensue. Lyle comes after Richard with a hammer, only to end up sprawled on his own store floor. As Lorenzo dashes in to drag Richard away from the scene, Richard cannot contain his glee: "Look at the mighty peckerwood! On his *ass*, baby—and his woman watching! Now, who you think is the better man? Ha-ha! The master race! You let me in that tired white chick's drawers, she'll know who's the master! Ha-ha-ha!" (75).

The conflict between Lyle and Richard is thus one that Richard chooses and pursues. He violates Lyle's space, insults Lyle's wife, and tries to dominate Lyle and his family in the way that whites have historically dominated and violated blacks. Because this struggle is finally a conflict that Richard cannot win, the price he has paid for setting himself up amounts to a different kind of braggadocio, one in which he perhaps never expected the result would be so final. When he tries to back off from Lyle in their final confrontation, insisting that they both have "things to do" (119), it is much, much too late; Lyle shoots him. While readers and viewers cannot condone that shooting, there is a measure of understanding that Baldwin allows for, especially given Richard's incredibly antisocial behavior and totally unnecessary aggression.

For Lyle, whose manhood is secure through his legendary status, his recent marriage, and his fathering of a son, there is nothing to be gained by confronting Richard. At almost every step of Richard's goading of Lyle, Lyle is reluctant to respond. Even when Richard comes into Lyle's store, orders a Coke, and makes fun of the Brittens because they do not have change for a twenty-dollar bill, Lyle initially only suggests that Richard leave before he gets into trouble; the physical scuffle occurs after Richard's repeated verbal taunts and refusal to leave. It is in the aftermath of that encounter in the store, when Lyle realizes how badly his reputation has been tainted, that he decides not to let the matter go.[11] When he and Richard leave Papa D.'s together, Lyle asks for an apology that Richard refuses to give. In this standoff, neither will back down, so the result is death. Even as death is certain, however, Richard resorts to the sexual arena in continuing to insult Lyle. Certainly, Richard stands up to what he perceived as the big, bad white racist, but he loses his life in the process.

It is important to Lyle that there not be any black spots, literally and figuratively, on his white manhood. As a white man in the South, he believes that he cannot allow a challenge from Richard to go unmet. In this modern-day duel of sorts, the challengers know their roles, meet, and act out the prescripted resolution. Lyle clearly knows that script better than Richard, and he is better prepared to accept the outcome. Lyle has a precise understanding of why it was "necessary" for him to kill Richard: "I had to kill him then [after Richard professes his carnal knowledge of white women and tells Lyle to keep his "old lady home" because she might develop a preference for having sex with black men]. I'm a white man! Can't nobody talk that way to *me*!" (120). What Lyle means is that no black person, especially not a black male, can talk to him that way.

It is noteworthy in this context that Lyle also admits that he killed Old Bill, and a similar rationale holds sway. He tells Papa D. that he will not allow Old Bill—or any other black male—to challenge him: "I'll shoot any nigger talks to me like that. It was self defense, you hear me? He come in here and tried to kill me. You hear me? . . . That's right. You don't say the right thing, nigger, I'll blow your brains out, too" (87). This scene illustrates that Lyle can be ruthless, but there is no occasion in the play—before the final shooting scene—on which he is ruthless toward Richard. He does not need to taunt Richard or harp on declarations of his own manhood.

Lyle, unlike Richard, is secure in the knowledge of who he is. Richard's fatal flaw is that he is searching, and he unfortunately searches in a venue that is absolutely unsympathetic to him. Further, he has a seriously flawed perception of whatever it is for which he is searching. On the other hand, Lyle knows what it means to be a white man.[12] His domination in the sexual arena as well as in the social arena is key to that definition. He also dominates in the legal arena, for he understands well the system under which he lives. "They'll never convict me" (13), he asserts early in the play. He can confess before Meridian, Parnell, and the others after a jury finds him innocent of the crime, for his guilt has never been the issue. Retaining the system of white domination that the folk tradition captures so vividly with the tale of Sis Goose has been the only concern of the court and the jury as well as Lyle's only concern. It is thus Richard's youthfulness, or his stupidity, or his fanciful dreams of transformation that have led him to think otherwise. In his attempt to replace fear with challenge, Richard loses everything.

While Richard has complained about Meridian's response to Richard's mother's death, he similarly has no definite course of action. He is just as lost for expression of manhood as Meridian has been. He understands the position Meridian has been in in insisting that Richard go north after his mother's death. "You didn't want me to look at you and be ashamed of you," Richard observes to Meridian, "[a]nd you didn't know what was in my eyes, you couldn't stand it, I could tell from the way you looked at me sometimes" (35). In order for the father not to see his own lack of manhood reflected back to him in his son's eyes, Meridian had sent Richard to New York. Still, the path that Meridian must follow is perhaps more fearful than the one Richard chooses.

Meridian remains in the South, and by doing so he must have his lack of manhood reflected to him in a dozen ways almost every day. He is seen as a "good nigga," the preacher comparable to Gabriel Grimes during his southern days in *Go Tell It on the Mountain*. White people come to Meridian to find out what is happening with black folks, and they expect him to lead black folks in the "right path" of acquiescence to white supremacy. In other words, Meridian has for the longest time not disturbed the waters of race relations in his small town. Richard's death is a turning point for him, but how much he will turn is not revealed in the play. He does, however, offer his understanding of the difficulties of being a black man in a white southern environment. In response to a question from the State during the trial, he offers: "I am a man. A *man*! I tried to help my son become a man. But manhood is a dangerous pursuit, here. And that pursuit undid him because of *your* guns, *your* hoses, *your* dogs, *your* judges, *your* law-makers, *your* folly, *your* pride, *your* cruelty, *your* cowardice, *your* money, *your* chain gangs, and *your* churches! Did you think it would endure forever? that we would pay for *your* ease forever?" (103). Strong words indeed, but the impact they will have is beyond what Baldwin depicts in the drama, perhaps because he had no realistic resolution for how black manhood could be represented on southern soil. From Meridian's comments, however, that manhood is almost purely reactive (black men can only be black men if white men let them), which is problematic in and of itself.

Fear of the destruction of the black male body and fear of the denigration of black manhood guide Baldwin's creative genius. Always at the center of those concerns is black male sexuality, which black men sometimes embrace to their destruction and which white men almost invariably see as problematic and challenging. When the history of race relations in the South is added to this psycho-sexual-physical realm, destructive consequences inevitably result on southern soil. To let Baldwin tell it, blacks and whites in the South do little except act out their primal conceptions of and stereotypes about each other.

Baldwin entitles his play *Blues for Mister Charlie,* but the title raises questions about its appropriateness and perhaps indicates yet another arena in which Baldwin exhibits discomfort with the South. Implicit in the title is a failure of representation, for there can be no blues, in the sense of an existential condition, for Mister Charlie (that is, white people generally). Although Parnell keeps trying to present Lyle as a troubled, misguided man who suffers as much as he dishes out suffering, the assertion is not persuasive. It is not the cultural prerogative of the white man to be soothed by the blues, and it is not the province of African American blues singers to try to comfort white people by offering them the essence of the blues. The blues offer catharsis by virtue of singing, which amounts to a release for the troubled singer, as Langston Hughes depicts so ably in "The Weary Blues."[13] There is no release in *Blues for Mister Charlie.*

Of course we could interpret the idea of "blues for Mister Charlie" as black folks determining to give Mister Charlie the blues, that is, to create difficult and untenable situations for the white man. Baldwin develops that idea in "Going to Meet the Man," where his embattled black demonstrators nonetheless garner the strength to keep on keeping on, to give "the Man" the hardest time they can possibly give him. In order for Baldwin's black characters to give the whites in *Blues for Mister Charlie* the blues, however, there must be some tangible measurement of their impact upon the whites. If we measure that, then it can be determined only in Parnell's decision, late though it is, to march with the blacks at the end of the play. That seems minimal, though, in the grand scheme of possibly bringing about change in this small southern town.

There is also the slight possibility that Lyle Britten has been given the blues in being pressured into admitting that he killed Richard as well as in his recognition that he can no longer count on Parnell as a friend who will always take his side of things. And if the narrative could be projected a few weeks into the future, it is likely that Lyle will feel the blues directly in the absence of income that will result from blacks boycotting his store.

Even with these possibilities, however, the title has more ring than substance to it. This is decidedly not a judgment on the impact of the play, for that impact is powerful. How the title directs possible reaction to the play is the issue. Blues, traditionally, are not conceived as a militant genre; they are conceived as a coping genre. Yet Baldwin seeks to graft militancy onto the genre if the more activist interpretation of the title is the one we accept.

If Baldwin were merely to accept the blues in terms of their coping strategies, he could perhaps see other possibilities for the lives of his black characters. While it is undoubtedly the case that many black people suffered and died on southern soil, it is equally clear that the majority of them did not. They lived and carried on in spite of the cultured hell of that repressive environment. Their lives were not to be pitied. They found time for creativity, as Zora Neale Hurston asserts, without thinking of repression twenty-four hours a day. In other words, they did not focus constantly upon white people and injustice, and they did not merely *react* constantly to white people.

Baldwin, however, is unable to think of the South without conflict between blacks and whites. In all of his essay commentary about the South, that conflict, especially with sexual overtones, is central.[14] For Baldwin racism defines the South; all actions of blacks and whites grow out of that basic assumption. Perhaps, in his inability to see beyond this context, Baldwin reflects some of the sentiments toward the South that Countee Cullen reflects toward Africa in his poem "Heritage."[15] It is mostly the book-learned or word-of-mouth mythology that guides Baldwin's perception of character. While that book learning might have some grains of truth, it does not provide the whole story. Perhaps, as with the Elvis character in Alice Walker's "Nineteen Fifty-Five,"[16] Baldwin kept returning to the South in his imaginative works in order to find something beyond the book learning, something that would reveal the essence of a part of the country to which he was consistently drawn but equally consistently without thorough understanding, something that would inspire him to see the South as beyond what Richard sees: "down here in the ass-hole of the world, the deep, black, funky South" (17).[17]

From another perspective, the South for Baldwin is sort of like homosexuality is for Rufus in *Another Country*. It is a "blacker blackness" in which one must immerse oneself in order to reach some enlightenment about the self as well as about the state in which one is immersed. That immersion can lead to a cleansing, as in washing one's hands of the situation, or to an embracing, in which case one arrives at some deeper understanding about the condition one is exploring. Whether Baldwin arrived at some deeper understanding about the South remains questionable. Even in his last works about the South, it remains a chimera, a jack-o-lantern looming in the distance, a warning sign for the dangers of psychological annihilation and physical destruction.

Although Baldwin made several trips to the South for civil rights work and for interviews during the disappearances of the black children in Atlanta, he was never quite able to reconcile himself to or sever ties with the territory that captured so much of his imagination. Nor was he ever able to escape the tremendous fear that accosted him every time he ventured south, which he documented in several of his essays. His inability to sever ties with the South is comparable to that of many black writers. In a bonding with black writers bred and born on southern territory, Baldwin, like other nonsouthern black writers, pays his dues, so to speak, to the periodic southern domination of his imagination. It is a domination that Southerner Ernest J. Gaines wears easily, though his male characters suffer through defining manhood as acutely as do those of Baldwin.

FEAR OF MANHOOD IN THE WAKE OF SYSTEMIC RACISM IN ERNEST J. GAINES'S "THREE MEN"

While Northerner James Baldwin imagines southern white male violence to black men, Ernest J. Gaines knows the environment intimately and lived under repressive Jim Crow strictures in Louisiana until, at age fifteen, he moved to California. However, he never left the South that shaped his literary depictions or the southern black men who are the substance of those depictions.[1] African American males confront systemic racism in almost all of Gaines's novels and short stories. They operate in the limited physical and psychological spaces that generations of white repression have assigned to them. Unlike Richard Henry, rarely, if ever, do they attempt to buck the system. One such instance of rebellion is *A Gathering of Old Men* (1983), Gaines's novel about a group of elderly black men who decide that it is time for them to speak out, to take a stand against the oppression that has shaped their lives. Mainly, though, Gaines's male characters contain the anger that causes Richard to explode; they hold their tongues, restrain their bodies, and endure the degradation that befalls them. Even in *A Lesson Before Dying* (1993), arguably Gaines's most popular novel (it supplanted *The Autobiography of Miss Jane Pittman* [1971]), the educated and disgruntled Grant Wiggins cannot muster enough self-confidence to challenge the white sheriff who treats him as if he were barely human. Certainly, Grant restrains himself in order to help Jefferson, the young black man falsely accused of murder, but the posture Grant adopts still harks back to early twentieth-century interactions between blacks and whites in which blacks invariably held the disadvantaged positions.

For most black people in the small-town South of the early and mid-twentieth century, safety lay in not distinguishing themselves from the quiet and acquiescent masses of blacks. To claim individuality, as Richard does in Baldwin's play, meant risking the possibility of imprisonment and/or physical harm. It was an action that brought fear to the hearts of relatives as well as to the heart of the one who dared to stand out. Codes of actions and interactions, as Richard Wright points out in "The Ethics of Living Jim Crow" as well as in "Big Boy Leaves Home," were well known by both races. Safe spaces and actions were delineated as clearly as safe patterns of interactions across racial lines. Such interactions meant that blacks and whites knew each other well enough to role-play in the drama to which both races adhered, as Richard and Lyle do. Those interactions might be a combination of stereotypes and truth, but reality dictated that they be adhered to nonetheless.

The scripted dramas that defined black and white interactions in the South were based in racial history, solidified by custom, and constantly reiterated in everyday occurrences. The glue that held the patterns together was the threat of physical and psychological violence. Gaines's major character in "Three Men" (1968) finds himself a pawn in a present situation where violence has been instituted by patterns in the past. For nineteen-year-old Procter Lewis, who turns himself in for killing another black man with a broken bottle, his encounter with the white policemen T. J. and Paul creates a scene that carries with it the burdens of race, violence, and history. Tension apparent in the scene derives from T. J.'s reputation as the ultimate racist cop and Procter's reputation as a violent black man who believes he can get away with antisocial behavior as long as he directs it toward other black people. The oppressively hot office that Procter enters at four o'clock in the morning mirrors the heat of racial interaction. How he engages the two white men makes role playing and racial history apparent.

As readers become aware later, there is a dramatic contrast between the Procter who has stabbed a black man with a broken bottle and the Procter who presents himself so acquiescently before T. J. and Paul. In the opening scene in the story, Procter casts himself as an image that lives in the imaginations of southern whites. His role playing is reminiscent of that usually assigned to trickster figures on the one hand and to Uncle Tom on the other. In the Uncle Tom portion of his disguise, Procter presents himself as physically deferential and practically nonverbal, which is a dramatic contrast to the swaggering Richard, who will not abide by the codes of cross-racial interaction even if he knows them. Procter is the instrument upon which he allows the whites to play instead of trying to create his own tune. He presents himself as a black man who is willing to follow their lead, play whatever role they think he ought to play. He does not speak unless he is spoken to, does not move unless he is told, casts his head and eyes toward the floor, and acts in all ways as if he were infinitely inferior to T. J. and Paul. His initial observations in the narrative indicate the role he is willing to play: "Two of them was sitting in the office when I came in there. One was sitting in a chair behind the desk, the other one was sitting on the end of the desk. They looked at me, but when they saw I was just a nigger they went back to talking like I wasn't even there. They talked like that two or three more minutes before the one behind the desk looked at me again. That was T. J. I didn't know who the other one was."[2] Self-referencing himself as a "nigger" shows the Uncle Tom infiltration of Procter's mind. He labels himself through the eyes of the whites, and he stands silently until T. J. asks, "Yeah, what you want?" (121). It is only then that Procter states that he has come to turn himself in for fighting "with somebody." He moves forward as T. J. orders him to "[c]ome in here" and tries as best he can to accommodate T. J.'s directives. He is especially careful not to let the little gate separating him from T. J. and Paul swing shut too loudly when he moves into the inner space of the office.

Guilty of the same tenets of white supremacy as Lyle Britten, T. J. requires a part of the tightrope walking to which many blacks, particularly young black men, in the deep South were subjected. T. J. orders Procter to show papers, and Procter takes out his wallet, but he knows that he "wasn't supposed to get any papers out" himself. Instead, he is to hand the wallet over to T. J., who "jerked it out" of Procter's hand. Procter is ordered to speak and then not to speak, with an ever-present threat hanging over his head. T. J. asserts that if Paul cannot make "that boy shut up," then he will. The interaction is designed to keep Procter on edge, to insult him without allowing him the option of responding, and to provide T. J. with the satisfaction of knowing that he is in charge. The reference to "boy" brings history into the present, as it does with Lyle referencing Richard; Procter is made to understand that, though he might have exhibited some standard of manliness in the fight with the black, large, and fearsome Bayou, he is still nothing but a "boy" to T. J. By forcing Procter to get "a swimming in the head" in the hot office and to feel "weak and shaky" (124), T. J. triumphs over him in the physical as well as the mental realm.

In this mixture of race and history, however, there is also the element of the trickster in what Procter has done by turning himself in. As a black male who has committed a crime, he is expected to run. When he does not, he circumvents at least a portion of T. J.'s perception of him; T. J. looks at Procter as if he were "crazy." When Procter fails to use "sir" as fervently as T. J. and Paul expect him to during the interrogation, he similarly pushes the limits of the patterns of interactions to which they are all expected to adhere:

> "A fist fight," Paul said. "Pretty good with your fists, ain't you?"
>
> "I protect myself," I said.
>
> It was quiet in there for a second or two. I knowed why; I hadn't answered the right way.
>
> "You protect yourself, what?" T. J. said.
>
> "I protect myself, *sir*," I said. . . .
>
> "You'll be sorry you didn't use your fists this time," T. J. said. "Take everything out your pockets."
>
> I did what he said.
>
> "Where's your knife?" he asked.
>
> "I never car' a knife," I said.
>
> "You never car' a knife, what, boy?" T. J. said.
>
> "I never car a knife, *sir*," I said.
>
> He looked at me hard again. He didn't think I was crazy for turning myself in, he thought I was a smart aleck. I could tell from his big, fat, red face he wanted to hit me with his fist. (123; my ellipses)

Procter's editorializing about T. J.'s responses to him also supports the observation about the trickster tactics he employs. He is mask and wearer, the Uncle Tom and the self-aware trickster, for the trickster registers his true responses to the situation as well as his resistance to the very role he has elected to play out for the white men. When T. J. asks, "What you think we ought to do with niggers like you?" and Procter is slow to respond, T. J. continues: "I'll tell you. . . . See, if I was gov'nor, I'd run every damned one of you off in that river out there. Man, woman and child" (125). Masking enables Procter to control his response: "I was quiet, looking at him. But I made sure

I didn't show in my face what I was thinking. I could've been killed for what I was thinking then" (125). Control of facial expression and self-censorship are crucial parts of role playing and mask wearing, and though Procter may buy into the stereotypical role at points, he can still separate himself from it occasionally.

Paul separates himself a bit from history and stereotype as he escorts Procter to the jail cell he will share with Munford, a repeat black male offender, and Hattie, a homosexual jailed for having public sex. Paul gives Procter "a pack of cigarettes and some matches," reminds him to say "thanks" and "sir," and warns him not to push T. J. too far, because "[i]t doesn't take much to get him started—don't push him" (126). Equally aware of history and problematic racial relationships in his world, Paul makes a small effort at mediation. He, however, is no less susceptible to what the volatile T. J. might order than Procter is to be the recipient of that order. With these sentiments as well, it becomes apparent that Paul has been masking during Procter's initial encounter with T. J. However, just as history and custom will not allow Procter to be anything but masked and layered, it will similarly not allow Paul to deny his white heritage, just as no white character in *Blues for Mister Charlie* can refuse to side with Lyle, even the so-called liberal Parnell, thus Paul's "liberalism," like Parnell's, is more useless than not. As long as Paul is a white police officer in the deep South, he is expected to carry out certain attitudes and actions toward black prisoners. If he does not, then he runs the risk of becoming a race traitor, an outcast status he is obviously not prepared to endure.

Once he is in the jail cell, the extent of the mask Procter has been wearing becomes clearer. He has time to reflect upon the scene in which he fought Bayou, a scene in which it is apparent that black and white notions of manhood and the arenas in which they get acted out are strikingly different. Procter and his friend Grinning Boy had gone to the Seven Spots juke joint where the fight occurred with the express intention of having a good time, of strutting in the peacock fashion that their notions of black manhood warrant. In this scenario, Procter is a virile young man who is willing to make himself available sexually to any desirable young black woman. He is active and aggressive, a far cry from the cringing Uncle Tom who presents himself before T. J. and Paul. When he sees an attractive young woman dancing with the man escorting her, he convinces himself that she really desires him. Her red dress, "two big dimples," and the way she "rolled her big ass real slow and easy" are all like red flags to the bull of Procter's testosterone. Although Grinning Boy cautions Procter with "poison, poison—nothing but poison" (128), Procter is in no mood to hear. "And I was looking down at them two big pretty brown things poking that dress way out. They looked so soft and warm and waiting, I wanted to touch them right there in front of that ugly nigger" (129).[3]

Procter gives the eyes that he must control in front of T. J. and Paul full freedom in this setting. So is he free in movement. Instead of waiting to be commanded to act, Procter approaches the woman, Clara Johnson, for a dance, which she refuses in front of her escort. Undaunted, Procter moves to the kitchen the minute Clara leaves her escort to seek refreshment and proceeds with the confidence of the well-practiced seducer.

> There was people talking out there, but I didn't care, I had to touch her.
>
> "What's your name?" I said.
>
> "Clara."
>
> "Let's go somewhere, Clara."
>
> "I can't. I'm with somebody," she said.
>
> "That nigger?" I said. "You call him somebody."
>
> She just looked at me with that little smile on her face—them two big dimples in her jaws. I looked little farther down, and I could see how them two warm, brown things was waiting for somebody to tear that dress open so they could get free.
>
> "You must be the prettiest woman in the world," I said.
>
> "You like me?"
>
> "Lord, yes."
>
> "I want you to like me," she said.
>
> "Then what's keeping us from going?" I said. "Hell away with that nigger."
>
> "My name is Clara Johnson," she said. "It's in the book. Call me tomorrow after four." (129–30)

Procter has no concern that the woman is with another man; he acts with the supreme confidence—and recklessness—that she will indeed give in to his charms. Like Richard, he measures manhood almost exclusively through his body. While Clara does respond to Procter, the scene is far less romantic than stereotypically scripted.

In this setting, black manhood, as Procter practices it, equates to sexuality that includes a healthy portion of verbal seduction. The nearly inarticulate Procter before the white men becomes the silver-tongued Procter at the

Seven Spots juke joint. Procter acts out his double life in a way that is usually nonthreatening, that is, by seducing a woman. However, his lack of restraint places him in a position that is almost as untenable as the one in which he places himself with T. J. and Paul, for Bayou, Clara's escort, barges out the kitchen door and into the scene just after Clara consents to see Procter. The sexual stereotypes inherent in Procter's presenting himself only as a stud and seeing Clara only as a sex object lead directly to the stereotype of black males violently dispatching each other in shady juke joints on Saturday nights.

Although Procter tells us that he tries to resist the battle, he has nonetheless provoked it by his actions. His disrespect for the woman as well as for her escort puts him in a position from which the onlookers will not allow him to escape: "You fight or you fly, nigger," someone says when Procter asserts that he does not want to fight; "If you run, we go'n catch you" (130). Bayou knocks Procter into the crowd, and they throw him back into the fray. The huge Bayou, who slugs away without speaking, joins Procter in living out the stereotype of the violent black man on Saturday night. Ruthless, unhearing of any explanation for someone talking to "his" girl, Bayou rushes headlong into violence. "But trying to talk to Bayou," Procter asserts, "was like trying to talk to a mule" (130), which anticipates the animal imagery that dominates conversation in the jail cell later. Bayou pulls a knife even as Procter keeps trying to tell him that he was only talking with Clara. Procter breaks a bottle for self-defense as he keeps telling Bayou, "Let's stop it" (131). And the inevitable happens: "He slashed at me, and I jumped back. He slashed at me again, and I jumped back again. Then he acted like a fool and ran on me, and all I did was stick the bottle out. I felt it go in his clothes and in his stomach and I felt the hot, sticky blood on my hand and I saw his face all twisted and sweaty. I felt his hands brush against mine when he throwed both of his hands up to his stomach. I started running" (131).

Stereotypes of violence here also extend to the crowd that is insistent upon the fight occurring and continuing. They toss Procter back into the fray with Bayou when Bayou knocks him down, and they chase him when he runs away. The unrelieved frustrations so typical of black people crowded into ghetto situations can be applied in this context. African American males who cringe before whites act out their "manhood" by perpetrating violence against other black men as well as women. All the anger in Bayou and the crowd, therefore, could probably be dissipated by the mere presence of a T. J. or Paul. The fact that Gaines allows such stereotypes to infect his narrative may be due to his attempt to portray as accurately as possible the social lives of Louisiana blacks who spent the majority of their time working on the plantations under conditions comparable to those he portrays in *A Gathering of Old Men*. The release, unfortunately, comes out in a false bravado that masks fear, the fear of trying to live as equals with whites in the deep South.

The fear of claiming manhood in any way but the stereotypical also defines Munford, who shares the cell with Procter. As he himself is aware, Munford is the epitome of the stereotype of the violent black man who takes out his frustrations on other blacks instead of directing aggressive energy toward whites, who are his true oppressors. Munford, who is about sixty, has been in and out of jail as long as he remembers. He has settled into a pattern of fighting on Saturday nights, ending up in jail, and being released on Monday mornings. He knows all the white judges, attorneys, and policemen in the area, and they know him; they often deride him about when they will see him again. Like Trueblood in Ralph Ellison's *Invisible Man*, Munford lives out a script that exists in the heads of whites about blacks, in this case that he is always drinking, cussing, and cutting. As long as he acts out his script of animalistic inferiority, he is a model example to illustrate white superiority. Just as Trueblood acts out sexual depravity that whites use to highlight white purity, so too does Munford serve as a negative example. According to the script that Munford perpetuates, it is not whites who are violent, but blacks. It is not whites who use knives and guns against their fellows at the slightest provocation, but blacks. It is not whites who end up in jail every weekend, but blacks.

Munford understands clearly the role he plays in this scenario, but his understanding has come at a late date, and he has not been able to step off the stage of presumed racial and interracial interactions. He knows that by having directed his violent actions toward other blacks, he will never receive the kind of punishment that will curtail such actions. At his core, he understands that a black man who hurts or kills other black men is really providing a service for those whites who believe blacks should continue to be at the bottom rungs of the society. "Can't stay out of here to save my soul," he tells Procter. "Been going in and out of these jails here, I don't know how long. . . . Forty, fifty years. Started out just like you—kilt a boy just like you did last night. Kilt him and got off—got off scot-free" (137). Having broken the law and been "forgiven" because a white man spoke up for him, Munford breaks it again and again. As long as he directs his violent actions toward other blacks, and as long as there is a white man to speak up for him, to claim him as his "nigger," he does not recognize any moral or communal boundaries that would inspire him to transform his behavior. By the time he truly realizes the cog he has been in the wheel of racism, it is too late.

> I kept on getting in trouble, and they kept getting me off. Didn't wake up till I got to be nearly old as I'm is now. Then I realized they kept getting me off because they needed a Munford Bazille. They need me to prove they human—just like they need that thing over there [Hattie]. They need us. Because without us, they don't know what they is—they don't know what they is out there. With us around, they can see us and they know what they ain't. They ain't us. Do you see? Do you see how they think? (137–38)

In his role as elder—even though a compromised one—Munford makes a lot of sense about how black men should try to live in this society, and he tries to give Procter advice that will prevent him from turning into another Munford.[4] He admits that he is caught in a repetitive pattern from which he is no longer able to extricate himself. Procter meets Munford's advice about staying put and not letting Roger Medlow, the owner of the plantation where his uncle works and where Procter lives, get him out of jail, with: "You got out" (138). Munford's reply is clear evidence of his inability to change, of the monster that history and racism have created out of him: "Yeah," he said, "and I'm still coming back here and I'm still getting out. Next Saturday I'm go'n hit another nigger in the head, and Saturday night they go'n bring me here, and Monday they go'n let me out again. And Saturday after that I'm go'n hit me another nigger in the head—'cause I'll hit a nigger in the head quick as I'll look at one" (138–39). Munford's volatile nature has been clear from the morning after Procter's arrival in the cell. Munford asks for a cigarette, and from Procter's perspective, "the way he said it, it sounded like he would've took it if I didn't give it to him" (135).

As a willing participant in the societal pathology that defines him and the other blacks with whom he fights every Saturday night, Munford is perhaps the last person from whom Procter should take advice. Nonetheless, he makes some good points. He tries to explain that the white males who have placed Procter in the cell are not men because they can subjugate the likes of Munford and Hattie, who are in turn not men. His point about how the society makes it nearly impossible for black males to become men echoes the sentiments of James Baldwin. One way to avoid that potential stripping,

Munford asserts, is for black males to claim themselves by standards other than the ones whites control, to step outside definitions superimposed upon them. Procter can do that by refusing Medlow's prospective offer of freedom and doing his time in the penitentiary for killing Bayou. That way, Procter can claim manhood by accepting responsibility for his action. Munford tells him: "You go, saying, 'Go fuck yourself, Roger Medlow, I want to be a man, and by God I will be a man. For once in my life I will be a man'" (141).[5]

Even as Munford explores, shifts, adopts, rejects, and retraces definitions of manhood and how it can be drained from black males, it is clear that, in some way, he considers himself a man. Inherent in his definition of himself as a man are stereotypes about black male sexuality. In addition to considering himself a man because he can best everybody else physically on Saturday night, he also names himself a man because he is not like Hattie, the gay black man in the cell. He believes that Hattie has been emasculated at birth, a fate from which he himself has been exempt. There is a conspiracy, he asserts in a narrative he relates, in which newborn black males are emasculated by the preachers who christen them. Munford faults preachers with sucking the manhood, through their penises, out of young black males. The narrative he relates locates the source of manhood in the very sexuality that has brought Procter to where he is in the cell. A man who chases women like a dog is preferable to Hattie, although Munford essentially contradicts a point he made earlier when he claimed that manhood did not depend upon how well a man could perform sexually. However, since sexual preference divides him from Hattie, he knows that he is a man because he does not prefer other men (although he teasingly [?] propositions Hattie). His and Procter's references to Hattie align Hattie with females, who, as far as Munford and Procter are concerned, are always to be subjugated.

In a narrative conspicuously titled "Three Men," it is engaging to note how Gaines positions Hattie, the homosexual black male. Is he also a *man*? Or does the title have other references? Although Procter allows Munford long stretches of commentary and philosophizing within his own narrative, Hattie's direct comments are kept to a minimum, and they are mostly insulting. Procter and Munford position Hattie as a disreputable black male, one who has dared to align himself with the actions of females. They thereby repeat the dominance of the society in which they themselves are caught by dominating Hattie. As far as they are concerned, he has no rights. Munford initially controls Hattie's movements, and Procter later controls them. As soon as Hattie speaks to Procter when he arrives in the cell, Munford yells out, "Get your ass back over there, Hattie. . . . Don't see how come they didn't put him with the rest of them whores" (127). Later, when Hattie is comforting the young black boy who has been beaten and recently brought to the cell, Procter orders: "'Get up from there and go to your own bunk,' I said to Hattie" (152).

Munford and Procter feel no remorse about yelling at or insulting Hattie, limiting his participation in their conversations, and slapping him around any time they want. Their disagreements and the age gap between them dissipate in the face of Hattie's homosexuality. Just as whites of all classes united to pursue and lynch black people, so Munford and Procter come together to persecute the gay Hattie. His positioning in the story raises questions about manhood as well as about the growth that both Procter and Munford profess to have experienced. Hattie becomes a scapegoat for their own masculine inadequacies.

Linguistically, Hattie is associated with "freaks" and females throughout the text. And since Procter relates the narrative, his uncensored evaluations of and attitudes toward Hattie are clear. Procter initially looks at "the freak laying on the other bunk": "[T]he freak stopped smiling, but he still looked sad—like a sad woman" (133). Procter repeats the "freak" description of Hattie three times within the next several paragraphs and several more times during the course of the narrative. When Munford propositions Hattie, and he rejects him, Procter observes: "'My God, man,' Hattie said. He said it the way a young girl would've said it if you had asked her to pull down her drawers. He even opened his eyes wide the same way a young girl would've done it" (139). When Munford reiterates his proposition later, Procter comments: "Hattie looked up at him just like a woman looks at a man she can't stand"(141), and "Hattie rolled his eyes at Munford the way a woman rolls her eyes at a man she can't stand" (142). Hattie's voice is "high-pitched . . . like a woman" (143). Once an officer releases Munford, Procter is clear that he "didn't want have nothing to do with that freak" (145). He does not resist, however, when Hattie asks for a cigarette and gets it when Procter does not respond: "His fingers went down in my pocket just like a woman's fingers go in your pocket" (146). Procter's boiling point with Hattie comes, however, when the young boy is brought to the cell and Hattie comforts him: "'Shhh now, shhh now.' Hattie was saying. It was just like a woman saying it. It made me sick a' the stomach. 'Shhh now, shhh now,' he kept on saying. . . . I hated what Hattie was doing much as I hated what the law had done. . . . He started rocking the boy in his arms the way a woman rocks a child" (149, 150, 151). After tolerating the scene through the hour-long decision-making process where he decides he will indeed go to prison, Procter throws Hattie across the cell away from the boy and takes over the role of comforting him.

In that space of "the freak" is what Procter and Munford both fear—the possibility that they may not be the men they have claimed to be.[6] Labeling Hattie a freak not only erases his humanity but also separates him from any definition of manhood. Freaks, at least the way Procter thinks, can never be considered men. The label is thus a way to dismiss Hattie from the tenuous brotherhood that Munford and Procter are forming as well as to dismiss him from any male kinship. They reduce Hattie to outcast, barely shy of "thing." Placing him so allows Procter and Munford naming power over him and gives them steps on the ladder to their own problematic claims to manhood. If they can humiliate and prop themselves up by denigrating Hattie, then they can fit into the same pattern that T. J. fits into by denigrating blacks and that Ellison's upright citizens fall into by denigrating Trueblood. It is a shaky superiority at best. Also, to add to that shakiness, it is uncertain if Munford's propositioning of Hattie might not have had fruition in a different setting.[7]

Putting others down to stay on top is a recurring pattern in the story, and the black males are as guilty of it as are the white males. Both Procter and Munford are afraid that the tar brush of homosexuality will paint them, so they hide their fears by asserting a more forceful brand of manhood than is apparent in Hattie's actions. Procter is as repulsed by Hattie as T. J. is by him. Procter could just as easily gather up all homosexuals and toss them into the same river, with the governor's permission, into which T. J. wants to toss blacks. The pattern of domination is the same even if the stakes are different. So are the methods of control; both Procter and Munford threaten Hattie physically, just as T. J. threatens Procter. The force that Procter uses against Hattie is the same kind of violence that he anticipates T. J. and the other policemen will use against him once he states his intention to go to prison, to become a "smart aleck," instead of bailing out of jail as T. J. expects him to.

Lest sympathy turn too unqualifiedly in Hattie's direction, however, let me note that he is decidedly not a saint. Whereas Procter and Munford are capable of physical violence, Hattie is comfortable in the realm of verbal insult. He highlights the comparisons to animals that pervade the narrative. By viewing his fellow black males as more animalistic than not, Hattie reverts to some of the same stereotypes that whites apply to blacks for the Saturday night behavior of black males such as Munford. He refers to Munford as a "jungle beast" (128). While Munford is certainly not a likable character and while he certainly insults Hattie, the fact that Hattie retaliates in kind adds to the slippery slope of manhood that adheres throughout the story. Just as Procter and Munford attempt to reduce Hattie to the category of "thing," so Hattie is similarly intent upon reducing them to nonhuman status. The fact that reader sympathy may be with one side or the other is not the issue; the point is that all the characters resort to the same tactics, which make them equal in their attempts to degrade each other.

Once Hattie introduces the animal and jungle images, he draws upon them several times in the narrative. His mouth, therefore, is just as danger-ous as Procter and Munford's fists in damaging black males. He later refers to Munford as "just an animal out the black jungle" (139). Intensifying "jun-gle" with "black" in reference to Munford illustrates yet again how far all three of the men in the cell are from respecting each other and themselves, for blackness is at the source of all their problems; making it animalistic only suggests the extent to which their minds have been controlled by external forces. Indeed, Hattie uses comparable animal imagery to describe what the white policemen have done in beating the young boy: "The bunch of ani-mals. Not one of them is a man. A bunch of pigs—dogs—philistines" (150). When Procter grabs his shirt and throws him across the cell and away from the boy, Hattie's imagery collapses in responding to white and black males. "'Philistine,' he said, 'Dog—brute'" (152); these references place Procter and the boy's tormenters into the same category. For Hattie, male roughness is animalistic, no matter the color in which it comes. The politics of language, however, makes the conclusion far more damaging to the black males. Hat-tie's references show that Hattie selects homosexuality over race just as Procter and Munford's references suggest that they select notions of man-hood over homosexuality and race. Hattie may be victimized, but he is also capable of victimizing. Any attempt to excuse him from the cycle of insult ultimately fails.

In this climate of fear, accusation, denial, and general ugliness, it is inter-esting to contemplate the possible growth of characters in the process. Mun-ford understands how the society has shaped him and how he has acquiesced in that shaping. He enters and leaves the cell in the same state of mind. What he has said about manhood and saving the self might have implications for Procter, but they have none for him. Hattie holds far less of the spotlight than

Procter and Munford, and there is little indication that he is in any way dissatisfied with his life; thus, there is no need for him to contemplate change. As the first-person narrator and the character who has gotten himself into such a predicament, Procter is the site where potential change can occur. Just before he takes over Hattie's role of tending to the wounded boy, he is convinced that he will go to prison and serve his time. A close reading of his position prior to this decision suggests that the position he takes, as he realizes, is one shaped by words, not by the trial of violence.

Initially, Procter has killed a man, even if he did so in self-defense.[8] Nowhere does he show remorse for his deed. And not only does he not show remorse, but he is not willing to grant to Bayou the very humanity and manhood that he wants so desperately for himself. Jail gives him time to reflect, and it is always possible that reflection could lead to transformation. With Procter, however, reflection reveals that jail brings mere inconvenience, not transformation. His attitudes toward Clara, Bayou, Marie (his regular girlfriend), other women he has dated, his parents, and Hattie all indicate that he is in many ways like Munford—a perpetual adolescent who envisions but can never truly approach the status of man.

Procter consistently views women as things, as objects to satisfy his lust or to provide a service for him. For example, his mother should have lived and taken care of him instead of dying and leaving him to fall into the situation he is in now. He values Clara for nothing more than her breasts, dimples, and hips. Her body captures Procter's imagination, and it is the stimulus to which he feels he must respond. He expects that, because he is so eager to have her sexually, she should feel the same way. He feels no sense of loyalty to Marie, his regular girlfriend, and he has little respect for women in general. If readers can respect Procter for anything, it is for his honesty in naming his own lapses, especially in his reflection upon Marie and the possibility that she will not help him in his current situation. "Hell, why should she stick her neck out for me. I was treating her like a dog, anyhow. I'm sorry, baby; I'm sorry. No, I'm not sorry; I'd do the same thing tomorrow if I was out of here. Maybe I'm a' animal already. I don't care who she is, I'd do it with her and don't give a damn. Hell, let me stop whining; I ain't no goddamn animal. I'm a man, and I got to act and think like a man" (144). Words and actions remain contrasting issues in Procter's assessment of his life. He has treated Marie "like a dog," yet he claims manhood, a manhood again that is rooted in the sexual. Women only mean climaxes for him, and there is no indication that he has a change of heart from this point to the end of the story several pages later. Procter even views prison in terms of the lack it would cause in his ability to have sex. "I couldn't make it in the pen. Locked up—caged. Walking round all day with shackles on my legs. No woman, no pussy—I'd die in there. I'd die in a year" (144).

His benediction on Marie comes in his reflection upon love and whether or not he has ever loved anyone. Again, the honesty creeps in in spite of Procter:

> I never messed with a woman I didn't love. I always loved all these women I ever messed with. . . . No, I didn't love them. Because I didn't love her [Clara] last night—I just wanted to fuck her. And I don't think I ever loved Marie, either. Marie just had the best pussy in the world. She had the best—still got the best. . . . Maybe I ain't never loved nobody. Maybe I ain't never loved nobody since my mama died. Because I loved her, I know I loved her. But the rest—no, I never loved the rest. They don't let you love them. Some kind of way they keep you from loving them . . . (148–49; ellipses in original)

Eschewing responsibility in relationships just as he eschewed responsibility in the fight with Bayou, Procter changes without changing, admits his faults without moving to the higher level of moral introspection that such changes might warrant.

Lack of transformation and remorse are also apparent in Procter's attitude toward Bayou. He blames Bayou completely for placing him in the situation in which he finds himself. In the process of doing so, Procter violates one of the staunchest taboos in African American culture: he curses the dead. Surrounding that curse is more meditation on the nature of manhood:

> That black sonofabitch—that coward. I hope he didn't have religion. I hope his ass burn in hell till eternity.
>
> Look how life can change on you—just look. Yesterday this time I was poontanging like a dog. Today—that black sonofabitch—behind these bars maybe for the rest of my life. And look at me, look at me. Strong. A man. A damn good man. A hard dick—a pile of muscles. But look at me—locked in here like a caged animal. . . . That black sonofabitch—I swear to God. Big as he was, he had to go for a knife. I hope he rot in hell. I hope he burn—goddamn it—till eternity come and go. . . . Five years [the usual sentence for killing a black man] for a rotten, no good sonofabitch who didn't have no business being born in the first place. (144, 145)[9]

There is apparently no discrepancy in Procter's mind between acting like a dog, which he does voluntarily, and being caged like an animal, which he blames on the powers that be. Nor is there any recognition of his own involvement in instigating the fight; he is merely the innocent upon whom malignant forces have acted. Locating his manhood in his penis, muscles, and sexual prowess, he moves no further toward growth in these reflections than he does at any other place in the text.

A scene near the end of the text might presage some growth for Procter, but it is surrounded by his ugly treatment of Hattie. That scene is the one in which he washes the beaten back of the young boy, washes the boy's shirt, and takes over the nurturing role that Hattie has been performing. While supporting the young boy might be worthy of applause, arriving at that state over the bruised body of Hattie is ultimately unacceptable. The text would have us conclude that, in the hour before Procter tosses Hattie across the room, he has come to the decision to remain in the cell and accept the beatings he knows will surely come. That moment of potential growth—standing up as a man—is undercut by Procter's resorting to the same methods of violence against Hattie that the policemen will probably use against him.[10] In a world in which violence and threat of violence are the norm, Procter has shown no desire to move away from it. He even forces the boy to smoke a cigarette in a perverted ritual of initiation into manhood. The boy has never smoked before and chokes on the smoke, but Procter forces him to continue smoking. If he can steal, Procter maintains, then he can smoke. Forcing an initiation and using physical violence against Hattie continue to place Procter in the realm of the perpetual adolescent whose true growth into manhood is short-circuited primarily because there is little clear definition of what manhood is in the text.[11]

While Procter has been insulted and repulsed when Hattie comforted the young boy, he takes over and defines nurturing in masculine, gruff terms. Hattie has merely rocked the boy; Procter orders him to take off his shirt and hold still while he washes his back. He also orders him to smoke the cigarette. With Procter and the young boy as with Hattie and the young boy, a male is attending a male. And although readers can conclude that Procter is also tending to the boy "like a woman," the difference is in the stereotypical aura with which Procter overcasts his actions versus the aura in which he casts Hattie's actions. If men can nurture, what difference does it make that one is homosexual and one is not? For Procter, it makes all the difference.

Whereas Hattie merely held the boy, Procter must enlist him in the decision he has made. He asks the boy to pray for him every time he hears Procter being beaten when the policemen take him away. Sexual prejudices are clear even here, for Procter further instructs: "And I don't want you praying like a woman, I want you to pray like a man" (153). The imagined scene anticipates the conclusion of *A Lesson Before Dying,* in which Grant Wiggins has his students on their knees praying as Jefferson is being executed. It is noteworthy, however, that Jefferson is innocent of the murder for which he is sentenced to death.

Procter is intent upon establishing with the boy a rough-and-ready masculine community from which Hattie is excluded, even though that community might contain elements of a softer side of masculinity, such as nurturing and praying. The fact that Hattie is excluded from the scene undercuts its potency in terms of transformation and accepting responsibility, for just as Procter never accepts responsibility for killing Bayou, he never accepts responsibility for mistreating Hattie. Of course we can argue that Procter's decision to allow the policemen to beat him is indeed accepting responsibility. However, his reasons for remaining in jail and undergoing beatings are not immediately connected to Bayou. It is the boy who prompts Procter's decision.[12] When the boy is brought into the cell, other black inmates are absolutely quiet. Procter joins Hattie in dehumanizing other blacks when he comments: "Like a bunch of roaches, like a bunch of mices, they had crawled in they holes and pulled the cover over they head" (151). He avows: "I didn't want have to pull cover over my head every time a white man did something to a black boy—I wanted to stand" (152).[13] Perhaps his desire, revolutionary in this instance, is genuine, but it is still forged in an arena outside the immediate one that has led to his incarceration. It is also noteworthy that Procter's attack on Hattie comes immediately after this so-called revelation.

The ability to stand has long been touted as a central trait of Gaines's characters. They do not aspire to earth-shattering changes or to bringing about community-wide revolution; instead, their heroism rests in their ability to make small but excruciatingly difficult decisions. Grant Wiggins, for example, goes forward with teaching Jefferson how to be a man in spite of the humiliation that he must undergo every time he enters the jail where Jefferson is housed. The old men in *A Gathering of Old Men* agree to stand their ground, literally, in the face of possible death when a white man in their community is killed. And it is the least likely suspect, a groveling, acquiescent black man, who is pushed to the limit and takes the stand to kill that white man. Procter joins their number in taking the stand to face T. J. and his fellow officers. Unlike what happens to the others, however, Procter's stand remains untested at the end of the narrative.[14]

That unchallenged open-endedness reinforces the flaw in Procter's decision as well as in his personality. Whether or not he is a man is still floating somewhere just beyond his reach. Yet Gaines entitles his story "Three Men." The title invites speculation about the three men to whom it refers. There are three possible clusters that could carry the weight of the title. The first is the scene in which Procter enters the police station. He, T. J., and Paul could be the three men of the title. Interpreted this way, the title serves as blatant contradiction to T. J.'s implicit assertion that he and Paul are the only men in the room and that Procter is a "boy." In this instance, the title thus equalizes males across race and culture.

A second possibility for the title's reference, and the one most often accepted, is the configuration of Procter, Munford, and Hattie in the jail cell. Again, a blatant contradiction holds sway. If the three in the cell are indeed "men," then the attitudes that Munford and Procter take toward Hattie are undercut. If the title refers to Hattie as a man, then he shares equal status with Procter and Munford. Their attempts to dissociate from him are therefore useless, which means that the title locates manhood in gender, not in sexual preference. The third possibility for the title's reference also comes with contradictions. The last three males in the cell are Procter, Hattie, and the beaten boy. If these are the three men, then Hattie makes the cut in spite of his homosexuality, and the boy makes the cut in spite of his youth. Perhaps Procter is eager to "grow" another man by forcing the boy to smoke so that he can counteract the beleaguerment he feels with Hattie.[15]

Problematic definitions of manhood also arise in considering how the characters view black people as a whole. This is especially the case with T. J., Procter, and Munford. All of them categorize the masses of blacks as things. "Nigger" is the operative word for that designation. For T. J., it serves to illustrate how he joins hands with his ancestors in the denigration of blacks; if blacks are things, "niggers," comparable to "freaks," and therefore lesser in the society, then T. J. can define his manhood, as Munford points out, by being "not them." He can thus easily advocate their elimination from the society. "Niggers" therefore help him to understand how he thinks of himself as a man.

Procter begins the narrative by referring to himself as a "nigger," and he does not evolve from that essential place for the remainder of the narrative. If he is a "nigger" whom T. J. and Paul can ignore for two or three minutes, then he is accepting—or seemingly so—the inferior status to which they have assigned him. The seeming part of this equation gets compromised, however, when later—without the intimidating presence of T. J. and Paul—he also refers to himself as a "nigger" who would not garner concern from anyone who could help him get out of jail. He refers to the "niggers' cell block" (125) and the "nigger trustee" (133), asserts that he is not an "Uncle Tom-ing nigger" (144) like his uncle, and derides Bayou many times as the "nigger" who has caused all his problems. Placing himself in and out of the category of "niggers," accepting that status and rejecting it, Procter consistently recognizes that blacks are expendable, close to things, and ultimately not even worthy of his consideration, let alone the consideration of someone like T. J. Procter is in part a man because he is not an "Uncle Tom-ing nigger" and in part a man because he has bested "that nigger" who had the audacity to pull a knife on him. Either way, there is total devaluing of black life and a healthy amount of self-hatred attendant to Procter's easy use of the word, a lack of introspection that makes his progression toward manhood all the more problematic. Like Richard Henry, Procter seems to have internalized a portion of the hatred that whites direct toward him.

Self-hatred is also the case with Munford. He is a man, he thinks, because he beats and cuts other "niggers," and he, like Procter, is as prejudiced against them as are the whites. Also, he values them no more than whites do. When he learns that Procter has killed another black man, his response is, "You killed another old nigger. . . . A nigger ain't nobody" (136) and later, "[A] nigger ain't worth a good gray mule. Don't mention a white mule: fifty niggers ain't worth a good white mule" (141). Munford clearly acts out this belief in his aggressions against other black men and, in the process, devalues black life in the same way that T. J. devalues it in declaring that all the local blacks should be tossed in the river. If claims to manhood are based on violence that maims or destroys those who look like one's self, then where is the health and sanity in that process?

Given these complications, perhaps there are no men in the text, at least no complete or whole men, which would mean that the title is ironic in any context. Consider a roll call of the characters in the text. T. J., who apparently has the most brute power in the story, locates manhood in intimidation and the potential threat of violence. Procter has encountered the legal system enough and seen T. J.'s handiwork enough to know the character: "He was a mean, evil sonofabitch. He was big and red and he didn't waste time kicking your ass if you gave him the wrong answers. You had to weigh every word he said to you. Sometimes you answered, other times you kept your mouth shut" (122). Even Paul is unwilling to challenge T. J. and warns Procter not to do so. The potential to subjugate, however, cannot be equated to manhood. Both T. J. and Paul are implicitly afraid of what it would mean to operate in a different way in relation to blacks. The pattern they follow, therefore, is but a fraction of what any full-bodied definition of manhood entails.

Munford, as already pointed out, has sadly misguided views about what it means to be a man. Locating manhood almost completely in his body, he has no notion of what a nonaggressive definition of manhood looks like. Procter shifts from the physical to the emotional in his engagement with ideas of manhood, and it is not clear that he has a concrete and workable definition handy even by the end of the narrative. Hattie has opted out of traditional notions of black manhood, but he retains an empathetic trait—in spite of his insults—that is admirable. Also, in nurturing the boy, both Hattie and Procter take on "feminine" roles, a movement that dovetails with Hattie's conception of himself but one that distorts Procter's self-conception.

With all these questionable models of manhood, Gaines is perhaps suggesting that the southern racist environment he depicts is not a fertile ground for the growth and development of either black or white men. Such a position would align him yet again with James Baldwin, who posits in *Blues for Mister Charlie* and elsewhere that the South emasculates more than it does anything else. Black Richard Henry and white Lyle Britten are both caught in a cycle that makes it impossible for either to rise to a true definition of manhood; they can react to each other only from the limited superficiality of their maleness. For Procter Lewis, meditations upon manhood and manly actions do not erase the image readers have of him as an acquiescing Uncle Tom or the one they get later of the frightened male whose own identity is so fragile that he must beat a homosexual to show his masculine superiority. Procter is finally desperately trying to label himself a man in a world where mere mention of that word in the wrong context could get him killed. The uncertainty he shows at the end—"I'll just have to wait and see" (155)—mirrors the uncertainty he has exhibited throughout the text. Munford made the point earlier that everybody in this southern society, black and white, had a role to play in the "culture" that defined it, and part of Procter's role is to know where to draw the line that defines his notion of manhood from that of the major shapers of that culture. In this cultured hell of the South, Procter remains a cog in the wheel of racism, seldom certain as to whether he is boy, man, or potential homosexual. How black women see themselves in this cultured hell is a task that Octavia E. Butler and Sherley Anne Williams, both Californians, take up in their explorations of antebellum black/white relationships in their neo-slave (freedom) narratives of the 1970s and 1980s.

THE IRRESISTIBLE APPEAL OF SLAVERY

Fear of Losing the Self in Octavia E. Butler's *Kindred*

Juanita may be onstage in *Blues for Mister Charlie*, but that play is ultimately as male centered as is Gaines's "Three Men." Following the 1960s, women writers change that pattern with their female-centered creations. This is especially true in the novel form. Toni Morrison, Alice Walker, Toni Cade Bambara, and a host of others privilege female consciousness in works published in the 1970s and later. This general pattern is especially prominent in a subcategory of the novel form, that of the neo-slave (freedom) narrative, the majority of which black women writers have published.[1] By planting their female characters on southern soil—*antebellum* southern soil—these writers tunnel through the history of slavery to explore different possibilities for existence, resistance, and survival in the cultured hell of the South.

The neo-slave (freedom) narrative, by its very nature, is about desire. The recently labeled genre represents the desire on the part of twentieth-century African American writers to rewrite history or, given the problems inherent in that endeavor, to reenvision what might have been possible during slavery in the United States. Having intimate knowledge of the lack of agency of persons of African descent who were enslaved in America, writers imagine what alternative possibilities might have existed. Indeed, they perhaps hope to intersect with a portion of unwritten history, with some of the stories that did not get told about how black people lived during slavery. Their desire to believe that more black people resisted slavery than traditional histories tell us, that more escaped to the North, that more were literate, or that more exemplified impressive humanity and agency is the impetus behind their tunneling through the violent history of the South and attempting to find the glimpses that could have presaged a happier future for persons of African descent.

That desire is apparent in the works of many contemporary African American writers, including J. California Cooper in *Family* (1991), Charles Johnson in *Oxherding Tale* (1982) and *Middle Passage* (1990), Toni Morrison in *Beloved* (1987), Ishmael Reed in *Flight to Canada* (1976), Margaret Walker in *Jubilee* (1966), Sherley Anne Williams in *Dessa Rose* (1986), and, for my purposes here, Octavia E. Butler in *Kindred* (1979). How these novelists manage that desire is all about slavery and its consequences. We know that fast on the heels of slavery came a series of formal and informal social and legal systems that kept African Americans in subservient positions. Sharecropping, ostensibly a boon to white landowners and recently freed black folks who needed work, ended up being just as mentally, financially, socially, and emotionally restrictive as slavery had been. The detrimental effects were probably felt more dramatically because black folks knew they were supposed to be "free"; those effects lasted well into the mid-twentieth century, as Alice Walker demonstrates so well in *The Third Life of Grange Copeland* (1970). The peonage and convict lease systems served as additional measures of titular enslavement for black people. Black males reputed to be indigent in cities in the South were routinely rounded up, imprisoned, and then leased out in the late nineteenth and early twentieth centuries to white farmers in the areas where they were captured. That system inspired the literary imagination of playwright August Wilson in *Joe Turner's Come and Gone* (1988). Herald Loomis, the brooding character in search of his wife, was jailed and forced to work for seven years just because white Joe Turner, law officer and brother of the governor of Tennessee, had the power to enforce his will upon Loomis. Black Codes that evolved into Jim Crow also exhibited kinship to slavery in the physical restrictions they enforced, strictures that governed public transportation, housing, education, and a host of other arenas. Figurative manifestations of the remnants of American slavery, therefore, unquestionably governed the lives of many black people in the twentieth century. None, however, was *exactly* like slavery.

But . . . what if literal American slavery could intrude into the twentieth or twenty-first centuries? What if a young black woman in southern California in 1976 could be transported back to 1815 Maryland and actually experience life as an enslaved person? What if that person found herself totally without agency in whether or not the transport occurs? What if she discovers that her life is so tied to one of her white male ancestors that any time he experiences life-threatening circumstances, he can call her across time and space to save him? That is the situation in which twenty-six-year-old, recently married Edana (Dana) Franklin finds herself in *Kindred,* as California-born Butler joins other African American writers in paying obeisance to the South.[2] The southern domination of her literary imagination leads to an engaging tale in the speculative mode of science fiction and shows the workings of the neo-slave (freedom) narrative in a different mode.[3]

Kindred enables Butler to undo one of the components of the Great Migration, that is, that portion in which black people left the South for California (just as they left the South for midwestern cities such as Chicago and Detroit and eastern cities such as Philadelphia, New York, and Boston). By having Dana return to 1815 Maryland, Butler reverses time just as easily as she reverses freedom and all the accoutrements of twentieth-century living. Dana, married to white Kevin Franklin, who shares the profession of writing with her, is fairly complacent in her California lifestyle. Although she and Kevin have managed to find each other and find love against the backdrop of explicit familial and implied societal disapproval, they are nonetheless happy. There is no immediate ugliness of history that intrudes upon them, and California, with its traditional expansionist connotations, provides them a kind of safe haven against less-accepting states, of which Maryland would probably be one. Dana's life in California, then, is antithetical even in the twentieth century to what she may have experienced in Maryland. Imagine the intensified contrast between twentieth-century permissive California and nineteenth-century hyper-restrictive Maryland, and the clash that leads to good fiction is apparent. Dana, like her creator Butler, truly has to tunnel through the history and practices of slavery in order to survive the cultured hell of the South.

Going back to the past to save the future gives *Kindred* a *Terminator* effect. In three movies starring Arnold Schwarzenegger, first as villain and then as savior, the *Terminator* narratives show a rise of machines that men created that are now bent on destroying humankind. As these intelligent machines take over more and more of the planet, a lone man steps forth to counter their evil intent. His name is John Connor, and, in some futuristic time, he is slowly making progress against the machines. That is when the plot thickens. A terminator, the Schwarzenegger character, is sent back to the twentieth-century past to kill Sarah Connor before she can give birth to their archenemy, John Connor. It is mind-bending to contemplate the ins and outs of the thesis, but it makes for great cinema. It also makes for great literary fiction. The only way Dana can live in the twentieth century is to make sure that one of her key ancestors in the nineteenth century stays alive long enough to impregnate the woman who will become her great-something or other grandmother. While that white ancestor, Rufus Weylin, is obviously not aware of the reason he can call Dana from the twentieth century, his power nonetheless enables Dana's existence. That power is even more complicated by the fact that Rufus is the white plantation owner's son and that he must essentially rape the woman who becomes Dana's black ancestor.[4] This form of the neo-slave (freedom) narrative, therefore, imbues Dana with the agency and desire to save her own future, indeed her own existence.

For Dana, the shock of being snatched inexplicably out of the comfort of her twentieth-century life and plopped down on a plantation in Maryland comes with a series of fears. How can she anticipate when Rufus will call her? How can she get back home?—"The fear that had followed me from home flared now. What would happen to me if I didn't go back automatically this time? What if I was stranded here—wherever here was? I had no money, no idea how to get home" (20). What if she cannot rescue Rufus in time?— "Still, now I had a special reason for being glad I had been able to save him. After all . . . after all, what would have happened to me, to my mother's family, if I hadn't saved him?" (29).[5] Is there any preparation that she can undertake that will enable her to endure in the nineteenth-century South? How can she escape sale, whipping, or death in the slavery environment—*if* she can? Can she trust her mind and her body to behave in ways that normally enslaved black people would? After repeated calls to the South, and after an extended stay there, how can she prevent herself from being attracted to the life that snares so many plantation owners, especially when, as a reader for Rufus and later for his mother, she has a relatively "good" form of enslavement? Can her husband Kevin survive the taint of slavery for the five years he is accidentally stranded after he clings to Dana when she gets one of her calls from Rufus? Will Rufus or Alice, the woman Rufus will rape, betray Dana? How far will Dana go in betraying Alice? Is this a world where morality governs in any way? Can Dana become an executioner, even when that seems the only course open to her near the end of the novel? Can the past be kept out of the future, or is it, as Faulkner asserts, not even past?

The only sign to Dana that something weird is happening to her is when she feels faint and dizzy as she and Kevin are unpacking boxes in their new home. That faintness and dizziness will be future signals to her that she is about to be out of control of her own life, as similar symptoms will with Elizabeth "Lizzie" DuBose in Phyllis Alesia Perry's *Stigmata* (1998). Initially, the disorientation lands Dana in Maryland where a four- or five-year-old Rufus is about to drown. She, following an instinct similar to that of Grange Copeland in trying to save the drowning white woman in the pond in Central Park in *The Third Life of Grange Copeland*, immediately rescues Rufus. Her ingrained, instinctual response leads her to perform CPR on Rufus, which in turn earns her the enmity of Rufus's doting mother, who does not have a clue as to what this strange woman, who appears out of nowhere, is doing to her son. It also earns Dana a near–shotgun blast from Rufus's irascible father. That life-threatening second enables Dana to disappear and return to California. Just as Rufus can call Dana when he is threatened, so she can "free" herself and return to the twentieth century when, in turn, she feels her life is in danger.

Barely at Rufus's house long enough on her first trip to know where she is or what is going on, Dana quickly learns on her second trip that slavery is the reason Rufus refers to her as a "nigger" and that she is somewhere on the eastern shore of Maryland. The dynamics that will govern her life for the next several weeks have been firmly set in place. It is important to note that while only days may go by in twentieth-century California, time moves much more quickly in nineteenth-century Maryland. A few minutes or a day to Dana can be years for Rufus. Indeed, the second time Dana rescues him, he is nine or ten, then seventeen the next, and twenty-five the next; in California, only a matter of minutes, hours, or days go by. Dana is able to recognize Rufus on her second visit only by the striking red hair she observed on her first visit.

What Dana must most come to fear initially is herself. The product of postintegration, postsegregation, and generally post everything connected to restrictions on black movement in the United States, Dana has no models for how to respond physically or mentally to slavery. Historically, black people in the United States were well aware of the sense of place that governed their lives, place manifested physically in all their surroundings and mentally in the attitudes they knew they could or could not display in front of whites, as is crystal clear with Gaines's Procter Lewis. Mask wearing as a strategy of survival is not second nature to Dana, as it is with Procter and as it most assuredly was to many of her southern black ancestors. She is therefore set adrift in an alien though familiar territory; alienation controls the process by which she gets to Maryland and her lack of intimate knowledge with slavery, and familiarity controls her understanding of a system in which she did not participate but about which she has some knowledge. This betwixt-and-between state means that Dana must be adaptable and flexible; she must, in other words, improvise upon and use the strategies that enabled her ancestors to endure slavery, segregation, and general second-class citizenship in the United States.

Dana cannot, then, allow her mind and body to become her enemies in the alien and enslaving territory of the South; she must control them. Having no experience of the South even in the twentieth century, Dana is especially ill prepared to tackle it in the nineteenth century during slavery. As a product of the twentieth century, Dana's very mannerisms are her enemy. She has not lived a life in which she had to bow and scrape to white people, one in which she lowers her eyes as Procter does in order not to be accused of being impudent, or one in which she is not free to move as she wishes. While she may have instinctively saved Rufus from drowning, she is far removed from the instinctual behaviors that governed enslaved people. She may therefore *think* an action is appropriate or inappropriate, but if her body does not immediately convey that understanding, she can reap loads of trouble. Consider, for example, Dana's initial mistake in not referring to the child Rufus as "Master" (30) and not calling him "Mister" when she is speaking to other enslaved persons on the plantation (72). In both instances, her tongue could get her into trouble, either through Rufus telling his father on Dana or through one of the black people on the plantation telling on her, as Liza will do when Dana tries to escape. Dana realizes that she "didn't quite catch" herself in time to say "Mister Rufus," but this realization does not enable her to catch many of the mind/body slippages in the text, which means that she is constantly in danger, constantly walking a tightrope of doing something wrong in terms of speaking and acting.

That unrelieved pressure is apparent on numerous occasions, especially the ones on which Dana refers to Rufus with the affectionate nickname

"Rufe" (not noting when his father might appear), the occasion on which she talks back to the patroller (41) and engenders her violent return to the twentieth century, and the times when she stares (66, 214) or "glares" (212) at one of the whites. She attempts to correct her behavior as often as she can, but her body sometimes acts in opposition to her mind. For example, when Dana returns on the occasion when Rufus breaks his leg, and Rufus asks, "Mama, can I have some water?" (69), Dana is slow to realize that it is she, not Margaret Weylin, who is expected to respond to the request: "The woman turned to look at me as though I had offended her. 'Can't you hear? Get him some water!'" (70). It is only Dana's ignorance of where to go to get water that sends Margaret out of the room in a huff to get it herself. Consider as well when Weylin stares at Dana on her second visit, perhaps trying to remember if she is indeed the person he has seen at the river who saved Rufus from drowning or perhaps speculating on her "resemblance to Alice's mother," and Dana comments: "After a moment, I realized that Weylin was looking at me—staring hard at me. . . . At first, I stared back. Then I looked away, remembering that I was supposed to be a slave. Slaves lowered their eyes respectfully. To stare back was insolent. Or at least, that was what my books said" (66). Reliant upon twentieth-century book knowledge in a situation in which her life could be taken on a whim, Dana is in a precarious position that becomes increasingly clear to her. If she can maintain the vigilance that is second nature to Procter, then she may be safer than not. How well—or not— she is able to manipulate nineteenth- and twentieth-century knowledges of using mind, voice, and body keeps her in a constant state of uncertainty, aggravation, and fear.

The pressure not to speak or act foolishly is especially apparent during the occasion, after several trips to the plantation and several years during which the occupants have known her, on which she literally shouts at Tom Weylin, Rufus's father. On her fifth trip to rescue Rufus, Dana duels verbally with Weylin when she thanks him for writing to Kevin to inform him that she is back at the Weylin plantation, and Weylin responds:

> "I didn't do it for you."
> My temper flared suddenly. "I don't give a damn why you did it! I'm just telling you, one human being to another, that I'm grateful. Why can't you leave it at that!"
> The old man's face went pale. "You want a good whipping!" he said. "You must not have had one for a while. . . . Rufus always said you didn't know your place

any better than a wild animal," he muttered. "I always said you were just another crazy nigger." (200, 201)

Dana's overstepping her bounds with Weylin anticipates Dessa Rose's overstepping her bounds with Miss Rufel at Sutton Glen. Both reflect desire in the neo-slave (freedom) narrative: to give voice to the historically voiceless. While Dana fears Weylin, she is nonetheless too often incapable of containing herself sufficiently to ever get in his good graces—even if he did not dislike her so much. Her lack of containment, however, always carries with it the risk of violence. And she makes the mistake of assuming that Weylin could ever recognize a measure of humanity in her, which he obviously cannot, just as Adam Nehemiah cannot straightforwardly acknowledge Dessa Rose's humanity. By this time, also, it is worth noting that Weylin knows Dana has saved Rufus on several occasions, and he is less volatile than he was when she first appeared. That is perhaps the only reason Weylin does not invoke white power and punish this uppity "enslaved" woman. Nonetheless, Dana's own voice and movements continually work as dangerous adversaries to Dana on the Weylin plantation, and she is in constant fear of being punished with whipping or worse.

With these clashes of body and mind, Dana has to learn slavery: learn how to be invisible, learn how not to offend, learn how to erase herself even when she is standing before a white person, learn how to walk the very fine line of exhibiting agency in a world that grants her none. Learning these habits is compounded by the fact that Dana wears pants, which is a recurring sore spot with everyone she encounters; it makes even the other enslaved people feel sorry for her that her "master," Kevin, has not provided her with better clothing. Clothing, then, becomes as much an issue for erasure as some of the other things Dana must learn. Erasure in the behavioral arena could be served by the traditional African American defense mechanism of mask wearing, but it necessarily goes beyond that because Dana has no experience in adopting and wearing the mask. It is a strategy that she is schooled by experience to learn, for she must be constantly on guard, constantly aware that a moment out of character, so to speak, can have dire consequences for her. Dana must also learn more practical things, such as how to cook on an open fire (which she learns from Sarah and Carrie); indeed, she learns it well enough to take over an evening meal for Sarah when she must leave dinner preparations to attend at the birth of Carrie's first child (159).[6]

It is understandable that Dana fears being killed, whipped, owned, sold, or otherwise abused during slavery. Even before she knows she is in slave territory, the fear for her life is apparent when Weylin aims his shotgun at her immediately after she saves Rufus from drowning. Her innate response to having her life threatened enables her to transport back to the twentieth century, a pathway that she later discovers only through discussion with Kevin. Dana overcomes this fear in part because she recognizes it as her only link to her home in California. If her life is in danger, or if she can *believe* that her life is in danger, then she can go home. In fact, she finally uses that fear to transport home when she slits her wrists to leave the Weylin plantation.

Perhaps more dramatically poignant than the fear of death is the fear of punishment by whipping. Dana knows that fear of death will get her home. Unfortunately, she comes to understand quickly that whipping will not kill her, for many of the other blacks on the plantation have been whipped, have had their wounds attended, and have survived. Dana's fear of whipping, therefore, is informed by a revulsion to violence shaped by her twentieth-century pacifist notions as well as by the literal bodily pain that she has no precedence for even remotely thinking she can endure. Having not come from a world where violence to the individual body is an expected part of normal everyday activities, an expected and normal punishment for not behaving in certain ways, Dana and her tiny stature are little match for nineteenth-century standards of slavery.

When Dana experiences her first whipping on the Weylin plantation, she is being punished for teaching enslaved persons to read and write, as well as for stealing books from Weylin's library to use as source material. She is so shocked by this initial whipping that she does indeed believe it will kill her: "All I was really aware of was the pain. I thought Weylin meant to kill me. I thought I would die on the ground there with a mouth full of dirt and blood and a white man cursing and lecturing as he beat me. By then, I almost wanted to die. Anything to stop the pain" (107). The fear of death causes her to transport home. Her second whipping, however, comes after her recognition that others have been whipped and survived; therefore, she cannot use it to transport from her situation. The pain Dana undergoes on that first occasion shapes her response to the second. When Rufus fails to mail her letters to Kevin, and she is targeted for a whipping after running away and attempting to reach the North on her own, her fear is almost primal. "No!" she yells and tries to run away. In response to Rufus's suggestion that she "take" her whipping and act like she has "some sense," Dana recalls:

> What I acted like was a wild woman. If I'd had my knife, I would surely have killed someone. As it was, I managed to leave scratches and bruises on Rufus, his father, and Edwards [the overseer] who was called over to help. I was totally beyond reasoning. I had never in my life wanted so desperately to kill another human being.
>
> They took me to the barn and tied my hands and raised whatever they had tied them to high over my head. When I was barely able to touch the floor with my toes, Weylin ripped my clothes off and began to beat me.
>
> He beat me until I swung back and forth by my wrists, half-crazy with pain, unable to find my footing, unable to stand the pressure of hanging, unable to get away from the steady slashing blows . . .
>
> He beat me until I tried to make myself believe he was going to kill me. I said it aloud, screamed it, and the blows seemed to emphasize my words. He would kill me. Surely, he would kill me if I didn't get away, save myself, *go home!*
>
> It didn't work. This was only punishment, and I knew it. Nigel had borne it. Alice had borne worse. Both were alive and healthy. I wasn't going to die—though as the beating went on, I wanted to. Anything to stop the pain! But there was nothing. Weylin had ample time to finish whipping me. (176; ellipsis in original)

Dana thus must endure the fear that she cannot control. That endurance is as much mental as it is physical, for she must reconcile herself to the knowledge that she does not matter to Weylin and his kind except as a piece of property that they can punish at will. Her success as a writer, respected for her mind that created ideas and her body that produced them in the twentieth century, is of absolutely no consequence to nineteenth-century slaveholders, even if they could remotely imagine such creative possibilities in a black person.

Another fear that Dana confronts is how *not* to become one of the slaveholders. Her special skills transported from the twentieth century make her an item of curiosity on the Weylin plantation, and since Weylin does not technically own her, she is free to take on whatever tasks she wishes. Indeed, her situation again anticipates that of the enslaved persons at Sutton Glen in Williams's *Dessa Rose;* they experience more freedom than the usual plantation would allow. Dana, like Frederick Douglass and Harriet Jacobs, thus lives under a milder form of slavery—in spite of her beatings—than most enslaved persons. She has sufficient food, is free to make choices about where she works, and is basically left alone until she deliberately defies Weylin by reading, teaching, and running away. Both Dana and Kevin, then, have to be on guard against the ease of identification with a place and time that are much simpler, in many ways, than their lives in the twentieth century. More specifically, Dana has to be on guard against using her status to further enslave other black people.

This is noteworthy in connection with her relationship with her ancestor Alice, whose unfortunate fate it is to be the sex and love interest of Rufus. Dana must negotiate the difficult terrain of helping Rufus seduce Alice while simultaneously identifying with Alice's degraded situation in being the object of her master. The conflict between race and gender thus informs the majority of the interactions between the two women. Add enslavement into the mix, and the morality issue becomes especially complex. It is a fine line that Dana must walk in order to ensure her existence without being totally complicit with slavery and slaveholders.

The first blow to Alice, a free-born black, comes when she dares to marry Isaac Jackson, who is enslaved on the Weylin plantation. That marriage leads to Isaac and Rufus fighting over Rufus's first rape of Alice, which in turn calls Dana from the twentieth century because Isaac is clearly getting the best of Rufus in the fight and may indeed kill him. Dana gets Rufus to agree to a concocted story of robbery by white men in order to ensure that Isaac and Alice get sufficient time to escape. However, no escape is possible in this territory, and Alice is not only brought back, but she is *bought* by Rufus after the couple is captured; Isaac has his ears cropped and is sold "down the river" into harsher slavery in the deep South. Not only must Dana nurture Alice back to health after she is severely whipped, but she must then convince her to be responsive to Rufus's sexual advances. It is a task for which she is uniquely and problematically positioned.

Dana's knowledge of her position in this triangle, which is not fully known to Rufus and of which Alice knows nothing, forces her to acquiesce in Rufus's request. Dana knows that, in order for her family to exist, Rufus must father a daughter, Hagar, by Alice. Hagar is the ancestor whose recordings in the family Bible that has passed down to Dana have enabled Dana to know as much of her family history as she does. When Dana arrives on one trip to discover that Alice has had a son Joe, then two miscarriages, but no Hagar, she is devastated: "I almost cried when I heard that. No Hagar yet. I was so tired of this going back and forth; I wanted so much for it to be over. I couldn't even feel sorry for the friend who had fought for me and taken care of me when I was hurt. I was too busy feeling sorry for myself" (208). So Dana must save Rufus and give him what he wants as much as is allowable for her in the boxed-in corner into which history and family have painted her. The books from which Dana has acquired knowledge of how to behave before whites in terms of eye and body movements must surely have also provided her with information about the exploitation of black female bodies that was the norm during slavery. To support that norm is for Dana to fight against herself.

We can view Dana's toleration of Rufus's repeated rapes of Alice as Dana's essentially raping Alice herself, which Dana recognizes. While Alice is recovering from the attacks by the dogs during her attempted escape and the beating afterward, Dana remarks: "I had thought that eventually, he [Rufus] would just rape her again—and again. In fact, I was surprised that he hadn't already done it. I didn't realize that he was planning to involve me in that rape. He was, and he did" (162). Dana assists in placing Alice in a position from which she has no agency. When Rufus demands, "Help me, Dana" and Dana responds, "I can't," he reassures her: "You can! You and nobody else. Go to her. Send her to me. I'll have her whether you help or not. All I want you to do is fix it so I don't have to beat her. You're no friend of hers if you won't do that much!" (164). Dana thus takes away from Alice the very thing that Dana herself longs for during her enslavement and everything she values in the twentieth century, that is, the right to be self-determining. The higher calling to which Dana is responding, that is, ensuring the continuation of her family, fades into the background in this moment of slavery, when she has to watch an individual woman experience the individualized trauma enacted on her body as she submits to violation. Dana hears Alice's complaints, knows how much she despises Rufus every time he has sex with her, and still must keep her silence about what that means in terms of using Alice and denying any individual will she may have.

What is the difference, therefore, in this instance, between Dana and Rufus in their relationships to Alice's enslavement? Barring the higher calling, there is none. Dana preaches enslavement in this instance as fervently as Rufus and his father preach it all the time—even if her preachings are not verbalized. Just as Rufus advises Dana to sacrifice her body, to submit to her punishment after she has run away, so too is Dana effectively telling Alice to be a willing victim in her own enslavement. It is understandable that Dana does not retaliate when Alice accuses her of helping "white folks keep niggers down" (167) and of being a "white nigger" (235). From the perspective of supporting slavery in the case of Alice, Dana may very well fit that description. Transportation from the twentieth century, under the peculiar circumstances under which she has been transported, turns Dana into the very thing she fears and despises: a slaveholder.

The problem, however, is that Dana tries to wash her hands of the implications of her actions. Consider her conversation with Alice when she informs Alice that Rufus wants her that evening:

> "Dana?"
> I looked at her.
> "What am I going to do?"
> I hesitated, shook my head. "I can't advise you. It's your body."
> "Not mine." Her voice had dropped to a whisper. "Not mine, his. He paid for it, didn't he?"... "Do you want me to go to him?"
> "I can't tell you that. You have to decide."
> "Would you go to him?"
> I glanced at the floor. "We're in different situations. What I'd do doesn't matter."
> "Would you go to him?"
> "No." (167, 168)

Dana is a liar and a hypocrite during the course of the conversation. Of course she can, in her twentieth-century smugness, say "It's your body" when she knows, absolutely, that Alice's body does not belong to Alice. And Dana is simply lying when she asserts that she would not go to Rufus, for she knows that Alice must go to Rufus in order for Dana to achieve the objective for which she has been whisked from the twentieth century. The portions of herself that Dana tries to keep from being tainted by slavery and her desire not to have Kevin tainted by slavery are revealed as selective hypocrisy in the face of Alice, whose very existence is controlled by slavery. No matter our understanding of Dana's difficult dilemma, she is still a person of more agency than Alice in this situation, and she still plays an instrumental role in Alice's intensified enslavement. Having run once and been brought back more dead than alive, Alice does not have the strength to run away again—not quite yet anyway. "I'm going to him," she tells Dana, "He knew I would sooner or later.

But he don't know how I wish I had the nerve to just kill him!" (168). But she cannot—and Dana cannot allow that, at least not until Hagar is born.

Dana seemingly tries to thrust aside the import of any guilt she may have as a result of Alice's committing suicide. Once Hagar is born, Alice takes her son Joe and Hagar and tries to run away again. Dana, who has been working with Rufus's mother, Margaret, provides Alice with some of Margaret's laudanum to keep the baby quiet. Caught and returned to the plantation, Alice is told that her children have been sold, which leads her to hang herself. In reality, Rufus sent the children to his aunt in Baltimore as punishment to Alice. Dana is called back from the twentieth century because Rufus is contemplating suicide in response to Alice's death. Again, Dana blames Rufus for what has happened to Alice. "You killed her," she tells Rufus, "Just as though you had put that gun to her head and fired" (251). While there is no denying that Rufus is guilty, so too is Dana. In this scenario of enslavement and death, her hands are not clean. She has played her role in becoming a slaveholder, at least titularly, equal to Rufus.

While there is deliberateness in the sequence of events that leads to Dana's acquiescing in Alice's enslavement, Dana's presence inadvertently causes another of the black folks on the Weylin plantation considerable distress—and further enslavement. The comfort in the relationship between Dana and Rufus increases with her repeated visits, just as the tension increases. Rufus grows increasingly possessive of Dana, which makes his earlier comment that she "can't leave" him even more pertinent. Familiarity also seems to be leading toward Rufus developing a sexual interest in Dana.[7] When a black man on the plantation speaks to Dana at Christmas and smiles at her at Easter, Rufus notices and plots against it. Although Dana asks Carrie to warn the man, Sam James, not to speak to her again publicly, he ignores that warning to approach Dana about teaching his younger sister and brother to read and write. That is sufficient cause for Rufus to sell the man away from the Weylin plantation and to hit Dana when she dares to object. The encounter might have been "innocent—completely innocent," "but three days later, a trader led Sam away in chains" (238). When Dana pleads, "Please, Rufe. If you do this, you'll destroy what you mean to preserve. Please don't . . . " (239; ellipsis in original), Rufus hits her, which leads her to slit her wrists and return to the twentieth century.

Much more willing to admit her role, innocent though it may be, in what happened to Sam James, Dana has, more often than not, tried desperately not to be co-opted—and not to have Kevin co-opted—by slavery. She has been especially fearful that slavery will corrupt Kevin when he accompanies her on one of her trips to the past: "A place like this would endanger him in a way I didn't want to talk to him about. If he was stranded here for years, some part of this place would rub off on him. No large part, I knew. But if he survived here, it would be because he managed to tolerate the life here. He wouldn't have to take part in it, but he would have to keep quiet about it. Free speech and press hadn't done too well in the ante bellum South. Kevin wouldn't do too well either. The place, the time would either kill him outright or mark him somehow. I didn't like either possibility" (77–78).

What is noteworthy in this commentary is Dana's concern for Kevin. Implicit in her comment is the belief that she can somehow withstand slavery better than Kevin or that she will not be as poisoned by it as he could possibly be. Does that mean that she believes black people were stronger in their abilities to endure slavery? Does it mean that she is assuming a mammyish, protective role toward Kevin? Does she value Kevin more than she values herself?[8] While Dana can fear for Kevin, she is slow to recognize that she can be co-opted as well. The process is subtle and effective.

She and Kevin "became more a part of the household, familiar, accepted, accepting. That disturbed me too when I thought about it. How easily we seemed to acclimatize. Not that I wanted us to have trouble, but it seemed as though we should have had a harder time adjusting to this particular segment of history—adjusting to our places in the household of a slaveholder" (97). Not only do they adjust, but, in spite of Dana's asserting that they are "actors" (98), they start to get accustomed to the smells and sounds of slavery (98). Kevin even asserts that the place is not what he imagined slavery to be (100) and borders on outright acceptance of the lifestyle. While Dana remarks that she "never realized how easily people could be trained to accept slavery" (101), the truth of the statement is apparent with her. She becomes so acclimated that she begins to think of the Weylin plantation as home, especially since she and Kevin had been in their new apartment in Altadena, California, only a few days before she was first snatched. Upon one arrival in Maryland, she is "startled" to find herself saying, "wearily, 'Home at last'" (127).[9] Alice even complains that Dana has become overly acquiescent because of the whipping she received (220), which leads Dana to wonder: "Was I getting so used to being submissive?" (221).

Ultimately, the question is, How do good people manage to remain good in an utterly corrupt system, especially one in which they reap some benefits? How, in other words, can people of good intention not lose themselves in ugly situations and circumstances? Neither Dana nor Kevin manages it well. Kevin comments that it would be interesting to go west in the nineteenth century and see how the country developed. During the five years that he is stuck in Maryland and northern parts of the United States, he even develops a southern accent. For Dana, her propensity to forgive Rufus becomes increasingly troubling and, given her purpose, increasingly necessary. She even forgives him for not sending her letters to Kevin when she hears his reason for not having done so. He wanted to keep her in Maryland, and she understands: "However little sense it made, I cared. I must have. I kept forgiving him for things" (180). In a foreshadowing moment a few lines later, she asserts, "Somehow, I couldn't take from him the kind of abuse I took from others. If he ever raped me, it wasn't likely that either of us would survive" (180). When, after Alice's death, he does attempt to rape her, Dana gives in to the primal need to preserve herself. She becomes a killer. In spite of Dana's best intentions, in spite of her staying after Hagar is born to try to change Rufus, he, unlike Miss Rufel and her interactions with Dessa Rose, remains an unrepentant slaveholder.

Dana exhibits a kind of compartmentalized, functional morality in the actions that enable her to become an enslaver as well as a killer. Rufus was "like a younger brother" to her, she says; "Alice was like a sister. It was so hard to watch him hurting her—to know that he had to go on hurting her if my family was to exist at all" (180). She can allow herself to be complicit in slavery, but she can also stand back from that stance when it becomes a matter of saving her own body from violation by rape. We could also argue that Rufus is so monstrous by the time that Dana stabs him to death that her action should be applauded no matter what. Still, it is only when her own vagina is threatened that Dana kills Rufus. Hagar has been born for quite a while, and Dana could have devised a way to go home. Instead, she has remained on the plantation, teaching the children to read and write, encouraging Rufus to free as many enslaved people as possible. She goes on a mission of manumission, which, altruistic though it may be, places her in the position of becoming the evil that she has despised.

Throughout Dana's conversations with Kevin about whether or not she could actually kill Rufus, she has tried to make clear that there is a line that he can cross that will lead to that result: "I'm not property, Kevin. I'm not a horse or a sack of wheat. If I have to seem to be property, if I have to accept limits on my freedom for Rufus's sake, then he also has to accept limits—on his behavior toward me. He has to leave me enough control of my own life to make living look better to me than killing and dying" (246). Rufus ignores those limits in his attempt to rape Dana, and he pays for that overstepping of boundaries with his life. His attempt to substitute her sexually for Alice is that line to which Dana referred. The good person from the twentieth century therefore resorts to the same kind of methods of destruction that the slaveholder would—executing someone for behavior that goes beyond the normal bounds of cruelty. Dana kills Rufus as much in self-defense as to put an end to her time travels. He will no longer be able to call her from the twentieth century, and she can leave Maryland with the assurance that her family's future and her past are now safe.

Ultimately, Dana is more like Rufus than she might remotely have imagined. She withholds information from the enslaved, as he does. She manipulates Alice just as Rufus does. And she makes a decision on the basis of expediency when it is necessary to do that, just as Rufus sold black people when he deemed it was expedient to do so. When she says that Rufus is like a "younger brother" to her, that is perhaps truer than she realizes. At times they think alike, they plot alike, and they plan alike. What separates them finally is less morality than insult. If Dana were to allow Rufus to rape her, it would take away her individuality, for it is the image of Alice in her that attracts Rufus more so than Dana herself. To allow the rape would be doubling up on enslavement. Rufus manages to bring her back from the twentieth century physically, and she thinks that she has some bargaining power with him. To submit to the rape would be the mental component of the physical control of her body. It is the mind/body split that Frederick Douglass discusses during his enslavement; the body might be confined, but the mind can be free if the enslaved person frees himself or herself. Dana would truly be enslaved if Rufus violates the most intimate part of her body—her vagina through her mind giving its consent; there would be no secrets, no resistance left. So she ends his life and thereby the control he has over her. It is a selfish choice, for she realizes that enslaved people on the plantation will be sold and scattered, but it is a human choice.

It is significant that Dana's final transport to Maryland occurs on the Fourth of July. It presages her freedom, her final declaration of independence from a man who has controlled her life for months in California time but for many, many years in his own time (Dessa Rose's escape also occurs on the Fourth of July, another indication of the symbolic value that date has for many black writers who imagine freedom for the enslaved). To be free, however, is not to be rid of the past or of the consequences of having known Rufus. When Rufus lies dying, he grabs Dana's left arm as she is making the transition back to the twentieth century; that lands her inside her house with the arm stuck in a wall. She loses it from just above the elbow. That loss comes to symbolize the unforgettable nature of her experiences in Maryland. It also comes to symbolize the past living in the present. No matter that Dana has no police officers tracking her down for killing Rufus and no trial to go through; she still has this strikingly vivid reminder of (punishment for) what she and Kevin have experienced, the vivid indication that she will always be tied to Maryland and slavery of the early nineteenth century. Her previously complacent life in California is forever merged with a vibrant and violent history; both shape a future for her that will be dramatically different from her quiet life as a writer.

Dana's fears do not quite end with her return to the twentieth century, for the manner in which she returns lands her in the hospital and sends the police after Kevin. The novel opens in the present with Dana groggily trying to explain to the police that Kevin is not responsible for the loss of her arm—just as it effectively began the adventures in the past with the fear that Kevin would not believe the story she had to tell him when she returned from Maryland the first time. The severity of the injury causes the police to be skeptical, but there is nothing they can do in the face of her testimony to the contrary; it is a more intense version of her having allowed her cousin to think that Kevin had beaten her after one of Weylin's whippings. Once her arm has healed, Dana and Kevin go on a trip to Maryland, and she tries, through historical records, to determine what has happened to the people on the Weylin plantation as well as to the plantation itself. They encounter more questions than answers, but they resolve to move on with their lives.

As an interracial couple in southern California in 1976, Dana and Kevin have experienced rejection from Dana's uncle as well as from Kevin's sister, who he was sure would accept his black fiancée. That rejecting familial racial backdrop, against which the trips to Maryland stand out sharply in bas-relief, reseats race in a central position in Dana and Kevin's lives. Surely a part of Dana's fear of Kevin being in Maryland was that he might adopt some of the negative racial attitudes from white slaveholders. Their trips serve to remind them that race dominates the twentieth-century landscape in ways comparable to how it dominated the nineteenth-century landscape. Again, the past is not past, and love alone is not necessarily a buffer against racism. Dana's fears for Kevin are Butler's fears about the possibility of a world existing where race does not matter.

In order to limn the world where race definitely does matter, she, like James Baldwin and Ernest J. Gaines, located it in the South. The monstrosity that is slavery in *Kindred* reflects the fear of nonsouthern black writers displacing ugliness onto the territory that they almost subliminally align with the worst of violence and racism in American history. When Dana is "herded" (211) to work as a field hand after Tom Weylin dies and Rufus blames her for it, the overseer beats her for not knowing how to cut stalks properly and fast enough. She finally gives up and passes out face down in the dirt. She awakens believing that she has transported back to the twentieth century only to discover, upon hearing Rufus's voice, "I was still in hell" (213). The hell she is in, with its books on the one hand and its sales and beatings on the other, is indeed a representative of the cultured hell of the South that consistently claims the imaginations of African American writers. Though Butler may have cast hers in the "What if . . .?" mode of speculative fiction, the kinship to the reality of southern history and culture is sufficient to place her solidly in the tradition of those writers born outside the South who feel compelled to tunnel through the South in their writings. The South claims Butler just as effectively as the Weylin plantation claims Dana, and neither is able to resist the attraction.

OWNING THE SCRIPT, OWNING THE SELF

Transcendence of Fear in Sherley Anne Williams's
Dessa Rose

Sherley Anne Williams joins her fellow Californian Octavia E. Butler in expressing the desire that is inherent in the neo-slave (freedom) narrative, which means that she also mines the South for the precious ore of African American history. Daughter of migrant farm worker parents who picked cotton in a California manifestation of a southern activity, Williams earned a reputation for her poetry as well as her prose. Keenly attuned to the nuances of black folk speech and the tradition of the blues, she incorporates both into *Dessa Rose* (1986).[1] The narrative works to give agency to an enslaved black woman, one whose story came to Williams as a result of her reading about two significance occurrences during slavery. Indeed, Williams makes it clear in the short "Author's Note" that serves as a prelude to the novel that her intent in creating the narrative was solidly located in desire, a desire to correct, transform, and transcend. She asserts that the novel ". . . is based on two historical incidents. A pregnant black woman helped to lead an uprising on a coffle (a group of slaves chained together and herded, usually to market) in 1829 in Kentucky. Caught and convicted, she was sentenced to death; her hanging, however, was delayed until after the birth of her baby. In North Carolina in 1830, a white woman living on an isolated farm was reported to have given sanctuary to runaway slaves" (ix). "How sad," Williams then thought, "that these two women never met." Her revisionist impulse, the fulfillment of her desire, is the sequence of events she recounts in *Dessa Rose*, in which she imagines that meeting, an extended and thoroughly engaged encounter. Like Morrison's similarly historically based incident in *Beloved*, Williams uses the events in *Dessa Rose* as a point of entry into a world where women, presumed to be without agency, find ways to act to the benefit of their families and their friends, both within and across races. That agency illustrates how black female characters navigate hell even as, under these extreme circumstances of slavery, they ultimately attempt to escape from it.

The novel, briefly told, is about Dessa Rose, who, as a result of losing the love of her life to her master's whim, escapes with a group of fellow enslaved persons. The very pregnant Dessa is captured and made the object of a book project that a white author, Adam Nehemiah, is undertaking with the hope of ingratiating himself to wealthy white planters. He conducts interviews with Dessa while she is chained in a cellar owned by Hughes, the local sheriff and Dessa's new owner. Nehemiah presents Dessa as the epitome of a wild, ignorant, illiterate, smelly, nearly subhuman enslaved person. Three of the persons—Harker, Cully, and Nathan—with whom Dessa originally escaped succeed in rescuing her from the cellar. They find their way to Sutton Glen plantation, located in northern Alabama, where Dessa must contend with the white mistress, "Miss Rufel" (Ruth Elizabeth Carson Sutton), and what her largesse in allowing runaways to live on the plantation means in terms of reevaluating a life's worth of perceptions of white people. Dessa begins the novel in loss, suffers through the majority of it in indignity and humiliation, and finally finds the peace that westward movement promises.

Although Williams had two southern states identified with the incidents she recounts and thus two possible settings for her narrative, she nonetheless chose yet another southern state, Alabama, as the site on which to locate her story. That choice serves at least a couple of purposes. Initially, Alabama, as a deep South state, has a more formidable connotative connection to slavery than perhaps Kentucky or North Carolina. It is one of the states to which enslaved persons could have been sold away from the upper South; thus it has intense connotations of repression and lack of recognition of black humanity. Second, by setting her narrative in northern Alabama, Williams essentially denies the easy coastal route to possible escape from slavery. In a way, she strands her characters in a no-man's-land of slavery, placing them hundreds of miles inland and far away from any expectations of "enlightened" forms of repression. To discover white humanity in such a setting is thus more gratifying, and to have black persons escape from such an out-of-the-way place is equally gratifying. In other words, the mountains these characters have to climb in order to claim themselves make that claiming all the more valuable.

And the mountains are indeed high—and fearful. As an enslaved person, Dessa, like so many of her historical and literary counterparts, is always on the alert. She is alert to the possibility of separation from Kaine, the love of her life. She is afraid that he is too much into the habit, from the master's point of view, of believing that he is human and acting accordingly, whether he is playing his handmade banjo or working in the mistress's garden. When Dessa retaliates for her master's bashing in Kaine's head with a shovel, she fears for her own life; then—upon escaping—she fears being recaptured. She has to worry about being claimed by Nehemiah after she escapes from the cellar of the new master who buys her, and she is fearful of being caught when she, Miss Rufel, and several others execute their schemes in planning for escape.[2] Perhaps Dessa's greatest fear, however, is being slimed by Nehemiah, being dehumanized and having her story stolen and told in a voice and with an intention that is antithetical to her very being.

In the first long section of the novel, entitled "The Darky," Williams makes clear the rationale for the neo-slave (freedom) narrative. The segment is presented primarily through the third-person, limited point of view of Adam Nehemiah, with segments of the narrative being directly in his voice and a portion of it following Dessa's memories as well as her thoughts as Nehemiah is interacting with her. Nehemiah is a reluctant white "specialist" on "the Negro question," reluctant because he desires fervently to be a member of the planter class, not someone who ministers to them. His objectification of Dessa is in the vein of traditional historical presentation. Dessa is merely "the darky," "the wench," or a host of other names that ignore the flesh-and-blood human being chained before Nehemiah occupying herself by sharing portions of her story.[3] Nehemiah epitomizes all the bad history from which the complexity of African American lives has been erased, all the history that engendered a need for the development of the neo-slave (freedom) narrative.

As a perversion of his biblical namesake, Nehemiah wants to build walls around all black people, confine them to spaces, places, and designations that he determines. In the book of Nehemiah, the altruistic title character, identified as "cup bearer to the King," is distraught when he learns that the walls of

Jerusalem have been destroyed. He gets permission, which the king allows, to travel to Jerusalem to rebuild those walls. With the help of many tribes and thousands of workers, the task is completed in a mere fifty-two days, which is a great insult to the neighboring rulers. They had assumed that the task of rebuilding would be too great and that the Jews were truly defeated.[4] The parallels to *Dessa Rose* place Nehemiah in the role of building a wall of containment and black people, especially Dessa, in the position of creating fissures in that structure as much as possible, whether those fissures are in language or in actions, both of which are apparent with Dessa.

Initially, however, it seems as if Nehemiah has the upper hand. To Nehemiah, Dessa is barely human, let alone literate enough to answer intelligently the questions he puts to her about her role in the uprising on the coffle from which she escaped and has been recaptured. Nehemiah has the power of naming that whites used to degrade blacks, to attempt to make them less than human, and to seal their own so-called superiority by so doing. Comparisons that come naturally to Nehemiah when he thinks of and interacts with Dessa Rose make his animalistic and dehumanizing connotations clear. He refers to her as "a wildcat" (16) and uses words such as "rump" (13), "flanks" (13), and "whelped" (15) to describe her body and her impending motherhood. He refers to her squatting "poised on her haunches" (37) or sitting "back on her haunches" (41). He reduces the effect of Dessa's reputation as a "devil-woman" who had fought for freedom to that of "a wild and timorous animal finally brought to bay" (15). He laments that Dessa's new owner, who allows him to interview her, fails to understand in permitting Dessa to take a bath that results in illness that "darkies" are "subject to the same chills and sweats that overtake the veriest pack animal" (27). For all the uprisings he hears about that yield a loss of black life, Nehemiah counts the loss in monetary rather than human terms (14, 21). In another reference, he compares Dessa to a "cow" (31) that could fall asleep under almost any circumstances. When he tries to get her to talk, he comments at one point that her baby "seems to have dropped" and remarks that old wives' tales suggest that she will give birth soon; he then offers that he "knew no more about that sort of business than he knew about animal husbandry or the cultivation of cotton" (42). Dessa's singing reminds him of "the clucking of the hens or the lowing of the cattle" (48). The fact that Nehemiah professes not to want to own blacks is irrelevant in the consideration of his cultural conditioning to consider them subhuman.

He has been so conditioned, in fact, that he expresses surprise when he witnesses instances of humanity in Dessa. He notes at one point Dessa's "expressive" (33) face, then is surprised later that she can tell a joke (36) and that she can truly smile (38). Though he is mostly annoyed with the humming that Dessa does constantly, he is also pleased with her singing on at least one occasion (49). The surprise Nehemiah expresses upon learning that Dessa has emotions, in other words, that she is human, typifies how enslaved persons were treated. Nehemiah cannot *see* Dessa, just as Mr. Yacobowski cannot see Pecola Breedlove in *The Bluest Eye* (1970) or as the blonde man who bumps into the narrator in Ralph Ellison's *Invisible Man* (1952) cannot see him. To see Dessa would be to acknowledge her humanity, which, given his background and culture, Nehemiah is totally unwilling and/or unable to do. The reductionist position into which he places this individual black woman, then, represents the mythology of thinking about most enslaved black females. It is that field of vacancy, that tundra of insignificance, from which Williams enables Dessa to lift herself and claim the agency that history and slavery often denied black women. The playing field of humanity is similarly the one on which Dana attempts to get the slaveholding Weylins in *Kindred* to recognize her, to see that not only can she read and write, but she is far more intelligent than they.

Almost contradictorily—and true to history—even as Nehemiah labels subhumanity in Dessa, he still, almost inadvertently, recognizes sexuality in her as well as in other enslaved women. Consider this passage: "The woolly hair fitted her head like a nubby cap and for a moment Nehemiah fancied he could smell her, not the rank, feral stink of the cellar, but a pungent, musky odor that reminded him of sun-warmed currants and freshly turned earth" (34). His denial of the attractive, sexual smell in this instance is gainsaid by a later utterance. After joining a posse and chasing after a group of Maroons that is reputedly in the area, and after suffering through a drenching thunderstorm, Nehemiah longs for a return to comfort: "A bed will be most welcome—and, perhaps, I shall see also about something to warm it when we get back" (69). Steeped in the custom of the black female enslaved person who sexually warms the bed of white masters, Nehemiah is eager to have sex with a person that most of his actions and commentary would suggest is not human. "Darkies" and "wenches" he may consider enslaved black women to be, but he is not above copulating with them.

The power of naming is mirrored in Nehemiah's general literacy and specifically in his skills as a writer. Those skills become Dessa's enemy, just as white writing historically was often the enemy of black people.[5] One need but pause to contemplate the plethora of volumes published during slavery that asserted the subhuman or barely human status of blacks and the need to enslave them for their own good. A similar contemplation yields the number of volumes that were published to ensure that slavery had a basis in Christianity, as whites claimed that bringing blacks from Africa was justified on the basis of the need/altruistic impulse to "Christianize the heathen." The literacy that white people possessed during slavery, as Sethe Suggs discovers so brutally, was innately the enemy of black people. When Sethe discovers schoolteacher instructing his nephews to mark her animal and human characteristics on different sides of their notepads, that is the final straw that sets her running. Black squiggles on white pages can mean her no good. Nor do they mean Dessa any good. Nehemiah's history marks him as a citizen of secondary status in his society who uses his literacy to try to improve his social standing. His commitment is purely selfish and intrinsically commercial.

Nehemiah has earned a small reputation as a publisher of *The Masters' Complete Guide to Dealing with Slaves and Other Dependents* (17), a volume that has earned him a certain amount of status with what he considers "the better class of planters" (18). His ambition is to publish a new volume, which "would be an intellectual as well as practical achievement, a magnum opus, far eclipsing the impact of the *Guide*" (25). He tentatively titles the volume *The Roots of Rebellion in the Slave Population and Some Means of Eradicating Them,* for which he plans to have Dessa at the center, and which will, he hopes, "establish" him "as an important southern author" (19). Again the wall imagery is relevant in that Nehemiah wants to contain Dessa, his version of her at least, within the confines/pages of his anticipated masterpiece, which, with its planned focus, he believes cannot help but be successful.

That success will in turn enable him to earn enough to buy an impressive amount of land, which is the only way he can truly get into the good graces of that better class of planters. His status in the text, then, is as an exploiter, separated from slaveholders and auctioneers only by finances and the power of the word. To take Dessa's story and package it for publication would be comparable to what Ishmael Reed identifies as taking a man's gris-gris or what leads Myrna to try to chainsaw her husband's head off in "Really, Doesn't Crime Pay?," Alice Walker's short story about an African American woman in the South whose northern lover steals and publishes a story she has written.

With Nehemiah, therefore, literacy is something Dessa should rightfully fear. Nehemiah has the power to command her to speak to him, even if she does so reluctantly, and he has the wherewithal to send her story—what she tells him, at least—into strange eyes and minds. The ultimate objectification would be for Nehemiah to distort her story to the point where her love for Kaine is hidden under Nehemiah's stereotypical notion of what a black "wench" during slavery is all about (he can refer to Kaine only as a "buck").[6] Comparable to Reema's boy in Gloria Naylor's *Mama Day* (1988), Nehemiah has the power to make everything that matters to Dessa disappear under a mountain of words, to alienate her experiences from herself. Her intuitive distrust of the man is accordingly more than justified.

It is noteworthy, however, that even as Nehemiah considers himself superior to and totally in control of Dessa, there are slippages in the portion of the text mostly dedicated to him that suggest otherwise. Dessa's memories of Kaine compete with Nehemiah's representation of her voice, and the omniscient narrator follows her in third-person-limited sections of "The Darky." This structural seepage in the narrative is mirrored in what Dessa actually reveals in her conversations with Nehemiah. Dessa speaks to Nehemiah, she asserts, because talking prevents her from "counting and recounting the cost" (52) of losing Kaine, being sold onto the coffle, and losing more of her friends, as well as because "talking with the white man was a game" (58). There is also the matter of Nehemiah, after Dessa's initial reluctance to speak, having urged her new master to administer a saltwater treatment to her; for several days, she is denied food, and the salt water is the only thing she is allowed to drink.

Being forced to talk does not necessarily mean, however, that one is forced to reveal. Or, being forced to talk might mean that one reveals what one wishes the forcer to hear. Both apply to Dessa for, as she tells Nehemiah what has happened on the coffle, or so he believes anyway, she is ever aware of a dual purpose in revelation. Instead of answering Nehemiah's questions about what has happened on the coffle directly, Dessa chooses indirection, which, as a trickster mode of operation, goes along with her talking as a game. Like Charles W. Chesnutt in his stories in *The Conjure Woman* (1899), Dessa tells Nehemiah about enslavement, but she tells him much more than he wants to hear (at times he seems too dense even to realize it). Her snippets of narrative reveal agency for enslaved persons, a resistance to enslavement, creativity among enslaved people, and a hope for a place without confinement and without white people.

Dessa's narratives about Kaine show that he had about as much "freedom" as an enslaved person could envision. As an expensive gardener bought for his growing and caretaking skills, he illustrates that slavery has not destroyed creativity in African Americans. He illustrates that as well in his banjo making and playing. As artisan, singer, and gardener, Kaine defies the stereotype of the illiterate black person whose physical labor is the only thing by which he can be measured. In revealing Kaine's teachings to her about the behavior of white people as well as about places where black people are completely free, Dessa conveys to Nehemiah what he refuses to see in her own actions—that black people were not content with slavery.

That lack of contentment ultimately results in Kaine's death. It is emblematic of the resistance that characterized blacks historically. They resorted to as many "allowable" methods of protest against slavery as possible. Sometimes they succeeded, and sometimes, like Kaine, they may have lost their lives. In commenting on the milder forms of resistance historically, Lawrence W. Levine offers the following:

> The records left by nineteenth-century observers of slavery and by the masters themselves indicate that a significant number of slaves lied, cheated, stole, feigned illness, loafed, pretended to misunderstand the orders they were given, put rocks in the bottom of their cotton baskets in order to meet their quota, broke their tools, burned their masters' property, mutilated themselves in order to escape work, took indifferent care of the crops they were cultivating, and mistreated the livestock placed in their care to the extent that masters often felt it necessary to use the less efficient mules rather than horses since the former could better withstand the brutal treatment of the slaves.[7]

This trickery, reflected in the folktales of Brer Rabbit's outsmarting his adversaries or of the enslaved John getting the best of Old Master, is mirrored in Dessa playing with Nehemiah in what she is communicating to him. Yet he prefers to see only the image of her that he has in his head.

The subtext of Dessa's comments consistently highlights a desire for freedom. She recalls how Kaine recounts meeting in Charleston a black man from Africa; his descriptions of freedom in Africa provide hope for Kaine, which he then relates to Dessa, who in turn shares the narrative with Nehemiah. It conveys, again if Nehemiah could truly hear, that blacks desire freedom. So do Dessa's comments about running away from slavery or about the women who have knowledge of how to prevent pregnancy as well as how to get rid of unwanted pregnancies. Dessa also conveys the desire for freedom when she shares comments about not wanting Kaine's baby, despite the fact that she loved him. Her desire, like Sethe's, is not, from her own body, to perpetuate the institution of slavery. Nehemiah is so focused on Dessa's living up to the script that he has in his head about black people that he cannot hear her comments. He refuses to believe that Kaine would have attacked his master because the master broke Kaine's banjo. How can that possibly be the whole story? Nehemiah's hold on a racist reality will not allow for it. More likely, Nehemiah suspects, is another script, the one in which a black male, jealous of the master's attention to his black lover, went berserk as a result of that unwanted attention—instead of calmly taking it the way Morrison's Stamp Paid does (even this explanation allows for white male desire for black females, which Nehemiah alternately accepts and rejects).

In the journal he keeps about his conversations with Dessa, therefore, Nehemiah can concoct whatever narrative suits his fancy. Just as he has expanded Dessa's name to "Odessa," so he refuses to hear what she has to say about her life and the lives of those who shared the plantation on which she lived and those with whom she escaped.[8] Intent upon his grandiose notions of authorship, Nehemiah represents Dessa as antithetical to himself and those he considers cultured. In his journal, she speaks as if she were contemporary with Paul Laurence Dunbar's dialect-speaking enslaved persons—but without the grace and rhythm of Dunbar's dialect. Here, for example, is the first representation from Nehemiah that we have of Dessa's voice:

> . . . Was I white, I might wouda fainted when Emmalina told me Masa done gone upside Kaine head, nelly bout kilt him iff'n he wa'n't dead already. Fainted and not come to myself till it was ova; least ways all of it that could git ova. I guess when you faints, you be out the world. (9)

That jumble of dialect is a marked contrast to the first few sentences in "The Negress," Dessa's first-person narrative:

> I never *seed* such a thing! Nathan—laying cross that white woman—Black as night and so—so *satisfied*. It was like seeing her nurse Mony for the first time all over again. I was *that* surprised to walk in on them. (175)

One could easily conclude that these are the voices of two distinct human beings and two distinct educational levels. It is a shock to encounter Dessa's true voice after the representations readers have had to read through in the first two major sections of the narrative. It is absolutely imperative, therefore, that Dessa articulate and produce her own story.

That imperative is also underscored in one brief encounter between Nehemiah and Dessa. She is curious about what he is writing about her, and he deigns to share "an innocuous line or two" (41). When she asks, "I really say that?" he assures her that her reality has little connection to what he is creating. He will use the material in a book, he says, and then: "[G]irl, what I put in this book cannot hurt you now. You've already been tried and judged" (41). That conclusion to her ventures, he seems to imply, gives him license to write whatever he wants about her. And since she is scheduled for execution, why should she care? Nehemiah plans to appropriate Dessa's story without conscience and without a sense of obligation to reveal whatever truths may be inherent in it. He just wants to write a popular, commercially successful book, and Dessa is merely the cannon fodder for his culturally conditioned imagination, an imagination that keeps seeking culture in the hell of the South.

Nonetheless, in another instance of structural seepage, or crack in the wall of stereotypical representation, a window of hope does open during this section of the narrative when Nehemiah has to write down that Dessa escaped on July 4, 1847. He writes the date with "wearied surprise" (69) at the knowledge of Dessa's escape while he and the others have been out looking for the Maroons. Dessa truly makes the white folks' Fourth of July her own song of freedom. It does not matter that Nehemiah continues to try to keep her in the category of thing. She resists "thingafication" as easily as she slips away from the Hughes plantation.[9] Indeed, the surprise he expresses here is but the surface measure of the depths of his ignorance about black people and black lives.

Nehemiah, a one-dimensional evil force in the novel, is farthest removed from having black interests at heart. "Miss Rufel," the white woman who allows runaways to stay at and essentially run her plantation, is not writing a book and certainly is not antiblack, but she is also a force from which Dessa must ultimately rescue herself—or at least reshape significantly the idea of their relationship. Miss Rufel dominates "The Wench," the title of the second long portion of the novel. This section is a progression from "The Darky"; it becomes a necessary step on the path to Dessa's owning herself and her narrative. Once she is rescued from Hughes's cellar and arrives at Sutton Glen, Dessa experiences an extended period of near derangement following the difficulty of giving birth to her son Mony. During this period, a sequence of events contributes to how readers view Dessa and how she views herself. The narrative alternates between reporting Dessa's recovery and impressions of her new surroundings and the impressions we get through Ruth. Viewing Dessa much in the way that Nehemiah did, Ruth will gradually have a change of heart even as Dessa learns to see the world and black/white relations in ways different from what the five-mile radius of all her previous experience has allowed.

Ruth shares with Nehemiah the language of dehumanization of blacks even if she does not share the spirit of that dehumanization. On nearly every page narrated from Ruth's point of view, Dessa is referred to as a "darky" or a "wench," both verbally and revealed in Ruth's thoughts. She also refers, like Nehemiah, to Dessa sitting on her "haunches" (145). Ruth, also like Nehemiah, initially stereotypes Dessa as a hot-blooded "wench" who went after her master sexually and thus caused the tragic sequence of events that led to Kaine's death. Ruth asserts: "I bet she was making up to the master; that's why the mistress was so cruel. I bet that's what it was" (145). A negative script is a negative script, no matter who utters or writes it.[10] Her cultural breeding prevents Ruth from admitting the possibility that white men could lust after and rape black women. What saves Ruth from dismissal is the malleable nature of some of her beliefs, the naïveté that her encounter with Dessa serves to reshape. Even as she screams "darky," "wench," and "uppity, insolent slut" (128), she also refers to Dessa on numerous occasions as "the girl" and "the colored girl"; such humanizing references would never have entered Nehemiah's consciousness. Dessa has thus arrived at a crossroads in having herself scripted by others as well as a crossroads in her own possibility for development.

Sutton Glen becomes a time-out space in which the usual rules of enslavement do not apply. This is the space of possibility—the possibility for a slaveholder to be humanized, the possibility for those enslaved to change their minds about so-called masters. Absent the external pressures of slavery, Williams seems to argue, humanity slips through in those caught up in the system, just as assuredly as Dessa's indictments of slavery slip through the narrative form in "The Darky."

With Bertie, Ruth's husband and this plantation's most virulent representative of slavery, away from the plantation, many things are possible. Ruth can harbor runaways, those runaways can run a plantation more efficiently than one run with a white overseer, black women can talk back to the mistress of the plantation without incurring punishment, the mistress can become wet nurse to a black baby, and the mistress and an enslaved black man can enjoy mutual sexual fulfillment. In this world of slavery without the usual rules, a black woman who has been considered a thing can be reborn from a near-death experience to claim ownership of her body and the narratives scripted about it. Beyond the prying eyes of unqualified proponents of slavery, different kinds of futures can be written for black people—as well as for a white woman willing to challenge her breeding.[11]

Even in this progressive environment, perhaps the major obstacle to Dessa's reclaiming her body and herself centers upon her condition following childbirth, which results in Ruth's having to nurse Mony, Dessa's son. For fictionally enslaved black women, mother's milk is perhaps the defining feature of who they are. Knowledge that babies would probably be sold away from them never prevented the bonding that occurred in the few days, weeks, or months that a black mother had to nurse her child. For that brief period, she was indeed a mother. The importance of mother's milk during slavery is nowhere more vividly represented than in Toni Morrison's *Beloved* with Sethe Suggs. The one thing that keeps Sethe going in her plan to get to the North is the need to get milk to her not-yet-weaned daughter, which will enable her to claim motherhood in a society that seeks to deny her that status. One need but contemplate Sethe's desire to begin to understand how horrible Dessa feels when she cannot produce breast milk for Mony. Add to that horror the fact that Dessa's lack is Ruth's bounty, which she gladly shares with Mony, and Dessa's plight becomes clearer.

Black motherhood was an entangled issue during slavery. It came—historically and fictionally—with the mythology that black women were infinitely better mothers than white women. After all, black women were the wet nurses and mammies, not white women. To have that situation reversed with black Dessa and white Ruth is to upset the universe. Adding to the loss of Kaine, Dessa condemns herself for not being woman enough, mother enough, body enough, to supply milk for her own child. This knowledge, combined with the physical debilitation that occurs after Mony's birth, leaves Dessa in a state of doubt about her body as well as her mind.

It is a slow process for Dessa to reclaim both. She learns, in this world with flexible rules about slavery, that Ruth is not evil incarnate, that Ruth is just as tender, giving, and caring when she feeds Mony as Dessa herself would be. Progressing through stages of resistance, Dessa finally puts her mind at ease about the white woman nursing the black baby. "Dessa knew the white woman nursed her baby; she had seen her do it. It went against everything she had been taught to think about white women but to inspect that fact too closely was almost to deny her own existence" (123). For the first time, she accepts a mutual human dependence, not one defined solely by slavery.

The pathway to Dessa's reclaiming her body approximates, initially, a process of being reborn. She and Mony are both new to the world that exists at Sutton Glen. The childbed fever that brings Dessa near death makes her as weak and helpless as a newborn, and she must be nurtured as thoroughly as Mony is nurtured before she learns to use her body again. It will still be a while before Dessa can envision herself as beautiful and imagine the kind of love she had with Kaine, but the healing of her body and her move from Ruth's house to the quarters are significant steps in the progression "The Wench" section represents.[12]

Her desire to work in the fields instead of as a house servant also reflects Dessa's desire to reclaim herself, to write her body as one that moves beyond the privilege of the Big House, despite the fact that that privilege has been used in her favor. To want to work in the fields is for Dessa to see herself outside the realm Ruth has scripted for her, outside of being thought a wench who chased her master, outside of someone who is content to lie in feather beds or at least inside the comfort of the Big House. For Dessa to want to live in the quarters is for her to reclaim history as she remembers it, a history that includes corn shuckings and the music she identifies so vividly with Kaine. The *choice* of where to work and what to do with her body is the important step in the progression away from any definition others may attempt to impose upon her; Dana musters similar desire to make choices in *Kindred,* though hers frequently lead to her being more rather than less privileged. Within a limited context, freedom of the body is the necessary corollary to freedom of the mind that Dessa has to settle within herself before she can truly express who she is and what she wants.

The potential for that freedom is further expressed in Ruth's changing attitudes during the course of her encounters with Dessa. From calling Dessa a "darky" and a "wench," Ruth moves to labeling the trader "vicious" (144) who forced Dessa to march in the coffle in spite of her advanced pregnancy and in spite of her having spent time in "the box," a contraption designed to punish intractable enslaved persons. Later, "something in her wanted to applaud the girl's will, the spunk that had made action possible" (158) in reference to Dessa's escaping from the coffle and the cellar. After her confrontation with Dessa about their mammies, Ruth also revises her conception of Dorcas, the black woman who had primary responsibility for raising her. She begins to question having taken Mammy for granted and for having put her own childish and young adult concerns above any consideration for Mammy and her life story: "Had she a sweetheart? A child?" (136); "How old *had* Mammy been? . . . Had she any children?" (137). Ruth is "chagrined by her own ignorance" (139).[13] With Dorcas and with Dessa, Ruth finds that she can be outraged in contemplating imagined as well as real actions of cruelty that may have or have been committed against these two women. As a budding race traitor, a position that the deputy Paul could never contemplate in Gaines's "Three Men" and that Rufus fails at contemplating in *Kindred*, Ruth approaches the humanity that enables her to engage in a kind of competition with Dessa.

That competition approaches a leveling of the playing field between mistress and enslaved person. For example, Dessa yells at Ruth without considering the consequences of doing so during their discussion about mammies (as noted, Dana is also brash enough to yell at plantation owner Tom Weylin in *Kindred*). Dessa can be sullen and ignore Ruth instead of interacting with her, which would not be possible on another plantation. More important, Dessa and Ruth can act out a competition for the affection of a black man that would not have been allowable anywhere else during slavery. Ruth immediately assumes that Nathan and Dessa are a couple to explain Nathan's concern for Dessa. While Dessa has no romantic interest in Nathan, there is the competition she feels at the level of a brother, a comrade in arms, becoming a traitor with the white woman she initially despises. Even remotely thinking that the mistress has something that she wants, or showing anger about the situation, suggests a kind of competition that can occur only among equals of a sort, thus diminishing the distance between those enslaved and those not. And of course there is the competition implied in the fact that Ruth can be viewed as a better mother for Mony because she is able to nurse him when Dessa cannot; Ruth even allows herself a moment of gloating about this fact: "Wench still should have enough sense to know I wouldn't let him go hungry, she thought a trifle self-righteously; yet, she was rather pleased to realize that she had some real power over the wench and Ada" (138). While this expression may not be exactly the truth in terms of power, it nonetheless conveys the competition and the leveling. Bringing the two women to the basic human level of jealousy of mothering or of men is another feature of the transformed environment that enables Dessa to reclaim herself mentally and physically and assert her humanity in a world that traditionally has denied it.

Williams finally suggests, however, that the only way to transcend fear, claim agency, and assert humanity is to control one's own narrative. "The Negress," the third long section of the novel, enables Dessa to do just that. Through geography and chronology, as well as the assertion of voice and storytelling, Dessa pushes Nehemiah off the stage of her existence and places Ruth into a space of memory that best befits her. Dessa's claiming of her life story begins with the language in which it is presented.

What is immediately obvious about the voice we hear in "The Negress" is its striking difference from the dialect with which Nehemiah represented Dessa's spoken words. Surrounding this revelation is a history of distortion, beginning with sympathetic whites recording blacks on the Georgia Sea Islands shortly after the Civil War, coming through the early efforts of folklorists to collect material from blacks, and remaining visible in the WPA collected narratives as well as in the studies of blacks presented in such venues such as *The Journal of Abnormal and Social Psychology* during the 1920s, when much folk study of blacks was in vogue. Nehemiah makes a deliberate choice to have Dessa sound illiterate in the visual representation of her speech patterns. He therefore achieves, so he believes, a superior/inferiority dichotomy at the very level of linguistic representation, a pattern that many of his historical descendants also resort to in representing blacks in interviews and literary works. By overwriting Nehemiah's representation of her, by literally having the last word, Dessa's voice reigns supreme in the reader's mind and eye.

Dessa acquires that voice in part through a change of place. From Sutton Glen in northern Alabama, she and her fellow runaways have succeeded in moving west to the expansive territory of possibility. The fact that it has been difficult to convince the leader of a white wagon train to allow them to travel at the end of it makes the arrival in the West that much sweeter. Like the Exodusters historically and Pearl Cleage's characters in *Flyin' West* (1995) fictionally, Dessa and her companions arrive in a place where dreams are possible; indeed, the arrival itself is the fulfillment of a dream. On nonslave soil, Dessa can claim herself in ways that remained impossible on slave territory, no matter how Ruth might have allowed the runaways free range on Sutton Glen. The space of the West, therefore, parallels mind space, parallels what it truly means to own one's own body, finally to be free of definers such as Nehemiah attempted to be. In a way, Dessa and those who traveled with her are able to embrace the concept of the frontier about which Ralph Ellison writes. Western soil enabled black human beings to picture themselves as Renaissance people, Ellison asserted, able to do and be whatever they wanted to be. That space of possibility, which Kaine tried to get Dessa to envision, is what Dessa has sought throughout her life—even when she did not realize that she was seeking it. Any time she felt cramped by the five-mile radius of her existence, she was figuratively longing for the possibility that westward movement represents.

Chronology is also crucial to Dessa's owning her narrative. As "The Negress" unfolds, it becomes clear that Dessa is directing her narrative to an audience, almost as if she is sitting on a front or back porch and entertaining someone with the story of her life. It is clear that the narrative is therefore postescape. What is not clear until very late in the section is that the narrative is also postslavery. Indeed, little Mony now has children of his own, and Dessa is telling the story in part to and for them. This chronological distancing from the events of "The Darky" and "The Wench" underscores the fact that Dessa has survived and has thrived. She has, in effect, beaten slavery. And she has been talking about how she did so. The fact that the narrative has been repeated often is another indication of the ownership of the story. Just as Frederick Douglass practiced relating his narrative to antislavery audiences until he had it crystallized for publication in the 1845 *Narrative of the Life of Frederick Douglass,* so too has Dessa been sharing her narrative with those never enslaved and/or with those who shared escape with her. Her references to "children" and "honey" suggest more of an intergenerational audience.

Dessa has thus, like Douglass, achieved a smoothness of presentation that was honed in oral delivery. After so many oral tellings, she decides to write the story down. She therefore owns it at three stages. She has been the oral parlayer of her experiences, and now she has written them down. Her motivation for writing the narrative is to ensure that others will know—long after she is dead. She thus has a stake in how future African Americans will perceive slavery and efforts on the part of those enslaved to resist their dehumanizing status. Dessa therefore "owns" the past and the present, and she stakes a claim to the future. Her words take precedence over anything Nehemiah may have eventually written about her because, in that crucial scene at the jail when Nehemiah tries to expose her, it becomes clear that Nehemiah's notes from the time he interviewed Dessa in the cellar are "nothing but some scribbling . . . can't no one read" (255). From a woman who did not own herself to one who owns the words that will represent her for generations, Dessa has transcended all claims on her body and her mind. Space and time have been her friends in both instances.

Owning the narrative includes recognizing what one is writing against.[14] For Dessa, that is Nehemiah and his "scribbling" desire to represent her. When he captures her and takes her to the sheriff's office, his assertions chill Dessa: "'I know it's her,' Nemi say. 'I got her down here in my book.' And he reach and took out that little blackbound pad he wrote in the whole time I knowed him. I membered him reading to me from it; even in that heat, I'd turned cold when I learned he tried to write down what I said. The book made me fear him all over again" (254). To be rid of the fear is to be rid of Nehemiah and the power of words that he potentially wields, both written and verbal. The verbal scandalizing of Dessa's name occurs just before the above passage, when Nehemiah is trying to convince the sheriff that he does indeed know Dessa.

> The white man could talk, I don't deny him that, open his eyes all wide, use all kind of motions with his hands, spoke in a whispery voice so you had to listen real careful to make out what he said. Oh, he was something; Miz Lady couldn't seem to take her eyes off him. And I was sweating now; some of these was things I'd told him. "I got it all down here," tapping his chest again. I'd strangled Mistress, he said, and conjured the white mens and laid with all the "bucks" on the coffle; I'd called up the devil there in that cellar. A danger to womanhood, he called me. (250)

It is Dessa's good fortune that Nehemiah oversteps his bounds verbally and equally fortunate that he scribbles illegibly. Many others writing about the enslaved did not. Dessa's recognition of an alien self that Nehemiah would write and label her is crucial. It is instrumental in shaping her move away from Nehemiah's desire to control her image through words and leads to her shaping of her own words. Nehemiah serves as inspiration for her almost as much as her own experiences do. When she gets to the stage of composing her narrative, she will be in the position to label him. By referring to him as a "crazy white man" (247, 248) several times in the text, Dessa scripts Nehemiah as a person out of tune with his society and one whose social status is so diminished that no one, and especially not the white sheriff, need pay attention to him. Just as Nehemiah serves as inspiration to Dessa, so he will serve as inspiration to future generations of black people by encouraging them not to allow themselves to be controlled by a white social climber like Nehemiah, one who is intent upon using black people to economic advantage. Dessa's writing, therefore, serves in part to undercut the economy of slavery—just as her escape serves the same purpose. Transcendence through body and mind is thus an essential component of Dessa's controlling her own narrative.[15]

Owning the narrative also includes mentioning one's blemishes, documenting how one has grown over the course of the telling. As an authorial voice, Dessa presents herself with the reservations that defined her early in her encounters with Ruth and charts the path by which she worked through them. From her jealousy of Ruth for sleeping with Nathan and violating their brother/sister relationship, to her unspoken but angry objections to Ruth nursing Mony ("It chafed me to be so beholden to her"—177), to her resistance to the plan of escape simply because Ruth—"a crazy white woman" (197)—is involved in it, Dessa documents her blemishes. That honesty serves well to establish credibility with her listening as well as her reading audience. She does not aspire to be saintly. What she does aspire to do is convince those willing to listen and read that no form of slavery was acceptable to her, not even the "progressive" form that existed at Sutton Glen. While not exactly presenting herself as a woman warrior (she generally pauses at being considered the "debil woman" on the coffle), she does present herself as a determined woman, one who could envision a future beyond what Nehemiah and slavery thought appropriate for her.

The ease with which Dessa owns her narrative is apparent in her relationship to her implied audience. As she gets more and more into telling her story, the audience becomes increasingly visible, and signs of dramatic monologue become more and more apparent. Seven pages into "The Negress," when Dessa exults, "We had *scaped,* honey!" (181), it is apparent that readers are but one of her audiences. References such as "you know" (183, 187, 192, 205, 207, 212, 226, 245–47), "you know what I mean" (220), "see" (191), "you understand" (193, 210, 250), "understand" (220), "honey" (219, 225, 229), "Oh, I tell you, honey, slavery was ugly" (226), and "You see what I'm saying?" (224) illustrate how important it is that Dessa's immediate audience see, hear, and perceive things in the manner in which she is directing the narrative. Her metatextual calls for their understanding responses highlight awareness of the telling and the tale. Dessa's situation is not unlike that of Janie Crawford in Zora Neale Hurston's *Their Eyes Were Watching God* (1937), in which it is crucial to Janie that Phoebe, the recipient of the tale she tells, fully understand its total import.[16]

The postslavery vantage point of Dessa's tale is obvious from internal references as well. There is a clear *then* and *now* in the narrative. In that interval, Dessa has come to make peace with the past and reflect on the adventures of *then*, which she can safely enjoy in the safety of *now. Then*, others attempted to shape her; *now*, she shapes herself. "Back in them days," she tells her immediate audience, "about all you had to do was put a rope and a collar on a negro and seem like every white person in seeing distance want to make an offer for him" (225). This she offers in explaining how the trick of selling and buying persons in their group could work so well. "They tell you now about the gloried south," she says later; "south wasn't so gloried back then, honey" (230), because of some of the pathetic places the group had to pass through, so pathetic that they even dehumanized white people. The town in which Nehemiah had her arrested seemed large at the time, but she has seen Decatur and St. Louis since then and knows, "since that time, . . . Acropolis wasn't no real busy place" (236). Leisure of place and voice allows Dessa the time to relax and enjoy a good story, which was mostly impossible during slavery.[17]

The postslavery vantage point also allows Dessa to become increasingly appreciative of the trickery that a group of enslaved persons and an abandoned white woman enacted upon so-called masters. She has documented her initial skepticism about the scheme in which several of the runaways on Ruth's plantation would be sold and would then escape, rejoin the group, and be sold again. From observing that others "thought it was a good trick to pull on the white folks" (194), Dessa cautiously, then firmly, joins in the appreciation of the trickery. "What we used to do with fear and trembling, we now did for fun" (233).

> And Miz Lady was good; she could hold and pacify Clara [her daughter] and bargain over a slave at the same time, matter a fact, she liked to do that to throw peoples off guard; they'd be up there playing with Clara and she had closed the sale. She bat her eyes and the sheriff want to put up handbills for her. She smile and a planter raise his price fifty dollars, just to be what she called 'gallant.' All that bat the eye and giggle was just so much put-on now, and it give me a kick to see how she used these to get her way with the peoples we met. (226)

By incorporating Ruth into the trickery that characterizes so much of African American folk cultural memory, Dessa scripts Ruth as a honorary black person, one whose position in the narrative is much more important than her positioning in the real world. By appreciating Ruth's effective trickery, Dessa implicitly acknowledges and admires this white woman who wanted to "friend" with her. Dessa's narrative, then, can shape a cross-racial relationship that the world would not allow, thus fulfilling one of the desires inherent in the neo-slave (freedom) narrative. That relationship becomes a possible pattern of behavior for future generations as well. After all, Dessa can clearly indicate who the good white people are in the new territory where she and others who were formerly enslaved have settled.

In *Dessa Rose,* the first two large sections, "The Darky" and "The Wench," both have negative connotations. Historically, "negress" is not appreciably better. Yet, while "negress" might not be an especially attractive word in the twenty-first century, it is worth remembering that it was a term that would rarely if ever have applied to a black woman in a positive way during slavery. As a contrast to "nigger" and with its uppercased emphasis, the word takes on newfound meaning. It is tantamount to having a white man in Alabama call Dessa "Miss Dessa" in 1930. It would not have happened. To refer to Dessa as "The Negress," therefore, moves her to a status of expressed, individualistic female humanity. The features of her face take shape against the backdrop of the already preset tabula rasa with which Nehemiah views her and the blurring with which Ruth sometimes surrounds her.

"Negress" is also the term that Harker, Dessa's new love, applies to Dessa when he requests that she dance with him at a gathering at Sutton Glen. He explains that it is French for "black woman" (201). Harker's etymology of "negress" serves to lift Dessa from distorted definitions of womanhood and femininity that slaveholders seek to impose upon her. For a black man to make an alternative definition of black womanhood a part of his courtship ritual opens up other possibilities for reclaiming and renaming. Through owning her own narrative, Dessa shapes those possibilities to her new life. She discovers liberation in narration, the transcendent power to name and control, and breaks free of a history that would lock her into fear and submission. The positive state of her mental health, shaped by her experiences on southern soil, is duplicated in some literary characters that follow her and not duplicated in others.

10,000 MILES FROM DIXIE AND STILL IN THE SOUTH

Fear of Transplanted Racism in Yusef Komunyakaa's
Vietnam Poetry

As I have noted in various places thus far in this text, the consequences of slavery did not disappear immediately with the reading of the Emancipation Proclamation. African Americans struggled physically through the new system of sharecropping and legal restrictions endemic to Jim Crow, but they also carried psychic wounds from their experiences. If black persons captured and brought from Africa exhibited cultural practices and patterns of behavior, such as body movements and ways of carrying babies, that were documented hundreds of years later in their descendants in the twentieth century, then it is not far-fetched to suppose that African Americans who endured slavery would, over a mere hundred years from the day they were freed, pass on the marks of that condition to their offspring. Those psychic wounds, combined with the onslaught of Jim Crow requirements for subservience and acquiescence—such as those Procter Lewis exhibits and that Richard Henry resists—could reasonably have led, for some black persons, to an unabating awareness of their racial positioning. The awareness, though American in origin, could easily transcend space and time.

It is unfortunate but true that the history of race relations that plagues the United States and the historically expected patterns of interaction between blacks and whites do not disappear when black and white Americans find themselves on foreign soil. Americans do not simply carry their American-ness with them, as travelers from any country are prone to take their nation-alism with them; Americans take their prejudices with them, particularly their racial prejudices. These prejudices define Americans and their interac-tions with each other. A question naturally arises. Under what conditions can black and white Americans exist on foreign soil and forget the history and animosities that underlie their relationships at home? Barring everything else, would war provide that exceptional space? Would war provide the ideal circumstances under which blacks and whites could come together, forget their differences back in America, and truly, truly be brothers? Is war the great leveler of racial prejudices for black and white American soldiers abroad, or is it merely a new ground on which old uglinesses are acted out? Yusef Ko-munyakaa, born in Bogalusa, Louisiana, and having spent a stint in Vietnam, would answer the latter part of this last question in the affirmative. Not only are old uglinesses acted out on the imaginary landscape of Komunyakaa's Vietnam, but new ones are poured into the old bottles of familiar prejudices.

For Komunyakaa, the American South and its racial attitudes are just as portable as Americanness in general.[1] When Komunyakaa was called to Viet-nam in 1968, he served his time as an information specialist editing *The South-ern Cross*, a military newspaper. When he returned from Vietnam, he could not, he recounts, write immediately about those experiences. Indeed, it took him fourteen years after his tour of duty, until 1985 when he was living in New Orleans, to begin to put his thoughts about Vietnam onto paper. The result, published as *Dien Cai Dau*, which means "crazy in the head," by Wesleyan University Press in 1988, provides some of the most striking renditions of war poetry since Gwendolyn Brooks wrote of "Gay Chaps at the Bar" in 1945.

For Komunyakaa, Vietnam becomes a transplanted American landscape, specifically a transplanted southern racist landscape, a psychological mine-field that his narrators must navigate even as they are navigating the dangers of war, for there are as many clashes between black and white soldiers as there are between American soldiers and the Viet Cong. For author and personae, therefore, the consequences of slavery manifested in southern history and lingering into the twentieth century in the racist practices of Jim Crow are inescapable. In Komunyakaa's renditions, war is not hell—it's Dixie.[2] The physical and psychological terror that black people have experienced on southern American soil illuminates and mirrors the interactive dynamics of black and white soldiers in Vietnam. Potential brotherhood gives way to history, and camaraderie is but another name for one-upmanship against those of the other race. The Vietnamese get caught in this dynamic as they become another group of "niggers" to the white soldiers who exploit or abuse them as relentlessly as they do black American soldiers.

On Vietnamese soil, the hierarchies inherent in American racism are duplicated. There, as in the American South, everyone has his or her place— both psychologically and physically. Boundaries are not to be crossed. White men expect the same privileges that accrue to them in Vietnam as in the United States, and they expect that the power dynamic descended from Rufus Weylin, T. J., Paul, and Adam Nehemiah will hold sway there as well. They expect, for example, that they will be the preferred foreign soldiers, preferred especially over black soldiers. Instead of embracing, learning about, and exploring Vietnamese culture, white and black soldiers bend that culture to fit their ingrained senses of the powerful and the powerless, the more important versus less important people, the darker-skinned versus the lighter-skinned. They duplicate their racist value systems in a tangled web of interactions that makes clear the impossibility of ever fully escaping one's culture and history.

As representatives of America, the soldiers also exhibit the political and social attitudes of the times. The late 1960s were rampant with race riots and internal strife in America. Soldiers drawn from those populations understandably carried the pressures of American politics with them, whether those pressures were manifested in the sense of violence everywhere back home or in violence related to a specific incident, such as the death of Martin Luther King Jr.[3] As products of their American culture, therefore, black and white Americans on Vietnamese soil were living embodiments of the racial and political conflicts back in the United States. Their historical experiences serve as creative inspiration for literary representations of those experiences.[4]

Dien Cai Dau contains poems that document the experiences of soldiers from carefully staged ambushes in "Camouflaging the Chimera," which is the first poem in the volume, to meditating on the Vietnam Veterans Memorial in "Facing It," the last poem in the volume. In between, Komunyakaa explores dangerous situations in which soldiers find themselves ("Tunnels"), arrest and interrogation of the enemy ("Prisoners"), powers that save soldiers from sudden death ("Thanks"), diversions (visits, games, prostitution), thoughts of home ("Combat Pay for Jody"), entertainment (music, shows), mentally damaged veterans ("Losses"), and what it means to be a prisoner of war ("Eyeball Television," "The One-legged Stool"). Komunyakaa is far less concerned with the blood and guts of war than with the psychological trauma. He is also interested in contemplating the enemy, either as a prisoner ("Prisoners") or as a sex partner ("Tu Do Street," "One More Loss to Count"). Komunyakaa always explores the complexity of human engagement with war rather than the patriotic, gung ho, unquestioned response to war. Because Vietnam was such an unpopular war, Komunyakaa's ruminations seem engagingly appropriate. Through all of his concerns, Komunyakaa focuses on what it means to have black and white soldiers, separated by race and history, fighting together as comrades on Vietnamese soil. Throughout the text, then, the burden of race in America is as prevalent as the burden of war.

As several of the poems illustrate, portable prejudices make the very soil of Vietnam a perverted playground for American versions of racism. This is no more dramatically rendered than in Komunyakaa's "Tu Do Street," which could easily be read as "two door," because that homonymic designation makes clear the division between black and white soldiers. The poem focuses on the entertainment that is available to American soldiers in Vietnam, specifically music and sex. On a night out, black and white soldiers enter bar/brothel establishments to get to the Vietnamese women whose brothers, the persona asserts, they have recently battled. The Vietnamese owners and servers at these places have been taught—and have learned well—to be acutely aware of the prejudices that exist between black and white soldiers and are made uncomfortable by them. The black narrator in "Tu Do Street," who enters such a space frequented more by white than black soldiers, begins the poem in this manner:

> Music divides the evening.
> I close my eyes & can see
> men drawing lines in the dust.
> America pushes through the membrane
> of mist & smoke, & I'm a small boy
> again in Bogalusa. *White Only*
> signs & Hank Snow. But tonight
> I walk into a place where bar girls
> fade like tropical birds. When
> I order a beer, the mama-san

> behind the counter acts as if she
> can't understand, while her eyes
> skirt each white face, as Hank Williams
> calls from the psychedelic jukebox.[5]

Music serves as the impetus to flashback to Louisiana, as the preferred patrons in this setting are the lovers of Hank Williams. On Vietnamese soil, music becomes as sharp an indicator of racial difference as skin color. The mere "music equals whiteness" equation transforms the narrator into a small boy back in Dixie experiencing the implied trespassing that ignoring "white only" signs would cause, the kinds of signs that Procter Lewis knows all too well in Gaines's "Three Men." Thus the traditional, historical, and customary notions of place—both physical and mental—and spatial dynamics for black and white interactions on southern American soil have been transplanted to Vietnam. The narrator knows that he is "out of place," so to speak, for black and white American soldiers have carved out dividing lines as distinct as those on their native soil. The black GIs are "down the street" and "hold to their turf also."

The strikingly sad consequence of black and white prejudices against each other, however, is what they do to the Vietnamese. The mama-san's discomfort nonetheless illustrates her preference, for clearly she recognizes this as a place where white soldiers "should be" and black ones "should not be." American racism, the poem leads its readers to conclude, has poisoned this part of the world. The absurdity of liberating the South Vietnamese from the Viet Cong is pathetic when measured against its capacity to turn a Vietnamese landscape into streets dirtied with American racism.[6]

The reflective narrator makes the absurdity even more vivid when he closes the poem by observing:

> There's more than a nation
> inside us, as black & white
> soldiers touch the same lovers
> minutes apart, tasting
> each other's breath,
> without knowing these rooms
> run into each other like tunnels
> leading to the underworld. (29)

How amazing to contemplate that black and white soldiers who would rather die than touch each other, or who have a history of touching each other mostly in violent ways, essentially make love *to each other* on the bodies of Vietnamese women. It is arresting to contemplate the visual images implicit in such a rendering.[7]

One way of viewing this perverted sexual intimacy is to contemplate the dynamic that existed during southern American lynching rituals. In those rituals, white male members of the mobs who lynched black men routinely cut off their genitals or otherwise focused on that site of presumed black male potency. It is noteworthy in this context that the majority of lynchings that occurred were usually the result of some reputed sexual impropriety that the black male victim had taken with a white woman. Black genitals, therefore, were considered to be especially potent. In ritualistic literary representations of lynchings, white males are presented as trying to effect a transfer of that potency to themselves, as in James Baldwin's short story "Going to Meet the Man." A temporarily impotent white man, a sheriff, is able to perform sexually with his wife only after he recalls the lynching of a black man, a lynching that focused for an extended period on castration. The almost pornographic features of the eroticized lynching serve as foreplay for the sheriff.

In "Tu Do Street," therefore, these notions of sexual transfer get combined with degradation of female bodies that are deemed not especially worthy of consideration. Not only does the poem suggest the prejudicial exploitation of Vietnamese women, the hypocrisy of killing the male portion of the population and making love to the female portion, but the potential leveling that could lead to enlightenment rather than continued prejudice. If blacks and whites are sleeping with the same Vietnamese women, then how could there be such hatred between them? But that is comparable to asking how black and white men on southern American soil both slept with black women and never reached any more humane understanding as a result of it.

Black and white soldiers thus place the Vietnamese women into the position of the "colored" or "black" women who are used and abused by both groups back in America. It is noteworthy as well that, by so doing, they both label the women prostitutes, to be used only as sperm depositories. Such a scenario implicates black men as much as it does the white men, for neither has the innate respect for the women that enables them to transcend the exploitation that may be inherent in a human need, that is, the desire to have sex, when one is at war and a long way from home. On Vietnamese soil, black men, in this arena, are equally as superior as white men in transporting their American privilege onto foreign soil; with the power of the almighty American dollar, they can both buy the sexual favors of Vietnamese women. In spite of the sameness of their touching Vietnamese women, black and white soldiers remain as divided and as hateful toward each other as they would be if they were on southern American soil in the early twentieth century.

White soldiers treating Vietnamese women as if they are black American women is also the subject of Komunyakaa's "Re-creating the Scene," a poem in which three white soldiers gang-rape a Vietnamese woman who is carrying a baby in her arms. The men are flying "[t]he Confederate flag" that "flaps from a radio antenna" on their APC (Army Personnel Carrier) when they encounter her in a grotto and violate her. "The three men / ride her breath, grunting / over lovers back in Mississippi" (19). In this context, the connotations of "Mississippi" are historical, racial, and legendary. The name resonates with the most repressive conditions for black people in America, from slavery to Emmett Till. Mississippi is the icon of racial violence, and its connotative quality in the context of the poem serves much more effectively than Komunyakaa's home state of Louisiana would serve. Mississippi therefore stands for whiteness that respects nothing of nonwhiteness, whiteness that is powerful, pervasive, and unyielding in achieving its objectives, no matter the soil on which those objectives are achieved.

When the violated Vietnamese woman approaches MPs to report the violation, "a captain from G-5 / accosts her with candy kisses." To her threats that she will "inform *The Overseas Weekly,*" she disappears on the second day of the trial, either through bribery or violence, leaving behind the baby, grabbing "at the air, / searching for a breast."[8] Where the Vietnamese woman thought she had redress, she discovered that there is none, a situation not unlike that of countless black women in the South who were raped by white men and simply had to bear the children planted in them as a result of those violations. White male privilege over colored female bodies, whether in the American South or in Vietnam, runs its course. The soldiers are not punished, censored, or reprimanded. They rape the woman and are no longer the central focus of the poem. It is almost as if their effect is equivalent to the air during a windstorm—felt, but not to be contained or held accountable.

Komunyakaa even hints at direct sexual competition between black and white soldiers on Vietnamese soil. His narrator relates in "One More Loss to Count" how Be Hai, the Chinese lover of his sergeant major, shows up in his doorway while he listens to James Brown and Aretha Franklin. They talk with "their eyes," which apparently hint that she would prefer him sexually to the sergeant major (maybe she has heard the stereotypes about presumed black male sexual superiority?). Of course he has the option of refusing her advances. However, a southern factor along with memory informs the current action: "This morning Be Hai shows up / with a photograph of the sergeant major / & his blond children / back in Alabama" (22). That talisman of blondness and southernness is the impetus the speaker needs to consummate the relationship sexually. So the room is "caught up in [their] movement," and the last image the speaker records is of the photograph falling "from her hand / like the ace of spades / shadowing a pale leaf." The sergeant major and his blond children are the benediction to the sexual moment. We might conclude that the narrator is spurred to compete with the sergeant major once he sees the photograph; it perhaps makes tangible the competition he has felt all along in knowing that Be Hai is sleeping with this southern white male. Although this speaker apparently hails from California, he is no less able to resist the southern implications of American racial prejudice than black soldiers from the South.[9]

Again, as in "Tu Do Street," the yellow woman's body becomes the site of the mixing of black and white American sperm. Be Hai may *want* the encounter, but she is nonetheless serving a purpose in a racial war of which she can have only an inkling of understanding. And the narrator leaves us to draw conclusions about the photograph serving as sexual foreplay, for that is essentially what it does. Presumably, since he can never possess blondness, the black soldier can at least show a Chinese woman that he is better in bed than the possessor of those blond children. This means, therefore, that Komunyakaa runs the risk of reinstating stereotypes of black male sexual prowess—even when the black man believes it—on that Vietnamese soil tainted with American racism. The image of the "ace of spades" shadowing a pale leaf makes clear that the black soldier's blackness has pushed the white sergeant major aside. It is a triumph not only in the imagery of cards but in the imagery of color and race.

The sexual competition is played out at the physical level of bodies, which is perversely appropriate given the circumstances of war. In an arena in which black and white men are constantly aware that their bodies can be destroyed by gunfire or blown apart by explosions, they locate the source of their manhood in prowess also associated with the physical body. Keeping in shape to fight is one kind of physical demand of war, but keeping track of the native bodies with which one has slept is another marker. The practice can be compared to Westerns where men notch their guns with the number of their kills. These soldiers mark their physical conquests of yellow female bodies and call themselves men by the numbers of women with whom they have sex.

Just as we surmise that the speaker of "One More Loss to Count" is likely to be black because he is listening to James Brown and Aretha Franklin when Be Hai approaches him, so we follow Komunyakaa's uses of music to identify other black and white speakers, as is the case in "Tu Do Street." In "Communiqué," black soldiers are misled into thinking that promised military entertainment will be attractive to them, but they discover that they are to listen to Bob Hope and watch dancers called the Gold Diggers instead of hearing Aretha Franklin: "'I thought you said / Aretha was gonna be here.' 'Man, I don't wanna see no Miss America.'" (30). But Miss America they get, with the accompanying music, for the military cannot offer a release from oppression even in its selection of entertainers. The black soldiers can only sit in stunned silence, contemplating "music & colors," after a downpour forces the early departure of the entertainers.

Komunyakaa recognizes that, with or without music, with or without distractions, war can alter one's sanity. In "The One-legged Stool," he portrays, in extended block paragraph form, the thoughts of a black American, Thomas J. Washington, imprisoned by the Viet Cong. They use various tactics to try to convince him to talk, to break him, not the least of which are race based. As with the mama-san in "Tu Do Street," the narrator's captors are very much aware of American racism. They use it to try to create a sense of disloyalty to America in the speaker so that he will give them the information they want. In a desperate sanity-saving ploy that merely serves to reveal how close to insanity he really is, the narrator marks his awareness of what his captors are attempting.

> No, don't care what you whisper into the darkness of this cage like it came out of my own head, I won't believe a word. Lies, lies, lies. You're lying. Those white prisoners didn't say what you say they said. They ain't laughing. Ain't cooperating. They ain't putting me down, calling me names like you say. Lies. Lies. It ain't the way you say it is. I'm American. (40)

In an effort to save his ever-slipping sanity, the speaker clings to an abstract unity, an abstract brotherhood of American combatants united against a common foe. He tries as hard as he can to believe in the land of the free and the home of the brave. He hopes that the *ideal* of Americanness will save him from himself, will save him from the possibility of being broken down because he has believed his own history. His imprisoners know that they can work on the racial slurs, the presumed inferiority, and whatever else they have at their disposal that will convince this young black man that he is an outsider, a foreigner even *within* American borders, and that he should therefore hold no allegiance to a country that could disown him.

Thomas J. Washington's tormentors know how to manipulate American racism as effectively as the voice of the enemy in "Hanoi Hannah." Hannah has learned the language, the politics, and the racism of America, and she uses all three to wage psychological warfare against American soldiers, especially the black ones. "Why are you in Vietnam," she implicitly asks, "when your lives back home are in shambles?" Wives and girlfriends of the soldiers, Hannah claims, are in the arms of other men. And to really hit below the belt, she taunts the black soldiers with news of Martin Luther King Jr.'s death. "'You know you're dead men, / don't you? You're dead / as King today in Memphis'" (13).[10] In addition to tainting the memory of a black hero, Hannah uses black cultural forms such as music and the dozens as her playthings. She evokes a famous Ray Charles song to assert that "Yeah, / Georgia's also on my mind." She refers to the black men as "Soul Brothers" and questions what they are dying for in Vietnam. By highlighting the loneliness and uncertainty that any soldier who is at war in a distant land must feel, Hannah rubs the soldiers' faces in the social, political, and cultural events and practices from which they are severed. Her tirades inevitably lead the black soldiers to ask, "Why *are* we fighting in Vietnam alongside white soldiers when a white man has just killed Martin Luther King Jr.?" Adept at strategies of divide and conquer, or at least divide and psychologically destroy, Hannah turns the war into the absurdity mirrored in the minds of many of the men.[11] The Viet Cong who are playing with Thomas J. Washington's mind know American politics and culture equally as well as Hannah.[12]

The fact that Washington can be made to believe that the white prisoners have the power to shape his reality is another indication of portable racism. The speaker cannot transcend the slot into which he has been placed in America, cannot deny his history of being named and at times defined by whites. Although he recognizes that his imprisoners have "pitted [him] against them. Against those white troops over there behind those trees" (41), he cannot deny the impact of that pitting. He is still defining his reality, his behavior, in response to some notion of whiteness. Although he keeps asserting that he does not believe what he is being told, the tremendous energy he exerts in denial is testimony itself to the influence of the history of race relations upon him.

By constantly professing that he will not be broken, Thomas J. Washington, black if by no other indicator than his name, remains caught in a web of race and history.[13] Even as he reiterates his mission—"try to keep alive"—the South and racial history flood his memories:

> Yeah, VC. I've been through Georgia. Yeah, been through 'Bama too. Mississippi, yeah. You know what? You eye me worse than those rednecks. They used to look at me in my uniform like I didn't belong in it. (*Struts around in a circle.*) I'd be sharper than sharp. My jump boots spit-shined till my face was lost in them. You could cut your fingers on the creases in my khakis. My brass, my ribbons, they would make their blood boil. They'd turn away, cursing through their teeth. With your eyes pressed against the face-window, you're like a white moon over Stone Mountain. You're everywhere. All I have to go back to are faces just like yours at the door. (42)

It is unclear how close to total mental collapse the soldier really is. What is clear is that his ghosts have been born and bred in Dixie. He is aware of the history of black soldiers in various parts of the South who were beaten or lynched following the first and second world wars if they were caught on the streets in their military uniforms. It is a history that has found its way into much African American literature, including Richard Wright's *Uncle Tom's Children* (1938), James Baldwin's *Go Tell It on the Mountain* (1953), Alice Walker's *The Third Life of Grange Copeland* (1970), and, in a smaller reference, Alice Childress's *Wedding Band* (1966). While the soldier in Childress's play is only given a tongue-lashing, the others are brutally killed. It was a direct insult, so many whites believed, for blacks to dare to wear the uniforms of the American military. That history and Thomas J. Washington's awareness of it can only bring a sense of irony to Komunyakaa's speaker. His uniform, in the late twentieth century, has brought him no more freedom than those of the black soldiers in World Wars I and II. By imprisoning him and using racial psychological warfare on him, the Viet Cong are effectively attempting to deny the Americanness represented by the uniform just as white racists in the South did. For Thomas J. Washington to retain sanity in the face of this onslaught requires a strength that may be faltering at this point.

The speaker's memories also evoke a kind of competition that is implied between black and white soldiers in others of Komunyakaa's poems about Vietnam. The "sharper than sharp" speaker apparently sheds negative light upon working-class whites in Georgia and other southern states who might not have been literate enough or fortunate enough to join the military. That would have given rise to an additional animosity toward him. The situation is comparable to that Langston Hughes describes in his short story "Home," in which a young black man returning to the South is dressed so much better than local whites that they lynch him for that economic gap—although they superficially claim that he has made improper advances toward an elderly white woman, his former music teacher whom he greets on the street.[14]

Komunyakaa's speaker's references to Stone Mountain also elicit a history of racism, for that huge monument to the Civil War engraved on the mountain outside Atlanta is about racial repression more than anything else. In his insanity—or his clarity—the speaker comes to see that the manipulation the Viet Cong want to effect against him is comparable to what whites have done historically to blacks in America. This is one instance in which Komunyakaa seems to make the foreigners as powerful as American whites; however, that power is manifested in the very negative context of imprisoning and psychologically torturing a soldier.

References to the faces of his imprisoners reminding Thomas J. Washington of Stone Mountain might also reflect a different kind of movement in the poem. Since it is the last observation the speaker makes, and since he has emphasized his mission of trying to keep alive, perhaps his leveling of the Viet Cong to the same position of white Americans means that he has found a way to transcend the psychological warfare aimed at him. Perhaps their daggers of defeat will find no points of entry now that he understands that whiteness, manifested in Americans or in violent imprisoners, can ultimately have no hold upon him. Perhaps. But perhaps that is much more optimistic a take on the poem than Komunyakaa would claim.

No one is happy in Komunyakaa's Vietnam poems. No one is content. Even in the racially confining narratives of Baldwin, Gaines, Butler, and Williams, there are some hints of hopes; in *Dessa Rose* there is downright celebration. In Komunyakaa's poems, there are people who celebrate, but their celebrations, by contrast, result when they violate someone else's freedom or take someone else's life. The territory of war is not a space on which complex human exchanges occur devoid of the history that soldiers bring with them to the site of battle. Consequently, for its duplications of the dynamics of racism on southern American soil, Vietnam may well be the southern part of Mississippi. For those of Komunyakaa's narrators who originate on southern American soil, they can only look into the dust of Vietnam and see the cotton fields of Alabama or other southern climes. The violence of lynching and rape mirrors the violence of war and violation of yellow bodies. The possibility of exploration of a new culture is reduced to smearing that culture with the tar brush of Jim Crow.

Where, then, can one find comfort in Komunyakaa's Vietnam poetry? How can the reader leave the scene of reading and find something to affirm, something to grasp as a possibility for transcending the muck and mire of racism?

The answers to those questions come in part in response to Etheridge Knight's notion of the function of poetry, of art in general. Knight, one of the young poets Dudley Randall of Broadside Press discovered during the 1960s and the Black Arts Movement, asserts that writing poetry is a way of organizing chaos. Knight, who spent several years in prison for crimes he committed in support of his heroin addiction, maintains that his discovery of poetry "saved his life." Examination of his beautifully crafted poems gives some insight into how his life was saved. To achieve the artistry required in the poetic vein, to master the craft of poetry, it was necessary for Knight to control the chaos of his life and record it for his readers. Because of that control, we have richly textured glimpses into one man's effort to maintain sanity in a personal hell of a world where he was the cause of the insanity.[15]

So, too, we can argue, it is with Komunyakaa's portraits of Vietnam. The madness of war and racism are ever present, but Komunyakaa leaves us with the poems, with these beautiful constructions that enable us to glimpse an imagined view of an already troubled land whose troubles increase because of black and white American foreigners. The celebration is in the craft, in the artistry that enabled Komunyakaa to become one of only four African American poets who have won the coveted Pulitzer Prize for poetry. Along with Gwendolyn Brooks, Rita Dove, and Natasha Trethewey, Komunyakaa shares the superb talent for poetry that saved Etheridge Knight. It is in the experiences he shapes artistically for us that we appreciate Komunyakaa's Vietnamese landscape. We rise above the chaos to realize that one black poet who was a soldier in Vietnam returned from that battleground unscathed enough to etch it permanently on the sands of time. In a poetry that focuses on violence and violation, the transcendent beauty of creation is our most lingering solace.

For Randall Kenan and other writers I treat in the following chapters, form may be beautiful, but torment remains nonetheless. The mental anguish of being a living monument to racist indoctrination in Komunyakaa's persona is modified in Kenan's *A Visitation of Spirits* (1989) to become the mental anguish that African American communities impose upon their fellow members in an unforgiving and often hellish small-town southern territory.

FEAR OF FAMILY, CHRISTIANITY, AND THE SELF

Black Southern "Othering" in Randall Kenan's
A Visitation of Spirits

Randall Kenan is one of the black writers who present situations in which black people instilling fear in other black people on southern territory is the *primary* concern. Kenan focuses on small-town eastern North Carolina, where the legacies of slavery are somewhat quietly in the background, but where a sense of black family tradition has become so all-consuming that it is perhaps worse than slavery. In *A Visitation of Spirits* (1989), his first novel, Kenan created the fictional soil of Tims Creek, a mythical territory to which he returns for the short stories contained in *Let the Dead Bury Their Dead* (1992). Tims Creek is small-town United States, tobacco-growing and hog-killing country. It is a southern village where everybody knows everybody, where family means everything, where churchgoing is as expected as breathing, and where deviation from whatever the established norm is designated to be is at best stupid and at worst suicidal.

In Tims Creek, whites are on the fringes of black lives; it is mainly the well-established black Cross family that provides the frame for evaluating

This chapter, with a slightly altered title, appears as a portion of my essay in *Women and Others: Perspectives on Race, Gender, and Empire,* ed. Celia R. Daileader, Rhoda E. Johnson, and Amilcar Shabazz, 45–65 (New York: Palgrave Macmillan, 2007). Reproduced with the permission of Palgrave Macmillan.

other blacks. The novel centers upon sixteen-year-old Horace Cross, named after his great-grandfather. A precocious young man who has read more than most college students, Horace is an A student who turns renegade during the course of the novel. As a senior in high school, having experienced in a very short period of time what he perceives to be the debauchery of sexual experimentation with males and then complete indulgence in that sexuality, Horace realizes that he is an "abomination" in the eyes of his church and his family. He determines that the only way to escape his fate is to perform an act of sorcery that will transform him into a red-tailed hawk and thus enable him to fly away from his destiny.

In a classic dark night of the soul, Horace performs the ceremony that will conjure up the demon that can transform him; he realizes that the demon he has conjured cannot be controlled and is instead controlling him and, at the demands of the demon and his accompanying ghoulish host, wanders the territory of his life and the town of Tims Creek before he blows his brains out early the next morning in front of his cousin Jimmy, a pathetic minister-turned-principal who has been more successful in denying his homosexual tendencies than Horace. What leads Horace to this fate is fear of family, fear of Christianity (that is, the church and rules as practiced by his family, friends, and neighbors), and fear of himself as a result of internalizing the rules in spite of his desire *not* to abide by them.

One of the mistakes cultural observers frequently make is assuming that black communities are monolithic, that they all adhere to certain beliefs and follow in certain paths. What cultural watchers often forget is that black communities can be just as controlling of what they perceive to be deviance as other communities. For Horace, that control begins when his relatives believe he has sinned against family. Now, of course we could argue that families everywhere put pressure on their young members. In the small-town South, however, that pressure has unique qualities, and it comes with a history.

Most black folks who survived slavery never received forty acres and a mule. Set adrift without skills or resources, blacks wandered here and there, tried to locate relatives, and often settled in haphazard ways or in unanticipated locations. For the Cross family of Tims Creek, North Carolina, however, no such haphazardness prevailed. As early as the first few years of Reconstruction, the patriarch, Ezra Cross, managed—through legal means or otherwise—to acquire hundreds of acres of land in eastern North Carolina. That acquisition gave status and independence to his family. The Crosses became Tims Creek's version of the black elite comparable to early middle-class enclaves in Atlanta, Chicago, and Richmond. For a formerly enslaved black man to have succeeded so exceptionally well is prestige beyond prestige.

For the five generations leading up to Horace, therefore, the Crosses have borne the burden of black family success and black family history. Kenan assigns their surname to reflect their at-times troubled position in the community as well as the high standards they have imposed upon themselves. Small blots on the record, such as drunkenness or promiscuity, do not ultimately stain the name. The overall family tradition continued, and descendants always kept the land in the family. Even when Horace's father impregnated a girl of whom his family did not approve, his grandfather Ezekiel and his wife Aretha simply took that child, Horace, and raised him as their own. Upon his grandmother's death, when he is ten, Horace finds himself in the hands of his great-aunt Jonnie Mae, his grandfather Zeke, Jonnie Mae's daughters Rebecca, Rachel, and Ruthester (teachers all), and—as the tradition goes—a host of relatives and friends. All of them have high hopes for Horace, for, as one of Horace's classmates points out, "But don't you know it yet, Horace? You the Chosen Nigger."[1]

For a young man of sixteen, an only child, to live up to five generations of expectations is formidable indeed. However, Horace succeeds admirably well from a purely academic standpoint. With his straight A's and his intention to become a scientist/inventor, Horace is on track to do more than anyone in his family has done (teachers, preachers and lawyers are the dominant non-farming professions thus far). That bright future is hampered by a lingering awakening: Horace is increasingly apprehensive about and finally irrevocably convinced that, in terms of sexuality, he prefers men to women. One of his final reveries in the text makes clear how long that attraction has existed. Horace comments:

> I remember watching men, even as a little boy. I remember feeling strange and good and nasty. I remember doing it anyway, looking, and feeling that way. I remember not being able to stop and worrying and then stopping worrying. I remember the sight of men's naked waists. I remember the abdomen that looked sculptured and the sinews' definition. Solid. The way the dark hair would crawl from the pants and up the stomach toward the chest. I remember looking at arms, firm arms, with large biceps like ripe fruit. . . I remember the way my neck would prickle and my breath would come shallow. (248)

These thoughts are from a young man whose family is aggressively heterosexual, whose patriarchs surreptitiously applaud their erring sons for loving "pussy" (55) and who themselves commit adultery, and whose relatives plan futures for individuals that are acceptable to the entire family. Horace cannot possibly thrive in such a directive environment. In fact, he labels his sexual preferences a "disease" against which he does not know how to "fight" (160) sufficiently to return to health.

Thus the burden of family: how can a young black man, in the small-town South, knowing that relatives have raised him when his father and mother proved unable or unwilling to do so, escape the guilt he must feel upon recognition that he is not "normal," not what they think he is—or should be? If that family history were truncated, perhaps it would be easy to be an aberration. If his father had not been weak and his mother inadequate, it might have been possible to be unusual. But Horace owes too much to the people who have raised him and to the family history that those people represent for him to ever be content with the early sexual awakenings that he feels. Even after he acts upon those feelings, the burden of guilt always follows the sexual pleasure.

Horace moves toward transformation and escape from himself when he realizes that he has failed the people who have held such high hopes for him. On the fateful Thanksgiving Day of his senior year, his family make clear how they feel about any man who would have sexual preference for another man. To show solidarity with his recently acquired group of young white male friends, Horace pierces one of his ears and inserts an earring. Late for the traditional meal and wearing the earring, Horace finds himself the center of vocal and unrelenting family disapproval. All the people who have cared for him appear in this scene to reject him totally and completely. They refuse to allow him to explain his decision. The simple fact that he is wearing an earring places him beyond their notion of family and history. The fact that he calls young white men his friends is tantamount to betrayal. His great-aunt Jonnie Mae asks Horace if he has "lost" his mind, his grandfather Zeke concludes that Horace is "crazy," and his elderly cousin Rebecca—usually his defender—avows that he "ain't got a lick of sense" (183). Horace can only stammer out "I" and "But" before they insist that he remove the earring. When Horace is finally allowed to try to explain that "all the guys . . ." (184), his family then jumps on him for being stupid enough, as Jonnie Mae asserts, to do what "them white fools do." It is she, whom Horace holds in special esteem, who pronounces benediction on the violation. "He *just* pierced his ear," she says in response to her daughter Ruthester's suggestion that that is all Horace has done. "Like some little girl. Like one of them perverts" (183,

184). The conclusion to this scene is that Zeke maintains that Horace has "forfeited" his Thanksgiving dinner and orders him to leave the table.

This scene is crucial for making family influence clear in a couple of other ways, both of which involve adult males in the family. Horace is able to witness how Lester, Jonnie Mae's son, is treated and how Jimmy, the preacher, has little if any influence in the family—or little desire to have any influence. Lester's name already marks his difference from his siblings. All of his sisters have "R" names—Rachel, Rebecca, Ruthester, and Rose. He is thus nominally an aberration. Secondly, though his sisters have much to say about Horace's earring, Lester simply is not allowed a voice in the family discussion. When he tries to defend Horace by tentatively positing, "Well, I kind of like it, my—," his sister Rachel responds, "Shut up, Lester." When he comments, "It reminds me of—," his sister Rebecca offers, "Hush, Lester." Finally, after Jonnie Mae's pronouncement of Horace's betrayal, Lester tries again: "Well, I think . . . ," to which his mother Jonnie Mae replies, "Eat your dinner, Lester" (183, 184, 188), which effectively ends the conversation.

Lester's silencing by his female relatives is parallel to Jimmy's cramping by the same figures. While Jimmy might have more words in the conversation, indeed offering that many young boys pierce their ears and that he will "talk with" Horace, his place is barely more secure than Lester's. In fact, Jimmy provides a pathetic example of adult male development throughout the text. His lack of aggression in pursuing his wife Anne (he is her companion for months without making a single pass at her) and his inability to make love to her when she finally invites him into her bed, leads her to ask, "Are you sure you're not a faggot?" (176) and to refer to him as a "little boy" who is too romantic for the situation in which they find themselves. When he discovers her unfaithfulness and does nothing, Anne calls Jimmy a "Goddamn pussy!"(180). From his encounters with Anne, to his inability to sort out a fight between Zeke and Ruth, to his pathetic efforts at ministering, Jimmy has shadows hanging over his manhood. As with Lester, he ultimately cannot deal effectively with the women in his family, even the ninety-two-year-old Ruth.

This lack of traditional—perhaps even stereotypical—male effectiveness raises questions about the focus on homosexuality in the novel. The text perhaps inadvertently supports the misguided assumptions put forth historically that excessively strong females might have forced certain males into homosexuality. While that might not be Kenan's intention, it could certainly be argued that Jimmy and Lester, as failed male role models whose failures are shaped by the women in their lives, are counterparts in male weakness to Horace's perception of his aberration that he names homosexuality. Such an analysis places these black female characters on the side of castrating matriarchs who align themselves with white men in emasculating black men. The good intentions that might be inherent in keeping black men in line for fear of white violence nonetheless simultaneously contribute to their loss of visible manifestations of manhood.

On the other hand, what Jimmy and Lester offer could be perceived as the family-molded male images from which Horace should run for his life. From this perspective, his movement toward homosexuality is at least a movement away from the silencing and confinement that characterizes males in his family who are closer to his generation. Why should he uphold family tradition, if all he can do is end up like Lester and Jimmy? Lester wins no family approval; Jimmy does so only by slotting himself into the role of minister that his grandmother Jonnie Mae has carved out for him. Although he offers to "talk with" Horace about his earring, Jimmy ultimately has as little clue as Horace about how to fit himself into a demanding family obsessed with history and tradition. His witnessing of the verbal assault upon Horace at the Thanksgiving dinner enables him to see the rejection that he himself has missed by hiding behind respectability.

It could be argued that Horace never recovers from this rejection. It occurs in November; he dies before graduation the following year. What Horace encounters is a wall of family tradition, the harsh attempt to keep him in line. After all, Horace's father dropped out of the family notion of success. Horace cannot be allowed to do so. His collective family pressure is not unlike that Mama Lena Younger places on Beneatha in *A Raisin in the Sun* when she forces her to assert, "In my mother's house there is still God."[2] The difference here is the burden made possible by *black* southern family history. For this family to have achieved so much and then to witness it being threatened by Horace's befriending and identifying with the very forces that have oppressed them historically makes the family see red. If Horace can be policed only through rejection, then they will reject him.

One of the greatest ironies of the text—and indeed of black middle-class life in the South—is its modeling of success on those same forces that have oppressed black people, an observation the Cross family can apply to Horace but fails to see in its own patriarchal legacy.[3] Ezra Cross and his descendants model whiteness and white success even as they echo the patriarchs of the Old Testament's "begats." Black people emerged from slavery with clear senses of where power and success lay. If they could be like whites in acquiring property and making those acquisitions work for them, then perhaps their descendants would not suffer as they had. They claimed white models as quickly as they rejected what white people represented in terms of violence and repression.[4] It was a fine line to walk, that is, to take the shell without the substance, and few of them managed that balancing act. Ezra and his descendants inadvertently adopt some of the values of the people whose pattern they emulate. Family moral purity (at least superficially so) and family respectability are two of those values. In their desire to value reputation and success, however, the Cross family runs the risk of devaluing blood. The fear of loss of reputation is almost as tangible as the fear of loss of property.

Inherent in the family's actions at the Thanksgiving dinner, therefore, is a fear that Horace will embarrass them, that he will do something even more egregious than his father in placing a blot on the Cross family name. As with Beneatha, Horace can therefore not be *allowed* to be deviant. He must be kept in place even as whites kept blacks in place during slavery and afterward. The problem for Horace is that he cannot ultimately fall into line with his family's expectations. This is clear from a conversation he has with his cousin Jimmy one Sunday after church. Horace builds up the nerve to speak with Jimmy about his homosexual urges. To his comment that he thinks he is "a homosexual" (112), Jimmy's response is condescendingly dismissive.

JIMMY (*smiling, puts his hand on Horace's shoulder*): Horace, we've all done a little . . . you know . . . experimenting. It's a part of growing up. It's . . . well, it's kind of important to—
HORACE: But it's not experimenting. I like men. I don't like women. There's something wrong with me.
JIMMY: Horace, really. I have reason to believe it's just a phase. I went through a period where I . . . you know, experimented.
HORACE: Did you enjoy it?
JIMMY (*slightly stunned*): En . . . Enjoy it? Well . . . I . . . you know. Well, the physical pleasure was . . . I guess pleasant. I really don't remember.
HORACE: Did you ever fall in love with a man?
JIMMY: Fall in love? No. (*Laughs.*) Oh, Horace. Don't be so somber. Really. I think this is something that will pass. I've known you all your life. You're perfectly normal. (113)

But when Horace suggests that he might not be normal and wonders if it is okay to be as he is, Jimmy falls back on the Bible and lets Horace conclude that the Bible says "it's wrong." Jimmy insists that Horace will change, but Horace keeps asking, "But what if I can't change?" Jimmy has no adequate answer to that question. Unable to change, but recognizing that "the possibilities of being a homosexual frightened him beyond reason" (156), Horace is set adrift in a familial world of sexual and Biblical expectations that he can never fulfill.

It is ironic that the questing young Horace seeks advice from his cousin Jimmy, for James Malachi Greene is an ineffectual minister and one of the most inadequate human beings in the text. Jimmy is a card-carrying conformist, a born mediator who will take whatever course provides the least resistance. Zeke believes Jimmy is too deferential to Ruth, and it is clear that he is totally incapable of managing her, Zeke, or the arguments in which the two of them engage constantly. Jimmy is too unsteady in his position as a minister to dare chastise an ailing parishioner who deliberately drinks a can of beer in his presence, and he declares to another, "ain't no harm," though it is a blatant deviation from the local brand of Christianity. Jimmy then contemplates the rules that have placed him in this predicament: "I don't want to be a watchdog of sin, an inquisitor who binds his people with rules and regulations and thou shalts and thou shalt nots" (109, 110). Yet he reverts to the rules when Horace seeks advice from him. In spite of his own homosexual tendencies, Jimmy pushes Horace toward the traditional familial and church views on the subject. Search your heart, he advises Horace, and ask God for guidance, which to a troubled teenager is probably about as helpful as suggesting that he consult an oracle.

In the last few weeks of his life, Horace discovers, as his father did, that he cannot live by family rules. His quest to turn himself into a red-tailed hawk is couched in terms of escaping human, familial, and societal rules:

> But now he was buoyed by the realization that he knew how he would spend the rest of his appointed time on this earth. Not as a tortured human, but as a bird free to swoop and dive, to dip and swerve over the cornfields and tobacco patches he had slaved in for what already seemed decades to his sixteen years. No longer would he be bound by human laws and human rules that he had constantly tripped over and frowned at. (12)

How can a powerless teenager find freedom from "acceptable" tyranny? In Horace's world, that feat can be accomplished only through imagination and/ or a willful surrender of sanity, for the rules will not bend for him.

Horace's father, Sammy, was a wild young man who similarly sought to escape the rules. He would often stay out later than his father Zeke thought appropriate. On two occasions, Zeke laid down the law to his son. "There are rules to this house," Zeke says to Sammy when he comes in late one night, "If you live here, you live by them" (56). When Sammy continues to resist and comes in one morning at 3 a.m., Zeke announces, "Boy, this is my house and if you think you too grown to abide by my rules, then I spect you better get up and go" (64). Sammy's departure from the premises can only be surmised as Zeke's wishes being fulfilled. For Horace, the rules are equally too much, and he has no more success than his father in abiding by them. He can remain in his grandfather's house only as long as he hides who he really is.

What finally breaks Horace's will to live is his knowledge of the fact that he has shamed his family. By shaming the present generation, he has essentially broken with the past, with his now-dead great-aunt Jonnie Mae (who cared about him in spite of her refusal to approve his wearing an earring), as well as with the four generations of Crosses who made sacrifices to enable Horace to be where he currently is. Horace "suspected his family might object to his action [piercing his ear]. But he had no idea they would pronounce treason and declare war. From top to bottom, uniformly, they condemned him. It was not the piercing of his ear, it was what it represented, they said" (238). To Zeke, the issue seems to be that Horace is more influenced by his white friends than he is by his family: "By Jesus, you'd 'just kill somebody' if one of them white boys asked you to. Wouldn't you? Wouldn't you? It shames me right much, boy. Shames me to see you come to this. We come this far for this. I'm glad your grandmother ain't around to see it. Shamed" (239).[5]

Horace's family renders him "Other" by finally making him feel worse than a stranger. They would embrace and feed a stranger. They cannot, will not, embrace the homosexual Horace. Indeed, they consistently and adamantly refuse to see that Horace has a different sexual preference. Jimmy simply files the conversation he has with Horace away in some Paul D-like tobacco tin that will never be opened. In one reflective moment following the fateful Thanksgiving dinner, however, Jimmy seems to understand the destructive impact of family on the impressionable Horace:

> That is what finally got to Horace, isn't it? I keep asking myself. He, just like me, had been created by this society. He was a son of the community, more than most. His reason for existing, it would seem, was for the salvation of his people. But he was flawed as far as the community was concerned. First, he loved men; a simple, normal deviation, but a deviation this community would never accept. (188)

These are Jimmy's thoughts. There is no indication anywhere in the text that he shares them with anyone or that he acts in any understanding way toward Horace as a result of his analysis of the family's or the larger community's expectations of Horace. Jimmy remains just as silent on the issue of homosexuality as the Cross women force Lester to be quiet about Horace's earring.

Zeke completely refuses to reflect at all upon Horace's suicide or the reasons for it; there is absolutely no mention, anywhere in the text, that Zeke even remotely suspects that Horace might prefer males to females. Perhaps to do so would be to consider his own less-than-exemplary sexual life, for he cheated on his wife with several women and has at least two grown sons born out of wedlock. Horace's great-aunt Ruth suggests that the Cross family and what it represents have led to Horace's death, but it is not quite clear that she understands the true nature of Horace's demise. In response to Zeke's accusation—a year and a half after Horace's death—that Ruth drove his brother, Jethro, who was also Ruth's husband, to drinking, Ruth's response is: "Well, you'll see yourself one day, Ezekiel Cross. See what you and your family, your evil family have wrought. And it wont just on Jethro. It's on Lester. It's on this boy here [Jimmy]. It was on your grandboy. You all is something else" (197). Even without naming homosexuality, Ruth knows that the family's lack of understanding for and sympathy toward Horace have played significant roles in Horace's death. She refers to Zeke's sister as "the Royal Miz Jonnie Mae Cross Greene" who has made a "slave" (137) of her son Lester; that negative influence undoubtedly descended down to Horace.

Inherent in this lack of understanding is black people's stereotypical refusal to name suicide, yet another sin that Horace commits. To take one's own life can only entail silence about the act. Like the hog killing so vividly portrayed at the beginning of the text and the requiem for tobacco with which it ends, Horace passes through the Cross family line without making a perceptible dent in its reputation or presaging change for its future.

It is obvious that Kenan intended multiple connotations in assigning the name "Cross" to his protagonist family. They not only burden their members and force them to make tremendous sacrifices—such as taking land from Jethro, not forgiving Rose for having children out of wedlock, forcing Jimmy to become a preacher,[6] and treating Ruth as an outsider instead of an in-law—but they do so under the ironic banner of Christian goodwill. The largest cross they construct, however, they plop onto Horace's shoulders. He will be "the One," in that tradition of choosing black leadership and success to which Ernest J. Gaines refers in *The Autobiography of Miss Jane Pittman* (1971). The Cross family's externally imposed cross and the one that Horace bears because he knows the depths of hell to which his family and community will consign him for being homosexual make burden-bearing in the text approximate biblical proportions. This conjoining of the secular and the sacred will never yield a peaceful resolution for Horace in this life.

The irony is that Horace's sin, as he himself perceives it, cannot be forgiven, whereas the text is rife with sinners who self-righteously continue on their paths of presumed forgiveness. The difference between those sinners and Horace is that they engaged in *sanctioned* sins, whereas Horace's sin is unsanctioned. Adultery is a known practice in Tims Creek, so those persons who may be privy to Zeke's infidelity to Aretha do not consider that the end of a way of life. The most vivid example of this is the scene in which Jimmy comes home early one day and finds his wife Anne in bed with another man. He simply turns from the bedroom, goes out to the front porch stoop, and stares into space; later, he ends up puking all over the guestroom bed. However, neither his world nor his marriage ends as a result of this infidelity.[7] The same is true for persons who drink excessively. Ruth's husband Jethro neglected her and their children during his drinking sprees, but he was not cut off from his family because of it, and he was not deemed to have "shamed" them. Thus the line between traditionally "acceptable" sins and the unknown, unconsidered abominations such as homosexuality is sharply and irrevocably drawn in Tims Creek. It is Horace's misfortune that he falls on the wrong side of that line.

Though family is perhaps the primary source of fear for Horace, the more intense fear is the one that originates in the Bible and the practitioners of Christianity in Tims Creek. Horace, like most black youngsters bred on small-town southern soil, has church in his pores. From his earliest memories to his death, church and church activities have saturated his existence. It is understandable, therefore—and exactly what his family and community would have desired—that Horace sees himself through the eyes of Christianity as practiced by Reverend Barden, Reverend Jimmy Greene, and other members of his family and community. Their brand of Christianity is an exacting one in which the God of the Old Testament is much more prevalent than the forgiving Jesus of the New Testament. Hellfire and brimstone are the watchwords for these small-town black southerners, and anyone who does not follow the straight and narrow path is in danger of eternal damnation.

Biblical language, therefore, dominates the text and dominates Horace's references to himself and his condition.[8] He has been in the church for so long that, like a good baptized believer, he carries its strictures around in his head. Even if others did not condemn Horace for his same-sex preferences, he would effectively condemn himself, for he knows what is "right" and "wrong" as well as they do. It is that double burden—the external admonitions to do right combined with equally dominant internal injunctions—that leads Horace to suicide. Horace might have been able to survive if he had not believed so fervently in what he had been taught. He is thus, in the words of his fellow believers, condemned out of his own mouth.

During Horace's dark night of the soul, one of the places he visits is his church. The church is crowded with a scene from his youth, and he sees a young Horace sitting in a pew while the Reverend Barden delivers a condemnatory sermon on same-sex relationships. There is absolutely nothing normal about such a condition, Reverend Barden repeatedly iterates. It will send one to hell, and deservedly so. The same fear and trembling, then, with which one comes before God and confesses one's sins before being saved is the fear and trembling with which one is sent to hell for deviating from what God has designated normal sexual activity. Again at issue is sanctioned and unsanctioned sins, for numerous are the tales of so-called believers in Horace's community committing regular sins, which presumably would land them in hellfire as effectively as other sins.

What Horace hears from Reverend Barden is what has guided his attitude toward his own sexuality. "Unclean. That's what it is. Unclean. And you knows it" (79). The demon orders Horace to kill the Reverend as he is praying, but Horace, unable to respond, can only watch as one of the harpies accompanying him lops off the reverend's head, with the word "unclean" emitting from his re-dying lips. Horace sits briefly in the pulpits and hears—or imagines— the voices that represent his grandfather's brand of religion.

Then the voices started, first from this corner, then from that, from overhead, then from below.

> Wicked. Wicked.
> Abomination.
> Man lover!
> Child molester!
> Sissy!
> Greyboy!

Old men, little girls, widows and workers, he saw no faces, knew no names, but the voices, the voices . . .

> Unclean bastard!
> Be ashamed of yourself!
> Filthy knob polisher! . . .
> Cocksucker.
> Oreo. . . .
> Homo-suck-shual!
> Ashamed. Be ashamed.
> Faggot! (86–87)

With these monstrous accusations in his head, Horace has essentially "Othered" himself. As with his religious belief, there is no reason to have family or neighbors calling out derogatory names. He has internalized the names and therefore internalized his own rejection and ultimate suicide.

Fear of God is a primary directive in Christianity. To approach God otherwise is to run the risk of blasphemy, to border on committing the sin that Nathaniel Hawthorne's Ethan Brand commits when he goes looking, aggressively, for a sin that God will be unable to forgive. Such boldness is the epitome of rejecting fear, which no sane person in Horace's community would do. "Fear God, and keep his commandments," so one injunction goes, "for this *is* the whole *duty* of man."[9] And preachers from Jonathan Edwards to T. D. Jakes have reiterated that directive.

Fearing God is one thing and arguably acceptable in the tradition of Christian belief. Fearing the *people* who profess belief in God is a layered dimension that the text embroiders to indict almost all of those who make such claims. To be fearful of those who would invite one into the fold of Christianity is a paradoxical position in which to find one's self, for the standard declaration is that God is love. God's people, as they are represented in *A Visitation of Spirits,* are not loving or lovable. They are small-minded and self-ish, judgmental and insistent upon their narrow interpretations of the Bible. Their imaginations are limited by the strictures they place upon themselves as well as upon others. They are not tolerant. They are not forgiving. They attempt to confine God to their smallness and use him to beat down all op-position, including their own flesh and blood. Kenan indicts them again in "The Foundations of the Earth," one of the stories in *Let the Dead Bury Their Dead.*[10]

With this judgmental variety of belief, then, it is no wonder that Horace fears not only God but that he fears his family and his community. Through the prism of the Christianity that he has been taught, Horace recognizes his family as being as willing to consign him to hell as the Old Testament God would be. While Kenan does not give us extended interactions between Horace and his relatives, we see them sufficiently to know that their serious-mindedness about religion does not allow for even miniscule lapses. For Hor-ace to have lapsed so titillatingly into the pleasures of the flesh is something they could never condone. And because they have taught him well and he has believed their teachings, Horace realizes that he is finally, utterly, alone and that the beckoning grave may as well be inviting because he cannot undo what has been done, to garner either forgiveness or love from his family. The tears he sheds in his final few hours of life, tears that his family would have considered cleansing signs of repentance when Horace graduated from the mourners' bench, are now the benediction sealing his fate. He cries for himself as well as for what he can never be. He cries for what he has lost in the way of family. And he cries because he is alone, with not a single Christian soul to offer him comfort. "Suddenly life beneath the ground had a certain appeal it had never had before. It was becoming attractive in a macabre way. No more, no more ghosts, no more sin, no more, no more" (231). Echoing a spiritual, "Many Thousand Gone," which repeats the refrain "No more" and which contains the line "No more auction block for me," Horace's determina-tion to commit suicide is as much a release from the slavery of religion as it is a release from life.[11]

Horace fails his family much more dramatically than his father Sammy, but the difference of that failure is one of degree, not one of kind. Both have been subjected to rules by which they could not finally consent to live. When Horace confronts Jimmy at sunrise, just before he kills himself, and Jimmy asks why he is doing what he is doing, Horace's—or the demon's—response is "too many fucking rules" (252). As a part of his final reverie just before this scene, Horace comments: "Then I remember the day I realized that I was probably not going to go home to heaven, cause the rules were too hard for me to keep. That I was too weak" (251). Perhaps it is less a matter of Horace's weakness than of the inability of the family and community that have nurtured him to make a place for him. Implicit in the text is the argument that there ought to be a place in the small-town South where black Horace Cross, sixteen years old, could be homosexual *and* live. Nonetheless, the community, with its warped rules and values, has won, for once again Horace condemns himself out of his own mouth, a condemnation that his family and community have taught him well.

What is left for Horace to fear beyond family and church is the self that has been shaped by those forces. Indeed, it is reasonable to suggest that there is very little of Horace beyond family and church—except school, and even there he experiences more than his share of rejection, even as he dishes out rejection to Gideon, the first young man with whom he has sex. Given the state of his mind throughout the text, Horace would be hard put to say who/ what he is. He names himself repulsive, unclean, faggot. He names himself descendant of one of the most famous and powerful black families in the area. And he names himself "brilliant" (225), a designation that serves only to achieve his escape from the first two designations.

In America, it is difficult to be an impressionable teenager under almost any circumstances. But Kenan suggests that it is particularly difficult when one is surrounded, as Horace is, by sanctimonious relatives and neighbors who scoff at and reject the very budding identity that Horace is attempting to shape. It is difficult to make friends when the classmates with whom one most identifies are not of one's own race and even more difficult to feel the reverse rejection by black friends who assume that one has first rejected them. Underneath the calmness of the pretty boy, good boy, well-mannered, straight-A-student exterior, therefore, Horace is a building volcano of intense emotions and so severely truncated identity formation that his hurt and fear could well occupy several teenagers instead of a single individual.

What Horace has to fear most about himself are his mind and his hands— the mind that indicts his very existence, the mind that concocts the spell of escape, the mind that brings the demon forth or is itself transformed into a demon, the hands that he uses to masturbate into violent spasms of uncontrolled pleasure, the hands that gather the spell-casting ingredients, the hands that carry the shotgun throughout his long, miserable night. Horace's final night on earth is a night of war within his mind or between his mind and his body. Having condemned his body for its participation in illicit pleasure, his deranged or possessed mind carries him to the point of suicide and through that act. He reaches various points during the evening when it is clear that he cannot trust himself, cannot trust his perception of the world around him or his own feelings and analyses, but there is no one else upon whom he can depend.[12] In his agony, his self is transformed, abused, chided, derided, and violated, both psychologically and physically. His body becomes the enemy, the prison, from which he must escape. And escape he does.

Sadly, even Horace's escape is modeled on his Christian upbringing. Above all else, during his evening of searching, questioning, and revisiting his earlier life, Horace is looking for salvation (he is also perhaps looking for validation and/or exoneration). When the conjured demon orders Horace to march, he complies, and "he was happy, O so happy, as he cradled the gun in his hand like a cool phallus, happy for the first time in so, so many months, for he knew the voice would take care of him and teach him and save him." When the hellish crew shouts "profanity and blasphemies," "he smiled and joined in for this was his salvation, the way to final peace, and . . . he marched along aware of the gun that he held tight in his hand, glad to be free, if free was a word to describe what he felt" (28).

Concocting the idea of turning himself into a red-tailed hawk allows Horace to escape from the judging eyes of people and the unrelenting attractions of the flesh. Returning to church, school, and the theater where he worked one summer are similarly desperate attempts to find something that will inspire him to want to remain on earth—or perhaps something that will spur him on to remove himself from earth. Either would be a salvation that has not previously been available to him. Unfortunately, there is no kindly reverend waiting to welcome him from the mourners' bench, no smiling Jesus waiting to lift the burden of homosexuality off his back, no motherly, nurturing church sisters to embrace him as he emerges from the waters of a new baptism. He is completely alone.

In that aloneness, the fragile self that has had such difficulty in forming essentially dissolves. The shotgun blast to the brain is but the culmination of the dissolution that has already occurred. After his grandfather expresses "shame" toward Horace, the narrator ponders: "What does a young man replace the world with, when the world is denied him?" (239). The narrator comments further: "His loneliness led him into careless and loveless liaisons with men who cared only for his youth, and though he pretended not to care, he worried more and more for his soul, and his increasing confusion took on a harsher guilt and self-loathing" (240). By the time Horace casts his spell, calls forth his demon, and makes his final journey through Tims Creek, he is already dead to everything that matters to him and to everything that he wanted so desperately to cling to and in which he wanted to be affirmed.

In the final analysis, Horace discovers that he has no living mirrors. Persons around him, especially his family members, only reflect distortions back to him. It is appropriate, therefore, that on the night when he wanders back through his life and the theater in which he worked, he encounters an image of himself seated before a large mirror (219–20). That image is busily applying layers of thick white pasty makeup to the other Horace—obviously a reference to the duplicitous roles Horace has been forced to play. When the image forces Horace to confront the mirror, which reveals him madly making love with one of the visiting actors, which in turn leads to another series of memories, Horace shoots the image of himself: ". . . there on the ground he lay, himself, a gory red gash through his chest" (235). His efforts to convince himself that he has only killed a ghost or something that was not real do not suffice; he finally takes a permanent vacation from his own mind and succumbs to the call of life underground.

In effect, Horace "disappears" himself. There are no white men with dogs chasing him through a marshy swamp. No threats of lynching. No violent mob waiting for him to make a trip to an outhouse. Only Horace has the power to make Horace disappear. By the time he meets Jimmy at school on the morning of his death, "Horace did not know it was Jimmy. Horace was no longer there" (241). His disappearance is the culmination of so many assaults upon his very being that Horace finally gives in and voluntarily disappears into insanity and suicide. The fragmented self from which so many people demanded so much simply crumbles under the load of expectations. This disappearance of the mind is but the prelude to the disappearance of the body, and perhaps it is merciful that Horace's mind goes before his body. The war between mind and body thus ends violently, but, paradoxically, it also ends peacefully. Comparable to Pecola Breedlove in Toni Morrison's *The Bluest Eye* (1970), *A Visitation of Spirits* essentially posits that there is no viable alternative for Horace.

Certainly it could be argued that a young man declaring his sexual preference for other males is a difficult process any place in the United States. While that might be an undeniable truth, it is also undeniable that southern manifestations of such sexuality can be more acutely problematic in particular kinds of communities, especially in small southern black communities whose ability to name themselves respectable is so tenuous. Anyone who threatens that respectability is expendable. Blood may be thicker than water, but sexuality that is deemed to be perverse can break even the bonds of blood. Horace finds those bonds broken without anyone in his family ever having named him homosexual to his face; they simply let the innuendoes hang in the air long enough for him to receive the strong message of rejection that leads to him killing himself.

Fascinatingly, Kenan does not depict Horace's funeral (though he does depict the funeral of Horace's great-aunt Jonnie Mae). Such a depiction would perhaps have forced family members into discussion about the nature of Horace's death, and it would perhaps have unveiled the silence surrounding his homosexuality. In this instance, therefore, the text conspires with Horace's relatives and with small-town southern morality in keeping homosexuality the unspoken (perhaps open) secret that leads to suicide instead of acceptance. If no one can even broach the subject, or if broaching the subject yields the kind of reaction that Horace received from Jimmy, then it is no wonder that such small-town southern black environments induce a fear that can chill—or stop—the blood.

7

A HAUNTING DIARY AND A SLASHER QUILT
Using Dynamic Folk Communities to Combat Terror
in Phyllis Alesia Perry's *Stigmata*

Horace Cross is victimized by five generations of black family expectations that had their origins in a direct response to slavery. Randall Kenan, therefore, turns fictional concerns away from the direct impact of white slaveholders on black people to the psychic wounds that black people inflict upon each other as a result of their slave experiences. That pattern also appears in Phyllis Alesia Perry's *Stigmata* (1998) and Edward P. Jones's *The Known World* (2003). Conflict across racial lines shifts to conflict within black communities and within black households as a result of the legacies of slavery. This shift and the continuing fear it engenders are still rooted in a history of a frightening southern territory where slaveholders worked hard to create awe of themselves and where, for generations beyond direct white control of black bodies, blacks still exhibited those fears.

For Perry, those fears are rooted in history and superstition, which in turn are rooted in slaveholder attempts to manipulate black minds. A brief history of some of those patterns will serve to place *Stigmata* in this context, a history about which folklorist Gladys-Marie Fry is expert. In *Night Riders in Black Folk History* (1975), Fry illuminates the ways in which slaveholders, who early learned that black people had a tendency to superstition, used superstitious practices and fear of the supernatural against enslaved people. Fry writes:

> The master's technique of utilizing the supernatural for slave control employed three associated methods, the individual planter using any one or all three of them. The basic, and simplest, technique was the systematic use of simple narrative statements concerning the appearance of supernatural figures, such as ghosts and witches. To implement this imaginative base, the planter often designated as haunted places usually located strategically along heavily traveled roads. Of course, the final step in the methodology was to actually masquerade as ghosts in order to reinforce the belief in the supernatural.[1]

To prevent blacks from plotting attempts to escape from slavery or even remotely contemplating those possibilities, slaveholders told them that un- imaginable monsters lurked beyond the boundaries of the plantation and would devour any black who moved beyond those boundaries. To reiterate the rumors they spread, slaveholders would periodically kill a chicken or a hog, smear its blood in strategic places, and point to the scene as the site on which one of those monsters had indeed killed. Many of the tales relating such practices were recorded from formerly enslaved black folks during the WPA collection projects of the 1930s. Interviewees recalled slave masters tell- ing them about "something coming in and they saw it when it came in, and it had big eyes and black paws and all like that." Frequently what came was headless—"a mule coming in the kitchen with no head on" or a master see- ing "9 cows with no heads." To reiterate monstrous possibilities further, such slaveholders "would have a puddle of blood and claim that something came and killed someone. . . . Well, they would make as though there was probably some ferocious animal, or some spirit coming back. . . . [T]hey used all types of tactics to keep the people afraid down there" (65).

As noted, haunted places, such as "main roads, cemeteries, woods, houses" (66), were devised to control blacks as well, and when all else failed, the mas- ters would masquerade as ghosts. "Stage 'props' were generally limited . . . to the use of tin cans used as noisemakers, stilts to give the appearance of ghosts walking up off the ground, and a headless disguise. Concerning simulated headlessness, William Henderson stated: 'They used to formulate that kind, go 'round that kind of a way [headless] to frighten the people. . . . But the slaves believed that it was ghosts. But they got up that program to hold them down.' Headless disguises continued in popularity even after the Civil War and were later adopted with embellishments by the Ku Klux Klan" (70–71).

In a society where African Americans were mostly illiterate, where access to any kind of knowledge to refute the claims or actions of slaveholders was hard to come by, it is not surprising that many black folks believed what they heard and saw. If such tales and actions did not make them more docile, they certainly succeeded in making them less adventurous. We might argue that slaveholders used such concocted tales and night rides to scare black people "into slavery," into acquiescence to their reduced conditions of existence. We could argue equally that slaveholders were strikingly creative in their efforts to maintain control during slavery. Understanding how to instill fear, making sure that enslaved populations remained docile, knowing what it took to make people act like animals—these were the skills slaveholders employed time and time again. They succeeded well in making slavery a scary institution in which, for the most part, they retained the upper hand.

Enslaved African Americans also had their folkways in presenting slavery as a scary condition. Historians such as Lawrence Levine recount tales that African Americans told about slavery as well as on themselves as they existed under that institution. Whether those tales involved punishments or escape from work, trickster tactics or bolder practices, there is nonetheless a visible trail of African American commentary from slavery to freedom. In one instance, a feared older enslaved man, a good worker who has escaped punishment for the longest time by declaring that he will not be whipped, is tricked into getting drunk by his young master. As a result, he is "whipped . . . almost to death" by his young master and a group of "paddy-rollers" who have lain in wait for the whiskey to take effect.[2] In another instance, an enslaved man who complained about a toothache preventing him from working met an unforgettable fate. "In 1899 R. R. Moton related a story told to him by an old, toothless man who as a slave used to get out of work periodically by claiming he had a toothache. One day the master appeared with a pair of pincers and pulled out twenty of the slave's teeth and a piece of his jawbone as well. 'I ain't nuver had no mo' teefache from dat day to dis, dat I ain't,' the old man told Moton" (Levine, 129). Free from the watchfulness of overseers and owners, the formerly enslaved could converse relatively openly about their past experiences. What they recounted, in autobiographical or folktale mode, highlighted the precarious and frightening situations in which they existed. For many of them, their experiences were just as vivid in the 1930s as they had been in the early 1860s. The legacies of slavery manifested themselves in physical bodies and psychological conditions as well as in verbal art, crafts, and other tangible remnants. It would certainly have been nearly impossible for anyone who had lived through slavery to escape the impact of that condition.

If we shift from the historical world of the impact of slavery to the fictional world, imagine how much more impressive the shock of slavery might be for someone who had not experienced slavery, who had no memories to cushion the impact, no physical scars to evoke the pain, no missing relatives to haunt every waking moment. Octavia E. Butler gives us a glimpse of that shock when she sends her character Edana "Dana" Franklin from 1976 California back to 1815 Maryland in *Kindred* (1979). From freedom to slavery, from an interracial marriage to the segregation of a plantation, from having no fear of physical harm to her body to experiencing that fear every day, Dana makes clear that a young, twentieth-century black woman is ill equipped to be plopped down into slaveholding Maryland. Even less equipped is *Stigmata*'s Elizabeth "Lizzie" DuBose, a young black woman in Tuskegee, Alabama, to handle the slavery that comes to her in the 1980s as well as that into which she is drawn back in time (psychologically and emotionally but without physical transport at times and physically transported at other times). In the reversal of Dana's journey, Lizzie finds herself claimed, victimized, haunted, controlled, physically assaulted by events that occurred during the slave trade and slavery in the southern United States. The pain Lizzie suffers, however, is inflicted by her own black female ancestors, which gives her as heavy (if not heavier) a burden to bear as Horace Cross. Her life is a story of slavery wrapped—at times literally—in family history, pain, and folklore.

Perry, a native of Alabama, creates folk communities in the text to deal with the trauma and seepage of slavery. What I mean when I refer to *Stigmata* as having dynamic folk communities is that it has an original story—a haunting story about slavery—from which several narratives develop, both written and oral. It has various sites for transmission of those narratives, including Atlanta, Georgia; Birmingham, Tuskegee, and Johnson Creek, Alabama; and various places in the northern and western United States, including Michigan and Montana. It has multiple narrators of the tales, and it has both active and passive tradition bearers. It has central motifs and core beliefs. The story breaks from its original source and moves through multiple generations, especially every other generation. The story has the power to influence other narratives and in turn produce spin-off narratives. It has the power to spawn folk arts and crafts. This original story about American slavery, therefore, which was probably duplicated thousands if not millions of times between 1619 and 1863, has the power to shape, control, and destroy lives even as it has the power to sustain and encourage life.

Stigmata's original narrative is family folklore, and it begins with Ayo, an African girl kidnapped when she strays from the market stall where her mother, a master dyer of beautiful cloths, is engaged with prospective buyers. Ayo, whose name means "joy," knows very little joy in this world. She wakes to find herself on a slave ship bound for the new world, though of course she has no understanding of what is happening; all she knows is that she is separated from her family and wants to go home. She knows that "ghosts," Olaudah Equiano's "men without skins," are in control of her destiny.[3] Her responses are threefold—an almost inarticulate, unsubsiding terror, an abiding desire to return home, and, when she realizes that that is impossible, a desire to die, which she tries to accomplish by attempting to jump from the slave ship en route to the new world as well as upon its arrival. Prevented from killing herself, Ayo, who is renamed "Bessie" in the new world, finds herself sold, transported to a plantation, and surrounded by actions and voices that she does not understand. Her inability to comprehend the orders of the recently married, young white mistress of the plantation to which she is taken leads to the circumstances that pervade the book. Ayo insists that her daughter, Joy Ward, write the story, and this is what Joy transcribes from Ayo:

> So one day Im walkin in the backyard carryin water from the pump and Miz Ward lean out a window upstairs and screams somethin. So I just stop in my tracks. She screams again but I dont understand so I just keep walkin to the back door with the water and put it in the kitchen. Im on my way back to the pump when she comes flying out of the back door screamin at the top of her lungs. . . . Then she swat at me but she miss and then she run round the side of the house like a jackrabbit. . . . [S]he comes back with two men. Big muscular hands. . . . Shes carryin a whip and them two mens hold my arms while she whip me cross the back. Oh daughter she was laughin while she done it and them mens wouldn't look at me while I buck and try to get away. My dress fell away in big pieces and the blood ran down in the dirt . . .[4]

It takes weeks for the adolescent Ayo to heal, a measurement in pain and misery that makes clear the horror of the pain that Ayo's descendants will feel. Having had her wrists and ankles cut almost to the bone by chains and now having her back cut open, young Ayo again wishes for death and tries to bring it about by refusing to eat, only to discover her African mother holding vigil by the pallet on which she has been placed. This visitation is a signal to Ayo that she needs to live and remember. She eats, regains health, and moves forward under the weight of one of the most repressive female practitioners of slavery.

What we learn about Ayo is that she, like the presumed historical tribe of Flying Africans or Charles Johnson's Allmuseri that appear in his novels *Oxherding Tale* (1982) and *Middle Passage* (1990), has special gifts. "*I come,*" she later tells her daughter Joy, "*from a long line of forever people. We are forever. Here at the bottom of heaven we live in the circle. We back and gone and back again*" (7). In repetition that is at the heart of folkloristic transmission and the core motif that shapes belief, she reiterates that point later:

> *We are forever. Here at the bottom of heaven we live in the circle. We back and gone and back again.*
>
> *I am Ayo. Joy. I choose to remember.*
>
> *This is for those whose bones lie in the heart of mother ocean for those who tomorrows I never knew who groaned and died in the damp dark beside me. You rite this daughter for me and for them.* (17)

Reincarnation, immortality, circles of life and death thus become the driving force in the novel. Ayo's desire to write herself into immortality combines the oral and written traditions; she must tell the tale to a willing audience who will in turn make it available to audiences long after her death. Echoing historical African beliefs in reincarnation and fictional beliefs in immortality, such as those Toni Morrison's characters express at the end of *Paradise* (1998), when they claim that they are "down here in Paradise" even after death, Ayo sets in motion the family tradition, legacy, and narrative that haunt Lizzie DuBose in Tuskegee, Alabama, in the latter third of the twentieth century. Since a parent cannot give birth to herself, Ayo conveniently dies so that she can be reborn as Grace, her daughter's child. She says, "*[W]hen Im gone she* [Grace] *come to take my place*" (34). Grace is born a few months after Ayo dies in 1900. Grace in turn dies in 1958 so that Ayo *and* Grace can be reborn as Lizzie DuBose in 1960. In both instances the dying woman has known that she would have a granddaughter, and she has left a legacy for that granddaughter.[5]

The legacies Lizzie's great-great-grandmother and grandmother leave take the form of folk artifacts and oral history. Ayo tells her story to her daughter Joy and insists that she write it down. Like the women in Gayl Jones's *Corregidora* (1975), Ayo is insistent that the story of her dehumanization be told. However, the diary is also the plan, so to speak, for Ayo's rebirth. Joy, as the generation in between Ayo and Grace, is thus a tradition bearer through her writing skill as well as her editorial comments on the condition of her mother at various points of her life. Like a camera might record the facial expressions of someone who is telling a story, Joy editorializes about Ayo's mental and emotional conditions as she relates her story to Joy. For example, Joy makes comments such as *"She stop and look way over my shoulder like she werent even in the same room with me. Like she saw somethin off on the edge of the world. And her voice got deep and low and words roll off her tongue like water falling from a high place"* (7). On the night that Ayo tells Joy about her kidnapping in Africa, Joy prefaces the episode this way:

> *Mama be moanin in her sleep. She say its only old memory comin to visit. Last night she be in the next room moanin like that and cryin. . . . I went in and Mama just layin there in the moon beams kickin the covers. I just watch her Im afraid to get her up. Then she sit up in bed sudden and stare at me with sweat comin down her cheeks and forehead. For a while its like she dont no me then she grab my hand and yell rite this down! and I get up and run out to the other room. . . . When I got back to the room with the paper Mama is mumblin to herself. You rite fast Joy she say. I aint gon tell this but once. It too bad to tell more than once.* (71–72)

Ayo proceeds to relate, briefly, the tale of her capture in Africa. She faints when a man covers her mouth in the market where she has wandered away from her mother's work site, then wakes to find herself on a ship chained to people around her.

Ayo, Grace, and Lizzie might be artists in terms of the traditional creative arts of sewing and quilting, but Joy is an artist in terms of capturing human emotion in writing. Joy thus becomes the emotional barometer for the horrific impact of slavery upon her mother. As a member of the skipped generation, Joy cannot experience the pain of enslavement and whippings, but she can empathize with her mother's experiences and revelations and in turn reveal them to the generations following her. Her written accounts, therefore, have as much impact upon the oral tradition as Grace's quilt.

Joy also participates in the family tradition of folklore by being the audience to her mother's storytelling. By listening to and "riting" down Ayo's stories, Joy is ensuring the ritual of telling, the time-bound immediacy of revelation that cannot be captured on the page. A necessary part of folk transmission is the ear for the voice. Joy serves that role well for her mother. She also provides her daughter with another memory—that of her mother's handwriting.

When Grace, Joy's daughter, inherits her grandmother Ayo's diary and begins to experience Ayo's life in slavery, she finds the burden too much to bear. She abandons her husband, twin sons, and daughter Sarah in Johnson Creek, Alabama, and moves to the North, restlessly trying to escape the pain of enslavement and punishment that is heaped upon her body through the stigmata that epitomize Ayo's experiences. Her task in telling the story is to carry it on through folk art. Thus, Grace creates an appliquéd quilt detailing the story of Ayo's life; the quilt is to be passed on to Grace's granddaughter. A significant piece of that quilt is a small scrap of her mother's blue cloth that Ayo was clutching when she was snatched in the marketplace. Suspecting the specialness of the cloth, Grace finds an equally special place for it in the quilt. Grace then dies so that she can be reborn as her own granddaughter, Lizzie DuBose.

Although the trunk containing Grace's quilt and Ayo's diary arrives in Johnson Creek in 1945 and Grace dies in 1958, it is not until 1974, when Lizzie is fourteen and her Aunt Mary Nell dies that Grace's remaining sister, Eva, passes it on to Lizzie. Obviously hurt that the trunk has not been designated for her, Sarah nonetheless joins Lizzie in exploring its contents. The fragile diary almost falls apart in their hands, and the quilt merely seems a quilt with a narrative until Lizzie begins sleeping under it. Sympathetic magic ensues in which contact with the quilt transports Lizzie into the lives of the woman who designed and sewed the quilt and the woman who is its subject. In one of her first trips beyond her own experiences, Lizzie is the young Ayo on her way to the African market with her mother. A dream, perhaps? Perhaps—except that Lizzie wakes to the observation that "there is dust about" her feet (25). This is but the beginning of intertwined lives that will find Lizzie at the mercy of and drawn into multiple lives from the past.

This story of reincarnation and replicated pain dominates the female line of these southern families. Indeed, the men frequently seem not to have a clue as to what is going on, or the women deliberately protect the men from knowing, as Grace protects her husband, George Lancaster. The female line is also noteworthy, however, because it fits the pattern of the transmission of so much folklore throughout the southern United States. It is women who most often keep the legacies alive, maintain the family home places, and remember long-dead ancestors. Ayo thus succeeds well in ensuring the continuation of her forever line. However, because Lizzie becomes involved with a man with whom she shares her story, there is the slight prospect that there can now be a coed transmission of the story. Both Lizzie and Anthony Paul, her lover, feel that they have known each other before. It is finally revealed that Anthony Paul was the young boy that Ayo saw thrown overboard the slave ship when he was near enough to death to be deemed unsalvageable. He had looked at Ayo as he was tossed/sailed through the air to the sea. Ayo thought that he looked as if he were flying, and she wanted to join him. Her longing has thus brought him and Lizzie together in Tuskegee in 1995. His special history signals that men may now be incorporated safely into the female legacy of storytelling and reincarnation.

The only way the dead can stay alive or return is that the living not forget them, which fits into an African conception of time. As long as there is memory, there is life. In the case of the women in *Stigmata,* memory gives birth to life. The process that Ayo sets in motion on American soil (we do not get glimpses of its workings on African soil) may be necessary, but it could also be considered cruel. When Grace begins realizing that she is Ayo, she is a happily married woman in Johnson Creek, Alabama, in the late 1930s. That does not matter to Ayo. She strikes Grace with memories that lead to the manifestation of stigmata on her body in the same places that Ayo was chained on the slave ship as well as from the beatings she received. Fearful that she is going crazy from the memories, the pain, and the recurrent bleeding, Grace decides to disappear.[6] That was easier to do in 1940 than it is in 1980. When Lizzie begins experiencing Grace's memories, when she is transported into various scenes in Grace's life, and when Ayo adds on her pain and suffering, there is no place to turn—especially with a physician for a father—except to mental institutions. Dr. DuBose, therefore, has a role to play in the transmission of the story and the lives of the women even if he is unaware of it.

Still, we might ask why Ayo and Grace do not just politely tap Lizzie on the shoulder to get her attention instead of drowning her in pain and blood, for there are literally flaps of skin lifted from her wrists and gashing cuts into her ankles. When these are added to the Sethe-like scars that dominate her back from whippings Ayo received, the pain intensifies many times over. Yet

Ayo and Grace both believe this is necessary for their continuation, for them not to be forgotten as "forever people." Perhaps the intensity of their attention getting is warranted, for it takes Lizzie fourteen years in mental institutions before she stops running from the fear that her ancestors induce and turns to face the gifts they have to offer. Ayo literally whips her into submission, a submission that Lizzie finally understands, accepts, and uses creatively.[7]

The process of acceptance that Lizzie undergoes functions in a folkloristic way as well. She is the "audience," so to speak, for the tales that Ayo and Grace have to tell. She is their *only* audience. Ayo and Grace call; Lizzie responds. And readers, together with Lizzie's family, neighbors, friends, and doctors, are the audience for Lizzie's narrative. Lizzie draws readers into her story by strategic use of voice and person. When she succeeds in getting her psychiatrist to believe that she is cured, and he releases her, she silently exclaims: "Ah hah. I fooled you. I fooled you" (6). We are the only "hearers" of Lizzie's triumphant cry, the audience for verifying her sanity and her ordeal. Similarly, she draws us into her story with her use of "you" as well as with the invitation to evoke experiences we have had that are similar to hers instead of considering her crazy. "You know," she intones, "how sometimes when you're just about to fall asleep and sounds grow around you and maybe, just maybe, you hear your name floating by?" (9). That comfortable, soothing voice is not the voice of insanity. We also celebrate with her when she looks into the trunk after her release:

> A certain rush of happy relief surprises me; I am free, I remember [an echo of Ayo]. These things can't hurt me anymore. The story on those diary pages belongs to me, but they don't own me. My memories live somewhere spacious now; the airless chamber of horrors has melted into the ground. I guess psychotherapy, psychiatry and long-term residential treatment really cured me of something. Cured me of fear. Made me live with every part of myself every day. Cured me of the certainty that I was lost.... And Bessie became Grace, and Grace became me. Me, Lizzie. (46–47)

A conspicuous presence in a very middle-class family in small-town Tuskegee, Alabama, Lizzie can no more escape the attention she earns by going "crazy" than Grace can escape Ayo's calling; thus another layer of folk tradition is spawned as family, friends, and neighbors discuss what is happening with Lizzie. Her Aunt Eva, Grace's sister, knows what has happened to Grace and has been intimately involved in keeping the story from Grace's husband

George, and she is equally reluctant to share it with Dr. DuBose and his wife Sarah. Thus the Ward sisters, Grace, Mary Nell, and Eva, form a cluster of folk community in an early twentieth-century manifestation that will be duplicated with Eva and Lizzie in the latter part of the century. High school classmates form an additional folk community in speculating on the causes for Lizzie having gone crazy and where she has been for fourteen years of her life, but all their conjectures can amount only to rumor. Verbal tradition does not yield clarity or understanding to them, but it does yield segments of the story sufficient for them to keep a part of the folk tradition alive. Thus they inadvertently serve a role in documenting and perpetuating the original story that structures the novel.

Lizzie joins Grace in becoming a part of the folklore of Johnson Creek and Tuskegee, Alabama, for Grace especially captured the imaginations of the locals.

> A respectable woman disgraced is enough to provide *juicy talk* for decades. So by the time Grace died in 1958, before I was born, her *legend* was already well established. She never came back, but the trunk did—in 1945—accompanied by a mysterious letter to Mary Nell. . . . There were folks who still believed the *rumor* that Grace had run away with some jackleg preacher man who caught her eye, but Mary Nell and Eva apparently knew better. They always rolled their eyes and shook their heads whenever *that story* surfaced.
>
> They told the *story* the same way every time: First came the telegram from some man they didn't know and then the body to Union Springs. When the hearse arrived in Johnson Creek, everybody turned out to see the infamous woman who had abandoned her husband, George, and their children to run away "up the country somewhere."
>
> "Grace sho' gave 'em a show," Aunt Eva would say, smiling. (10; my emphases)

As a legend in and after her time, Grace captures the imaginations of countless raconteurs. By repeating tales about her, they inscribe her memory upon the life of the community even if they cannot connect all the dots. Indeed, *not* being able to connect all the dots serves as the very impetus to legend making. The mystery surrounding Grace is matched only by the mystery surrounding Lizzie, but obviously much more of Lizzie's story is revealed.

Validation of any folk narrative is a tricky business, as is validation of any extranatural occurrence, yet Perry includes such evidentiary material in *Stigmata* to provide objective, even if questionable, commentary on the truth of

Lizzie's experiences. Lizzie's cousin Ruth (another granddaughter who could have inherited the diary and quilt) is one character who is outside the circle of older adults who know the story of Ayo. When Ruth and Lizzie are visiting Eva on one occasion after Lizzie inherits the diary and the quilt, Ruth follows Lizzie as she goes sleepwalking one night. Caught up in Ayo's memories and believing herself back on the slave ship, Lizzie/Ayo dives off a bridge in an attempt to commit suicide, only to awaken to the discovery that she has dived into a pond on Eva's property, from which Ruth has rescued her. Ruth not only observes the facial transformations that Lizzie undergoes when she is taken over by Grace or Ayo, but she experiences the pain left by the shackle marks on Lizzie's wrists when she touches Lizzie. Ruth can feel the heat and the pain, which means that, although she has not been selected to receive the diary and the quilt, she is close enough to the family tradition to validate it. She is, in other words, a passive tradition bearer, the person folklorists identify as knowing the tradition well enough to know it, as Zora Neale Hurston would say, but not well enough to tell it. Ruth cannot experience fully what Lizzie is going through, but she understands that it is something beyond logic and empiricism.

In the older generation, Eva is the validator of the tradition. She has understood what was happening to Grace but has been powerless to do anything about it. With Lizzie, she tries to guide her as early as 1980.

> "The diary, see, is just the key, baby. The diary. The quilt. Just the keys that unlock the door to what you call the past."
>
> "So what are you telling me, Eva?" I watch her bustling from counter to table with cucumbers, tomatoes, chicken and cornbread, just reheated in the oven.
>
> "I'm telling you, *Grace*"—I jump when she rather pointedly says my grandmother's name and realize that I'd left off the customary "Aunt" when addressing her—"that this time you have to control this thing, these memories, or you're going to be in trouble. And you can't pack your bags and run away from it. You gotta stick here with it." (118)

Unfortunately, it will be fourteen troublesome years before Lizzie learns how to "control it."[8] This early in her inheritance of the diary and quilt, however, Lizzie is validated in her new role. Even when she is institutionalized, one of her moments of comfort is remembering Eva's validation: "I found myself strangely comforted by Aunt Eva; she called me by her sister's name and for the first time I had confirmation that Eva did understand, she knew who I was" (218). In the folk memories that Lizzie and Eva share, therefore, Eva serves to confirm the power of family folk tradition.

Validation of the tradition also comes through one of the patients in Lizzie's first mental institution, which is in Montgomery, Alabama. Lizzie will be silent for two years before she deigns to speak to one of her psychiatrists. During that period, she absorbs the memories and pains of Ayo/Grace and bleeds profusely, recurringly, from her wrists, ankles, and back. At the six-month mark of that silence, one of her doctors allows her out of her room. Another patient, a white woman who listens to the blues, sees Lizzie walking down the hall and asks her, "What in the world are you?" (162). When Lizzie does not respond verbally, the white woman pulls Lizzie into her room and offers her a drink before proceeding with this observation:

> "Now," she says, after taking a sip and settling into an old easy chair near the window. "I won't tell anybody. And I ain't afraid. I've heard about these things." She leans forward, whispering, "But I did see you, you can't deny that. First you were there, then she was. You look kind of alike but she's a little taller. Darker. Wearing a hat and gloves and carrying a suitcase. Pretty nigger girl. I saw her. Smiling and talking. Couldn't hear what she was saying, but saw her clear as day."
>
> This blows my mind, or what's left of it. She saw me. Us. Grace. I find myself wandering into the room a little further. (163)

The elderly white woman, with her entrée credential of the blues, has seen Lizzie as she looked when she went north as Grace and entered the first rooming house in which Grace had resided in Detroit. As Lizzie stepped into the hallway from her hospital room, she was experiencing Grace meeting her new neighbor in the rooming house, then moving to her room with her suitcase, when Mrs. Corday witnessed the incident.

Validation of folk legends is, as mentioned, always tricky business, which Perry elides by having Mrs. Corday be just as "crazy" as Lizzie. However, since readers know that Lizzie is not crazy, Mrs. Corday takes on the role of objective verifier that the vet serves in his supposedly "crazy" state in Ralph Ellison's *Invisible Man* (1952). Truth therefore transcends the purview of psychiatrists and the guards of mental institutions; it is located firmly in the realm of those who believe. Lizzie will come to believe more and more. Equally as important, she comes to accept what she believes. As a visiting priest tells her in the institution in which she spends time in Birmingham, "True faith is belief in the midst of unrelenting pressure" (232), which is certainly what

Lizzie's parents, especially Dr. DuBose, and the psychiatrists put on Lizzie. All of them want her to deny what she is experiencing. They prefer that she assert instead that she has been dreaming, that she has tried to commit suicide (though they can never uncover the instruments of that presumed attempted self-destruction), and that she make every effort to act normal and live in the latter part of the twentieth century in spite of all evidence to the contrary.

From another perspective, Dr. and Mrs. DuBose, Lizzie's parents, serve as validators of the folk tradition of which they are reluctantly a part by their very skepticism, fear, and insistence upon sanity. Every time Lizzie's physician father wants to insert rationality into the spaces where belief reigns, he succeeds in giving more credibility to belief. Every time he denies that Lizzie has actually bled involuntarily, he gives credence to the very possibility that he exerts so much energy denying. As a representative of the scientific approach to the world, Dr. DuBose is slotted into a position comparable to that in which Charles W. Chesnutt slots the northern white man, John, in *The Conjure Woman* (1899). The rationalist, by his very presence and insistence upon rationality, merely becomes the reaffirmer of the beliefs he denies.

Even more is this the case with Sarah, the abandoned child and skipped generation in the latter twentieth century. Sarah is so frightened of what is happening to her daughter Lizzie that she could easily have a breakdown under the strain. Every time she expresses that fear, she joins her husband in giving credence to the possibilities that fear engenders. Sarah, after all, is the daughter/mother of Lizzie/Grace and the great-granddaughter of Ayo. While she might not be gifted with the powers to transcend time, place, and experience that her female relatives have, she is perhaps close enough to those gene sets to sense what she does not fully understand and in which she cannot fully participate. Also, Sarah is the abandoned daughter in the scenario that privileges mother/daughter relationships. Her awareness of her mother Grace's disappearance and the emotional loss she has suffered as a result of that abandonment place her in a position close to mystery and legendary personalities.

Sarah's emotional state, her general ineffectualness in life (she is merely the doctor's wife, hosting her sorority parties with tea and little sandwiches), positions her as the primary target for recovery for Lizzie/Grace/Ayo once Lizzie learns not to fear the past. The circle of which Ayo spoke can be complete only when the relationship with Sarah is repaired, for that has been the primary tear in the mother/daughter fabric. Saving Sarah, so to speak, becomes the impetus for Lizzie's undertaking her own quilting project. Just as Grace told Ayo's story, so it is Lizzie's fate to tell Grace's story. By explaining in this narrative folk art form why Grace had to leave Sarah, and by being there to reclaim Sarah when she finally realizes that Lizzie is not only her daughter but also her mother, Lizzie brings the circle of the "forever people" to its natural conclusion. Once she faces fear, conquers it, and settles down to relive and value the experiences of Ayo and Grace, Lizzie is positioned well to ensure that her mother/daughter regains a sense of emotional health and that her yet unborn granddaughter will perhaps bear a less loathsome burden than Ayo/Grace/Lizzie and herself.

It is striking that so much of the story takes place in moonlight or with references to moonbeams (Lizzie even incorporates an image of "Grace reaching for the moon" [151] onto the quilt she makes). The moon is generally thought to govern the realm of extranatural happenings, of werewolves and heightened human emotions. Ayo's agitated kicks, for example, are reflected in moonbeams as she remembers being snatched away from her mother in Africa (71). Lizzie's first trip into Ayo's life occurs "when the moon is full" (24), and she wraps herself in Grace's quilt as "the moonlight bursts in through the window" (71). Grace connects Ayo's blue scrap with the moonlight and thus brings color and imagination into alignment with each other: "Blue. A closer look in the moonlight tells her it is that beautiful blue piece that her mother, Joy, had given her" (58). When Lizzie joins Grace in returning to the slave ship where Ayo was chained, which results in blood "drowning everything," she comes to herself as "the moonlight filters slowly back" (145) into her bedroom in Tuskegee. The folkloristic associations with the moon, therefore, overlay the novel with otherworldly and transnatural potential, all of it centered upon a reappearing body.

The shared body ("We hurt, our body hurts. Arms and ankles and back"— 56) and shared memories of these three women evoke folk stories of shape shifting (which frequently occurs during certain phases of the moon, especially the full moon), reincarnation, and ghostly possession. In many ways, *Stigmata* is an ultimate kind of ghost story, a never-ending one in which generations upon generations can be caught up. As the lives of the three women most directly affected in the novel make clear, however, the particular components of that never-ending story can vary and can have tremendously different impacts upon different individuals. Ayo's haunting, for example, is duplicated in the very diary structure of the novel, another ghostly way in which the women are tied together.

Beyond ghost stories, the title of the novel sends us in a slightly different direction. With its religious connotations, the word "stigmata" evokes godliness and belief. The power that Ayo exhibits to re-create herself certainly has a ring of goddesshood to it. From African sources in her background or simply from the sheer force of will power in a difficult world, Ayo wills herself into immortality. No matter how difficult that process is or how horrible it might initially be for others, she nonetheless sets it in motion, at least on United States soil. The "we" she identifies as part of the "forever people" is not clearly articulated with persons on this side of the Atlantic. The "we" might simply refer to what she *knows* is going to happen with her granddaughter and her great-great-granddaughter. Clairvoyance, therefore, is another component of the godliness that characterizes her. Her extranatural power might also be read in the context of witchcraft or sorcery, except that there are no overt signs of that in the text. Even if we thought of the diary or the quilt as being conjured, there is no strand of conjuration that would yield life from death across several generations.

Instead of some kind of sleight-of-hand conjuration, belief seems to be the key to understanding the situation in which the descendants of Ayo find themselves. As with much seemingly inexplicable phenomena in an otherwise rational world, whether or not people accept what happens with Ayo, Grace, and Lizzie depends upon their willingness to believe. This applies as much to the women themselves as it does to the people around them. We can chart Grace's growing belief of what is happening with her even as she questions her sanity. We can chart the same growth with Lizzie, even as she is confined in various mental institutions. She moves from witnessing the past to experiencing the past, from trying to separate herself from her ancestors, to realizing that they share the same body. Once she truly believes, she is strong enough to share her story with Sarah and to act as Sarah's mother in soothing the pain of abandonment out of her. And we can chart the belief with the resistant Sarah. Once Sarah lays out the completed quilt of the narrative of her mother's life and stands transfixed before it, Lizzie can step into that moment and reveal all to her mother/daughter. It is Sarah who then stitches the final piece of blue cloth onto Grace's quilt (as a scarf around Grace's neck), leading Lizzie to observe: "The circle is complete and my daughter sits across from me with the gap finally closed" (230). The section ends in this manner:

"I used to beg God to send you back to me," she [Grace] says trembling.

"I came as soon as I could."

The quilt slides to the floor as she puts her head in my lap. I stroke the hair out of her eyes. (230)

Skeptical Grace, through her prayers, has actually played a role in the cycle of reincarnation. More important, if the intensely skeptical Grace can be brought to belief, then it is possible to garner legions of converts. It is noteworthy that this final moment of reconciliation and recovery occurs on a Fourth of July, for it marks newfound independence and release for both Sarah and Lizzie/Grace/Ayo. Recall that that symbolic date also marks Dana's final return to California in *Kindred*, and it is the day on which Harker, Cully, and Nathan rescue Dessa from Hughes's cellar in *Dessa Rose.*

Stigmata, though, is also what the text is about in terms of its audience, both textual and extratextual. Throughout the text, the proponents of rationalism reject Lizzie's claims. Throughout the text, the women participating in the reincarnated lives must be brought into belief about them. And throughout the text, there are a couple of folks who are willing to believe—the priest who visits Lizzie, Mrs. Corday, Anthony Paul. As a narrative told to a skeptical extratextual audience, the concept of stigmata invites the potential for belief. It was the intensity of his belief, the priest tells Lizzie, that led a monk to bleed from wounds comparable to those of Jesus Christ. By surrounding a story of slavery with the context of Christian belief, Perry succeeds in overlaying her tale with multiple layers of veracity, and she gives Christianity much more positive possibilities than Randall Kenan does. The tales the women tell, the incidents they experience, are always told/read against the backdrop of one of the greatest human horror stories turned triumphant. If Christians believe in Christ's resurrection and in the possibility that others bleed as he did, then why not believe that a slave woman, who was so physically and psychologically violated, found a way to live again? By intertwining the secular and the sacred that so characterize African American folk traditions, Phyllis Perry locates her narrative solidly within those traditions and makes her tale of slavery, reincarnation, violence, and violation one worthy of continuing oral, written, and artistic transmission.

Transmission is a balm against terror, against southern horrors. Ultimately, her family tradition of stories saves Lizzie, gives her strength to continue living in the South and the power to know how to live wisely and effectively. It is a salvation that is unavailable to Horace Cross, who, in contrast to Lizzie, cannot stop his fate short of suicide. Unlike stories that are designed only for the imagination and the emotions, those that affect Lizzie are also designed for the body. They shape her identity as a Ward woman, but they also shape her body as a DuBose woman. Once she discovers her history, culture, and fate, and affirms the potential for health and wholeness, she, like Toni Cade Bambara's Velma Henry in *The Salt Eaters* (1980), can begin to envision herself as a cultural worker whose future is filled with possibilities for creativity, self-fulfillment, and familial/communal preservation. Hers is a hopeful future that echoes that of Dessa Rose. For characters who encounter slavery in Edward P. Jones's *The Known World*, the last text in this study in which slavery is a central focus, no such hopefulness exists.

DOMESTICATING FEAR

Tayari Jones's Mission in *Leaving Atlanta*

When African Americans were enslaved, they faced a visible, tangible evil. The horror of capture in Africa led to the horror of being paraded as things in front of eager buyers in auctions in the New World. From the auctions to the plantations or wherever they were enslaved, black people could not hide from the white people who professed to own them, the white and black overseers who drove them in the fields, or the whims of white mistresses who could make their lives miserable in the plantation houses. After slavery, tangible horrors continued in the sharecropping system and the convict lease systems. People of African descent daily encountered the forces that shaped their lives, indeed held their very lives in the balance. They experienced similar encounters with the court systems that could curtail their freedom or end their lives on a whim. In the face of tangible, visible evil, black people could devise strategies for fighting back. Through their folk traditions, they could pass down survival strategies by word of mouth, they could encode messages that only their fellow blacks could decipher when pointing to an escape route to the North, and they could devise whatever means necessary—within limits, of course—to fight back against oppression and confinement, as Gladys-Marie Fry, Lawrence Levine, and others have documented.

151

Knowing and *seeing* the enemy that controls one's life at least gives an enslaved or a repressed person the hopeful possibility that he or she can overcome, escape, or subvert the will of that enemy. But what if one cannot see the enemy? What if the enemy is not known or knowable? What if the enemy thrives on secrecy and the power to disrupt community and kill at will? What if the enemy, as invisible and imperceptible as the very air one breathes, glides in and out of one's community, selects victims, and kills them like ancient chimeras slaughtered their victims? Can there ever be a defense against an enemy that operates like air but is as destructive as a category five hurricane? These kinds of questions undoubtedly crossed the minds of many citizens of Atlanta, Georgia, and the surrounding areas between 1979 and 1981 when, depending upon the records one consults, twenty-eight, twenty-nine, or thirty-one young black people, most of them male, mysteriously disappeared from a section of southwest Atlanta. The youngest victim was seven and the oldest twenty-seven. They all disappeared from territory along Memorial Drive in southwest Atlanta that covered approximately a twelve-block area. According to police records, the bodies of the recovered victims were mostly "strangled" or "asphyxiated."[1] For twenty-two terrifying months, the people of Atlanta had no clue to the killer and no sense of the motive. What was clear was that young black people were dying—mysteriously, brutally, viciously.

The Atlanta Child Murders or "the Atlanta child murder case" nearly paralyzed the city of Atlanta. More specifically, it brought unprecedented heights of fear to the black people of that city. While American history may have taught black people well that they could die just for being black, the manner in which the murders occurred in Atlanta increased levels of fear exponentially. Experiencing that fear was young Tayari Jones, who was in the fifth grade at Oglethorpe Elementary School in southwest Atlanta when most of the murders occurred. As a young adult, Jones began to pursue in earnest the story of what had occurred in her community between 1979 and 1981. Her response is *Leaving Atlanta* (2002), a novelistic account of the impact of the Atlanta Child Murders on preadolescent children in that area.

The Atlanta Child Murders began with the disappearances of Edward Smith and Alfred Evans in the late summer of 1979. They ended (at least officially) with the disappearance and murder of twenty-seven-year-old William Barrett, who disappeared on May 16, 1981, and whose body was found shortly thereafter near his home. The disappearances and murders were understandably horrible, but what increased that horror was the pervasive uncertainty and fear surrounding the cases. As James Baldwin makes clear with the disappearance of Peanut in *Just Above My Head*, the possibility of disappearance is equally as horrible as the fact itself, for the realm of imagination can be infinitely more powerful than reality. To be in a situation where any form of self-defense was like fighting the air, black Atlantans lived in a terrified state of siege. At any time, any child—or any young adult—could be snatched. And, at any time, *anyone* could be accused of snatching a child. To illustrate how pervasive this fear was, consider the account that Tayari Jones provides of one of her father's errand-running outings.

> Just before Wayne Williams was arrested, my father returned home from a simple errand about an hour late. He was shaken, clearly upset. My parents weren't the sort who would discuss important matters before the children, so we were sent away. But I hung back, where I could listen.
>
> My father explained that he had become lost while finding his way home. He'd driven around on the back roads, looking for a familiar street sign. "What would have happened if the police had pulled me over? I'd been gone for almost an hour. I couldn't say where I had been. There was no one to vouch for me." I backed away from my secret eavesdropping space, having already heard more than was good for me.[2]

Jones's father's fear is understandable, given the fact that one of the investigators of the murders had publicly stated that black parents were killing their own children.[3] Jones's father could thus just as easily have been arrested and accused of the killings as Wayne Williams was a matter of days later. Uncertainty and fear, therefore, made potential victims out of people who were already victimized.

What made the situation more horrible was that information about the cases was not as forthcoming as the violence seems to have warranted. In the absence of such information, therefore, rumors, legends, and conspiracy theories developed to fill in the gaps. Turner, a folklorist who studies rumor and conspiracy theories, interviewed individuals in Atlanta following the closing of the cases and published her findings. Residents felt variously that the CDC (Centers for Disease Control), the FBI, the CIA, and the KKK were responsible for the murders. In 1979, there was much discussion of how interferon, a substance in the human body, could be used to cure cancer. Expendable members of the body politic (that is, black people—and especially black males), it was felt, were being killed and their bodies used in experiments to find a cure for cancer. The FBI, CIA, and KKK were just presumed to be in their usual roles of keeping black people down. Also, as Turner points out, since the first two agencies were linked—at least in the minds of the folk—with the assassinations of the Kennedys and Martin Luther King Jr., black folks were inclined to indict them in their perceptions of an overall antiblack sentiment at the governmental level. A few klansmen were interviewed about the cases, but reportedly no evidence led to viable pursuit of any klansmen.[4]

Other conspiracy theories centered on taxi drivers and policemen in Atlanta. The general feeling among blacks was that anyone with easy access and quick getaways from the section of town in which the murders occurred was suspect. It did not matter that those persons, such as the police, might have been authority figures. As history and folklore have captured, black people have never felt that they could rely upon the police for safety. Indeed, in many striking instances historically and contemporarily, the police have served as enemies of black people. One need but contemplate the instances in the South in which white sheriffs handed over black males accused of crimes so that mobs could lynch them. And one need but contemplate historically the Emmett Till case in 1955 in which officers were complicit with the killers, or, in more-recent times, the Rodney King case in California in 1991 in which King was surrounded and beaten by a group of police officers as he lay on the ground, or the Amadou Diallo case in New York in 2006 in which a black man was fired at forty-one times (nineteen bullets hit him) for reaching for his wallet. It is not surprising, therefore, that black people could just as easily imagine the police in Atlanta killing black children as they could imagine the KKK or other hate groups committing such murders.

To step into this complex recent history and render it fictionally is no small task, for it has not simmered over a hundred years or through the Emancipation Proclamation or other devices designed to change the situations of blacks in America. Yet that is precisely what Tayari Jones undertakes in *Leaving Atlanta*. She steps into raw, unhealed history, tunnels through the violence and emotion, and tries to make sense of what it meant to a group of children in the fifth grade in Atlanta when children were being snatched. She comments on her blog:

> As I write these words, I can understand those who would argue that reopening this case is "opening old wounds." But for many Atlantans, the memory of the child murders cannot be likened to an old wound, carefully sutured and healed.

For us, it is more like a bone poorly set—painful, crooked and gimpy. The events of 1979–81 so ravaged our community that we have been unable to speak of them in the years since. The arrest and conviction of Williams for the murders of two adults, and the subsequent closing of the children's cases, was neither balm nor tincture. Rather, it was just a plaster cast, ensuring that the fractured bones of our community would never properly mend.

Re-examining this case will cause great pain to Atlanta, the city of my birth, the place where my family still lives. I don't anticipate that this will be easy. Tempers will flare, as will old rivalries and grudges. But as we know, the only way to repair a bone badly set is to break it again, and then set it right.[5]

In the face of no new conclusions about the cases, Atlantans such as Jones must find solace in other ways. For Jones, that is the fictional re-creation of a moment in time and the fictional license to provide her own kind of closure.

In *Leaving Atlanta,* her first novel, Tayari Jones is less concerned about locating the villain or villains in the Atlanta Child Murders than in dealing with the consequences of fear. The city that was "too busy to hate" all of a sudden became a place where children wondered if they would be the next victims and where parents took extreme measures to ensure that their children were safe. Jones locates the fear in a classroom of fifth graders, in which a child by the name of Tayari Jones is enrolled. The adult Jones looks back on the childhood Jones with the eyes of analyst and participant who can re-create the sharpness of the fear the children experienced. But she does more than that. She takes that fear and essentially *domesticates* it. Ten- and eleven-year-old children worry about killers snatching them in the midst of worrying about whether or not their parents will get divorced, whether they will be invited to a party the neatest girl in fifth grade gives, and whether they can ever really please their parents.

Leaving Atlanta is divided into three parts, each of which utilizes a distinct point of view. The first section is devoted to LaTasha Baxter and is related in a traditional third-person-limited point of view. Tasha is the older of two daughters in her family. Tasha's father, Charles, having recently moved out to live "with his woman," returns home when the children start disappearing.[6] Tasha observes and tries to gather as much information as she can from her parents; she then parrots her father's comments in an effort to appear informed about the missing children in front of her fifth-grade classmates. The second section, devoted to Rodney Green, is related in a very unsettling second-person point of view. Like Tasha, Rodney's family is a nuclear one—with Father, Mother, and Sister (a younger sibling). Rodney's position in his family, particularly his fear of his father, influences the decision he makes to get into a car with a stranger at the end of his section. The final and longest section, related in first person by Octavia "Sweet Pea" Fuller, whose dark skin leads her classmates to call her "Watusi," ties up some of the loose ends of the first two sections. Living *near* the projects (as opposed to *in* them) with her single mother, Octavia is far more streetwise than most of the kids in her fifth-grade class, but there are still major issues with which she must deal. This section ends with Octavia on the verge of leaving Atlanta to live with her father and his new family in Orangeburg, South Carolina.

It is in the nuclear family of LaTasha Baxter, reconstituted because of the threat, that Jones spends most time exploring the impact of the murders upon families, as "Daddy" (Charles) and "Mama" (Delores) discuss the situation around Tasha and her younger sister, DeShaun. What is clear from Tasha's perspective is that all of the people and institutions that kids can usually count on for safety start to fall apart. The first of these is family. Tasha is initially humiliated at school when Monica Fisher, the most popular girl in the fifth grade, asserts that she has "let" Tasha win at jacks because her mother instructed her to be nice to Tasha because Tasha's parents are "separated" (7). Even before children are snatched, therefore, Tasha's lack of ability to rely on her parents, who have told her that they are "*living apart*" temporarily, begins the unraveling of areas of her life that she has earlier considered safe.

Her father's return provides only a temporary balm, for Tasha must witness the impact of the child murders upon Charles and register the implicit racism that informs his thinking about the killer or killers. His assessment of the situation parallels the conspiracy theories that Patricia A. Turner uncovered in her interviews about the cases:

> "It's got to be somebody white," Daddy said, shoving his peas around his plate with a slice of light bread.
>
> "Might be," Mama said.
>
> "Might nothing. Think about it. You ain't never heard of nobody black going around killing people for no reason. That's white people's shit.". . .
>
> "Think about it, Delores," he said. "Charles Manson, Son of Sam, all of that stuff. White folks."
>
> "I've known some black folks to do some ugly things," said Mama.

"I ain't saying that niggers are harmless. I know a black man will cut you in a minute on a Saturday night over his money or his woman, something like that."

"Yeah, a real good reason like that."

"Delores, I am not saying that it's all right to stab somebody for two dollars. I'm saying that *we* gotta have a *reason* for killing someone. White folks just kill for the hell of it." (35, 36–37)

This conversation supplies Tasha with information that she uses to try to gain status among the popular girls in her fifth-grade class. Since she is eavesdropping to get the latter portion of the conversation, it indicates the level of concern among adults that gets transferred to children.

Tasha really sees the impact of the murders upon her father after he returns home from a stint with a search party, in which several whites have also participated. Although his search did not yield any bodies, Charles is so disturbed and so sure that white racism is responsible for the deaths that he insists, over his wife's objections, upon telling Tasha and DeShaun about the church bombings in Birmingham as well as about the death of Emmett Till. Charles's shouting rants about "white folks burning niggers alive" (77) and a fist punch to the table lead Tasha to want comfort from her father, for him to step back from his own trauma to soothe her: "Tasha wanted him to hold her on his lap, kiss her forehead, and say that everything was all right. But he didn't even look at her" (77). The upsetting scene leads Mama to send the girls to their room, but, as usual, Tasha hangs back to gather whatever additional information she can. She listens as her traumatized father ends up on the floor with his head in Delores's lap, describing the scene during the search. Although he and the white man paired with him only found a dead dog in a trash bag, another group found the body of a girl. What makes it especially frightening is that the body was not "way north," where Charles's party searched, but very near the neighborhood in which the Baxter family lives. Charles is so distraught about the news that he has to be rocked "like a grumpy baby" (79). If parents are reduced to infantilism in the face of the violent murders, then what hope is there for the children? Charles has returned from living with his woman, but he has perhaps inadvertently created more anxiety in Tasha than he has relieved. Of course he is unaware that Tasha is eavesdropping, but the impact upon her is no less dramatic. She has heard/witnessed a meltdown of the authority and safety upon which she has previously relied. If the persons kids look up to to provide comfort and soothing words during this difficult time are themselves traumatized, then where can kids turn? Yet another of Tasha's assumed sources of safety, therefore, gets called into question.

Jones domesticates fear in the novel by showing the impact of the murders through the eyes, minds, and emotions of children. When children no longer play on the streets, when they have to huddle in a neighbor's house after school for fear of being snatched, the pervasive nature of the threat is compounded. In Tasha's section, Tasha and her sister try to come to terms with what the murders mean by likening them to scary things with which they are familiar. They also echo the title of the section by recognizing the impact of "magic words." Such words can ward against evil, but they can also create evil, as Tasha believes she does when she "curses" one of her classmates who is later snatched.

The girls' effort to understand what is happening around them is comparable to Claudia and Frieda's effort to understand the adult world in Toni Morrison's *The Bluest Eye.* When Mr. Henry touches Frieda's breasts and she believes that she has been "ruined," a condition that can be alleviated only through drinking alcohol, the girls create their own folk space, children's versions of folk traditions that will save them. So too does Tasha attempt to carve out a space of safety in the face of the possibility of being snatched. She and DeShaun move from sleeping with Delores on the first night that missing children's faces are splashed across the television screen to executing other ways that they can be safe. When they come home from school before their mother arrives from work, "they would go to their room, shut the door and put a chair in front of it as an obstacle for child murderers who might be lurking in the house waiting for sisters coming home alone" (32). Tasha realizes that the fear generated is "way worse than a swamp-monster with vague motives" (28), which is the result of her using movies to measure her previous levels of fright. After her father returns home and after the numbers of snatched children rises, Tasha posits the belief that it could be a creature snatching the children, and that the only thing "keeping the creature from getting us is Daddy" (42), because "those kids that got snatched, not one single one of them has a daddy" (42). The flawed logic here—comparable to alcohol-is-the-cure for being "ruined" conclusion that Frieda and Claudia reach—illustrates the child's attempt to deal with the unknown and the monstrous.

Tasha finally advises DeShaun that "if the creature tries to get you, all you have to do is say a magic word" (42). It is the belief in the power of words, their magic, that leads Tasha to conclude that she has contributed to the snatching and death of one of her classmates. Jashante, a boy from the projects, takes a liking to Tasha. Unfortunately, the popular girls look down upon Shante, thereby making it difficult for Tasha to show unqualified affection for him, even though she does like him. In a relay race at school, Shante causes Tasha to fall and rip a prized pink coat that her father has bought for her. In retaliation, she utters these words: "'I hope you die. I hope the man snatches you and . . .' She searched her mind for the word she had heard on the news. 'I hope you get asphyxiated and when they find you you are going to be . . .' What was the other word? 'Decomposed'" (45). Understandably, then, when Shante is indeed snatched and presumably killed (his body is not recovered), Tasha blames herself. Indeed, she is almost inconsolable when Shante disappears. While her "magic words" have certainly not been responsible for Shante's death, Tasha nevertheless reveals the pattern by which children engage with tragedy, how they try to make sense of the horrors that affect their world.

When DeShaun later asks Tasha for the magic word that will keep her safe, Tasha has a vague response: "'Oh, *that* magic word,' Tasha said, as if there were only one. Words could be magic, but not in the abracadabra way that DeShaun believed. The magic that came from lips could be as cruel as children and as erratic as a rubber ball ricocheting off concrete" (81). With her knowledge of what has happened to Shante, Tasha does not provide a magic word; instead, she gives DeShaun a charm: the Christmas tree air freshener that Shante has given to her. She admonishes DeShaun: "Put this under your pillow and you'll be alright" (82). In a world where there is no tangible protection, the realm of folk belief seems the only solace left to the girls. That is the note on which the section ends, as Tasha retains the role of big sister and protector to DeShaun.

Jones places the child murders and their impact upon Tasha's life on par with and sometimes trumped by other of Tasha's concerns. That is another part of the domestication of fear. Tasha is desperate to be popular with Monica Fisher and the group of girls that surrounds her. She practices jump rope and jacks all summer long to impress the girls, only to discover that they now consider jumping rope "baby stuff" (they are probably hiding the fact that they are not as adept as Tasha is by now). She selects her friends on the basis of whether or not they would be acceptable to Monica's group. She rejects Rodney Green, "the weirdest kid in class" (8, 44), because the other children do. When her father purchases the pink coat for her, she thinks that "Monica Fisher was going to pass out with jealousy" (34). When Monica's group rejects Tasha after she "curses" Shante, she is especially careful about where she sits at lunch: "If she sat with Octavia today, she could never eat with Monica and Forsythia again. Unpopularity was terribly contagious" (48). Tasha's overwhelming desire to be popular takes up as much if not more of her time and emotion than the missing and murdered children do. Jones thereby succeeds well in showing that horror can take up only so much space in an eleven-year-old mind. Everyday things with which children are concerned can be life stoppers as much as murderers can be.

Consider the case of Monica Fisher planning a party to which Tasha is hoping to get an invitation. The extended scene is unparalleled in emphasizing how regular events in the children's lives carry as much if not more weight than the snatched children. On the day that Monica brings the "nine pink envelopes" (53) to class, Tasha goes through a list of girls who might be invited to the party, including alternates. As the envelopes get passed from hand to hand, Tasha eliminates some of the alternates and holds on to the possibility that she might indeed be included. When the teacher's entrance into the classroom disrupts the passing out of envelopes, Monica has to wait until after lunch to pass out the final one. That gives Tasha even more time to stress herself out about the possibility of that envelope reaching her hands. Instead, it lands in the hands of Tayari Jones, with whom Tasha has been having lunch after she dumped Octavia. She convinces herself that Tayari, who is a "cutup," is "just playing" and will shortly "pass Tasha that pretty invitation" (55). When Tayari opens the envelope, "Tasha ran her finger down a column of spelling words, as if this week's quiz were the reason she was on the brink of tears" (56). Certainly, Tasha cries about Shante, but she also cries about being rejected by popular girls in her class. In this prepubescent stage, one pain is nearly as great as the other. By leveling the response between children being snatched and a child being rejected by the most popular girl in her class, Jones again contains fear. While she does not suggest that child snatching is as "normal" an activity as planning parties, she does suggest that the emotional impacts can be comparable.

Rodney Green, like Tasha, is part of a nuclear family. The family's middle-class status and issues surrounding it often seem to take precedence over the tragedy happening around the family. The fear that his father induces in Rodney is much greater than any fear he might have about being snatched by one of the child murderers. Also, as the most unpopular boy in his fifth-grade class, Rodney struggles with various inadequacies. Through class issues and peer pressures, therefore, Rodney's section becomes a meditation on power, authority, and victimization. They ultimately lead Rodney to get into the car with a man who he knows is masquerading as a policeman. This "passive suicide," as one of my students refers to it, makes clear yet again that, from a child's perspective, the Atlanta Child Murders only intermittently evoked the same responses from children as they did from adults.[7]

Readers may conclude initially that Rodney is the most expendable of the three children by virtue of the second-person narrative that Jones uses in his section. The effect is one of distancing—of the reader from Rodney, of Rodney from his family, of Rodney from just about everyone around him as well as from himself. Paradoxically and simultaneously, the second-person narration also locks readers into Rodney's situation. Forced to watch him watch his father and his family, as well as his classmates, we ponder the total alienation of this eleven-year-old from just about everything and everybody around him. Rodney is in a situation comparable almost to watching a movie of his life, with him being dragged along as the reluctant participant.

Rodney's problems begin with his middle-class family. "Father," "Mother," and "Sister" are perfect—echoing again the Dick and Jane myth of American nuclear families that Morrison unravels in *The Bluest Eye*. Father (Claude L) is a successful businessman, Mother (Beverly) spends her days shopping, taking yoga classes, and playing the role usually expected of the leisured middle-class wife, and Sister (Patricia) is the perfect little apple of her parents' eye. Rodney is the screwup, the misfit in this perfection. Although he has scored impressively high on standardized texts, he refuses to live up to his potential. His grades are poor, his mother does his homework, and he generally does not seem to care about very much at all. What gets most response from him is his father, and that response is measured only through his thoughts, for Rodney tries to remain silent as much as he can: "Since your words are almost invariably misinterpreted, you avoid speech in general and abstain entirely from rhetorical questions" (87) and "you are not shy. You simply have nothing to say" (98). *How* this child has arrived at this state is not completely clear, though there are some possibilities; what *is* clear is that Rodney is in a psychological, emotional, and physical hole that we can compare to how Richard Henry describes his life, for it seems rather more advanced than Rodney's young life would warrant.

The "how" of Rodney's condition is contained mostly in his relationship to his father. He believes that his father hates him. His father's mere presence evokes tension in Rodney, and he imagines his father planning, from early in the morning, ways to "berate" him over dinner. While there may be no objective verification of the father's hatred in the point of view that locks readers so closely into Rodney's perspective, a few things are apparent. Rodney's father is a "manly man," one who "picked cotton" and has pulled himself up by the bootstraps to owning a car repair shop. He has hopes of his son following in his footsteps, or at least appreciating the value of hard work. Unfortunately, Rodney is the classic nerd who wears glasses, is short, and is physically inept. When Tayari's older brother Lumumba sees Rodney trying to run at school one day, his comment is: "'Little man sho do run flickted'" (135), which is a curse in a world where Father would like his son to be as physically fit as he is.[8] Echoing Tasha's comment that the children who were taken mostly had missing fathers, the narration asserts from Rodney's perspective: "You have heard of an epidemic of disappearing black fathers, but you know you will never be as lucky. Yours comes home *every* evening . . ." (110). On one such evening when his father asks Rodney if he has done his homework, and Rodney shakes his head, the narration is: "Father exhales. He is disappointed that he has nothing better for a son. A boy who is not only too short but *trifling, lazy, sloven, and spoiled*" (127). On one early morning when Rodney's father sees him coming out of the bathroom and insists that Rodney have breakfast with him, Rodney must serve as a sounding board to his father's stories of growing up around his own father. Ever silent, Rodney finds his father's conversation and the breakfast so repugnant that he vomits as soon as he can reach the bathroom after the ordeal (132).

It is also clear that Rodney has failed to live up to Father's expectations as early as his fourth year of life. Claude L was determined to teach Rodney to swim; the effort has almost disastrous consequences:

> You nearly drowned when you were about four. . . . Father held his large hands under you as you lay, trusting, near the surface of the cool, chlorinated water.
>
> "Kick," he commanded, and you did.
>
> He laughed. "Look, Beverly," he shouted over his hairy shoulder. "This boy might be ready for the Olympics in seventy-six!". . .
>
> You sank. . . . Powerful hands with calluses softened by cool water lifted you through the blue glass. You twined your legs around Father's waist. Wiry chest hair scratched your trembling stomach.

"What happened?" he asked, prying you from his torso so that your faces were level. "You were swimming good until you saw that my hands were gone. Then you went under like a lead balloon."

He laughed a little bit, but you cried. "Oh, come on." Father gave you a rough shake. "Don't act like a little girl." (114)

This failure may account in part for Rodney's current relationship to his father. Immediately after the pool incident, when Rodney seeks comfort from his mother, who is pregnant with Sister, his father's comment is: "Beverly, you gonna make this boy into a sissy" (115). Notions of "sissification" are prominent in Claude L's relationship to Rodney in the sense that it is the opposite of sissification, the "manly manliness," that wins consistent approval from Claude L.

Rodney, then, is in a perfect family where his alienation is complete. He is frightened of his father physically as well as frightened of the authority his father wields over him. His father beats him when he gets bad grades and tells him that he is "never going to amount to nothing" (129). Rodney takes refuge in silence, mask wearing, and mentally applauding his father's small failures. For example, during a major thunderstorm, Claude L insists that Rodney go outside with him to repair a drainpipe. It is this moment in the text when fear of his father combines with Rodney's awareness of the missing children to brew a strange indictment.

Apprehension envelops you, permeating even your bones. Father never solicits your assistance in such decidedly male endeavors. What did rotund Officer Brown say? *If you don't know who it is, you don't know who it's not.* One dead girl was taken out of her window. The barbershop consensus indicts her stepfather. "Who else could get a child out the house without her screaming and carrying on?" the men wanted to know, as clippers buzzed against their necks. And who else besides a father, of some kind, could harbor such malevolence, you mused, sitting very still in the red-cushioned chair. (116)

Rodney imagines writing a note to Octavia: "*My father has taken me out of the house early on Tuesday morning*" (116). Of course Rodney's father is not one of the child killers, but the fact that Rodney even remotely entertains the possibility suggests how totally distrustful and frightened he is generally of his father. The only weapon he has is silent pleasure when his father fails to repair the drainpipe as efficiently as he anticipated: "Your feet are going numb from the cold stagnant water in your shoes, but you enjoy the pain as you witness Father's sheer ineptitude" (117).

The Officer Brown to whom Rodney refers had come to the fifth-grade class to provide information about the child murders. It is an occasion for learning more about the murders as well as for showcasing Rodney's mostly unused intelligence. When Officer Brown declares that Shante is "only missing. Lots of missing children are found each day and returned to their parents," Rodney's perspective is: "Not around here. Not this year. You now know, as undeniably as if you had read it in the World Book Encyclopedia, that Officer Brown has nothing useful to share. As a matter of fact, you are more fearful than ever to know that this man is all that stands between your generation and an early death" (93). When Shante's cousin asserts that his father says "it's the police that's doing it" (94), Officer Brown responds: "There may be some individuals *impersonating* officers of the law. But the imposter will not have this!" (95), and he proceeds to show a badge with raised letters, which are reputedly the distinctive mark of authentic police badges. Rodney's assessment is: "This man is clearly delusional, so you do not point out that a criminal who could steal an official police *uniform* certainly would not neglect to take an official police *badge*. Furthermore, it is nearly time for recess" (95). Rodney keeps his intelligence to himself, just as he keeps his fear to himself.

The fear that he cannot overcome, that is, the fear of his father, manifests itself in a scene that leads to Rodney's going voluntarily with a stranger. Claude L's friend, Mrs. Lewis, owns a store from which Rodney routinely steals candy, primarily because Mrs. Lewis enables him to do so; after all, "you are not the type of boy who steals" (102), a reference to class and economics that dominate Rodney's section of the novel. But Rodney *does* steal, and he is not merely competent at it; he has perfected it. When Rodney falls asleep after a recess on one occasion when he has stolen candy, his father comes to school and beats him in front of the entire class. The punishment is certainly for stealing, but it is more for not being in place and thereby tempting possible child snatchers. Throughout the ordeal, Rodney tries to claim the one thing at which he is competent, but the blows from his father's belt drown out his declarations of having stolen candy.

This "ritual of humiliation" (137) traumatizes Rodney to the point that he literally tries to disappear by putting his head down on his desk and not responding to the teacher's questions. This is the blow that leads him in "the direction opposite of home," which is the title of the second part of the novel. His desire to commit suicide is clear: "At Martin Luther King Drive, you dart across four lanes of traffic against the blinking warning of the cross signal. Car horns scream, but the drivers accelerate when you find yourself alive and disappointed on the north side of the road" (140). When a blue sedan pulls up with a "policeman," whom Rodney recognizes as "not a real policeman," and whose badge is "as smooth as chocolate and fake as a glass eye," Rodney nonetheless gets into the car at the driver's assertion that there has been a bank robbery and "we need to get all the civilians off the street" (140). Thus Rodney willfully gives up his freedom and his life. A difficult question arises: is acquiescence in his own death a cruel kind of happy ending for Rodney?

Consider Rodney's situation. His father makes it clear to Rodney every day that he is a disappointment to him. His mother is apparently too involved in her yoga classes at the Y and other preoccupations to pay sufficient attention to Rodney. As long as she completes his assignments for him—with no concern about the ethics of that act—she takes little other interest in him. His sister is not really an important part of his life beyond his escorting her to and from school. Rodney's classmates either ignore Rodney or deride him. The teacher, Mr. Harrell, is another male figure whom Rodney hates and believes to be generally inept. In Rodney's blighted familial and social landscape, only Octavia is friendly to Rodney. His humiliation by whipping leads him to give the last of his candy to Octavia before he heads in the direction opposite of home. There has been no positive reinforcement for Rodney, no network of safety that surrounded him, no appreciation for his existence as an individual, troubled child who may be just as frightened by the missing and murdered children as any other child. His middle-class status, as his parents seem to have thought it would, has not saved him. Nor has his father's punishments, Officer Brown's warnings, or anything else. Rodney has fallen through the cracks of his family, his school, and his community. They have made a scapegoat of him in much the same way that Pecola Breedlove is made a scapegoat in *The Bluest Eye.* Just as her state of insanity finally proves better for her than her existence in reality, perhaps Rodney has found something as well that he could not find in reality. First of all, he earns recognition and friendly conversation from the child murderer. It is noteworthy that, while he hesitates or stutters most of the time when he speaks in the text, he does not do so with the child murderer. Noteworthy as well is the fact that he says more words to the child murderer than he has said to any member of his family or to his teacher.

Second, that something Rodney has found or wins is his death and a grand funeral. Where people had ignored him when he was just another fifth grader, his disappearance brings with it a status that he has never had before. Police officers and members of the community look for him. Once they find his body, there is the attention that he gets from his parents, his neighbors, and his classmates. Most important, his father is now brought to grief. While Rodney cannot witness that grief, the fact that he took so much pleasure in his father's pain is sufficient evidence to support the assertion. Only in embracing his own death has Rodney managed to find a place in life. In preparation for this moment, Rodney had lain in bed one night "hoping for a peaceful prenatal memory to assure you that death is nothing to fear" (113). The fact that he achieves his objective through a child murderer brings the various themes of the novel into sharp relief—given the right circumstances, fear of an authoritarian father can be just as destructive as fear of a child murderer. Evil, from a child's perspective, can be warm and cuddly just as it can be cold and distant.

Third, by getting into the car with the child murderer, Rodney takes control of his life (and death). All his life, he has been driven by his father, who has made—and perhaps rightfully so—all the important decisions about Rodney's life; after all, Rodney is only a fifth grader. Now, for once, Rodney has the opportunity to make a decision totally, completely for himself, without anyone looking over his shoulder or without him having to look over his shoulder to see who is watching. In that moment when he opts, willfully, to get into the car, he is as free as he has ever been—without criticism, without censure, without acceptance or rejection. It is but a moment, and it leads to his death, but it is the crucial moment that enables him, figuratively, to "leave Atlanta" and all the horrors connected with his family life.[9]

Octavia Fuller, the child who actually "leaves Atlanta" and lives, is equally concerned about her family situation, but the concern is dramatically different from Rodney's. Octavia's single mother, Yvonne, works from eleven p.m. to seven a.m. and leaves Octavia at home alone. She is therefore perhaps more concerned about spending evenings alone than she is about being snatched, though that fear is certainly a concern. As the most streetwise of the three protagonists in the novel and as a much-maligned child, Octavia has had to develop a level of maturity not apparent in Tasha or Rodney. She has learned from the constant taunts of her classmates that she is not what they consider pretty, that her socioeconomic status is inferior to most of them, and that she is the least likely child with whom any of them wants to share a table at lunch. Her tough-skinned coping strategies have required that she get used to being alone and that she harbor absolutely no expectations of acceptance from her classmates.

Octavia's section of the novel, which Jones narrates in first person, is the longest. The first-person narrative draws readers into Octavia's isolation from her peers, her interactions with her mother, the taunts she must suffer at school, and a host of other situations. Her voice positions us to be sympathetic to what she relates as well as how she relates it. As a child who lives near the projects in a community where class is almost as important as race, Octavia encourages us to sympathize with her economic condition, for we can see that her mother works as hard as any lower-income parent can to provide for herself and her daughter. As a child who is very dark-skinned and who is constantly picked on for this natural condition, Octavia invites positive responses from readers for the times she stands up against her tormenters, as well as in her meditations on what skin color and class mean in her world.

As a child with a missing father, Octavia falls into the category that Tasha mentions as the most common for child snatching and for which Rodney longs. Octavia also sees Rodney's father as monstrous: "But if I had a daddy like Rodney got, he would have been the one ran *me* off. For real. He took that strap to Rodney like he was enjoying it. And Rodney is so quiet that he couldn't even cry. When it was all over, I thought the man was going to take a bow while my stupid teacher, Mr. Harrell, clapped. Rodney walked back to his chair, but it seemed like he was crawling. Then he just stayed there, all crumpled up like a dirty napkin" (149).[10] This additional view of the scene reinforces the traumatic effect the beating has upon Rodney and provides readers with a sympathetic understanding of why Rodney is pushed to make the decision that he does. It illustrates as well, as do many other scenes, that outcast Octavia has a keen perception about things that happen around her.

Octavia's mostly absent father makes an appearance at her maternal grandmother's house in Macon once a year and showers Octavia with gifts and awkward parent/child interactions. That situation is made even more trying because Octavia's grandmother considers Ray, her father, to be infinitely preferable in social status and looks to Yvonne and Octavia. The ever-present fear of child murderers, therefore, is set against a family pathology that lends itself to predators. Given the chances of Octavia's survival in Atlanta in the face of her mother's work schedule, the mostly absent Ray offers to take Octavia to Orangeburg, South Carolina, where she will join him, his wife, and their new baby. This trek will supposedly ensure her future and increase her class and social status.

Octavia's fears are perhaps the most domesticated in the novel, for she is most vulnerable. Thus she has to contain herself and remain functional in a society where many things are falling apart around her. In many ways, Octavia becomes the emotional barometer for the "Missing and Murdered Children," as they are referred to in her section. She marks feelings of distress, and she captures her own fear and grief as well as that of her community. When her mother forces Octavia to go to bed to ensure that she is sound asleep before she leaves for work at the Sun-Beam factory at ten thirty, the strategy backfires:

> It mighta worked if I didn't know that she was leaving at eleven P.M. Then I could sleep as sound as I do on her off days. But I can't get locked good into a dream because I keep waking up looking at the clock to see how much longer before I'm by myself. It's like the men that's about to be put in the electric chair. They always ask them what they want to eat. But I bet they bring them the fried shrimp or whatever and the men can't even eat it because they so worked-up about what's going to happen next. That's how I am at night. My stomach get balled up in a gooey mess like chewing gum stuck in somebody's hair. . . . The first thing I do when I get out of bed is put on my shoes. I get nervous and I like to be ready to run if I have to. I ain't never had to, but it's good to be ready. (150, 151)

Comparing her situation to that of a condemned murderer is domesticated by the reference to chewing gum in someone's hair, but they both serve to establish the emotional toll on a fifth grader left to fend for herself while a child murderer is on the loose.

In registering her emotional reaction to Rodney's death, Octavia again appears as one of the more-mature students in her class. She has expected to hear news of Shante's disappearance, she says, but when, on one of her treks out of bed, she learns of Rodney's kidnapping, it "caught me by surprise like a cheap trick"; "my crying came hard and sudden like a coughing fit. And the tears were hot as blood" (153). While she tries to imagine a different outcome than death for Rodney, such as his "having a good time with those child murderers. They might be giving him Big Macs and strawberry shakes to keep him from hollering and running for the police" (154), reality sets in when she views Rodney's photograph on television: "Kodak commercials say that a picture is worth a thousand words, but the one they showed of Rodney ain't worth more than three or four. Boy. Black. Dead" (155). "When the first kids got found," Octavia comments, "I was jumpy at night like after I seen *Night of the Living Dead*" (155–56), which is comparable to the movie comparison that Tasha uses to describe her fear. "Then," says Octavia, "I started getting over it. . . . When Jashante got took, I couldn't get no scareder" (156). Rodney's disappearance, however, intensifies her fear. If anyone can "catch" bad luck from someone, then she surmises that she might catch it from Rodney, because she is the only one with whom he has actually carried on conversations.

Here, as in Tasha's section, the role of television is important in keeping people informed about the child murder cases. Given the limited news coverage of the period, viewers had to wait from the six o'clock news to the eleven o'clock news for updates. Tasha had mentioned how important it was to get the news from Monica Kaufman, a black newscaster. That importance is mitigated somewhat, however, by the fact that the news media serves as much as rumors and conspiracy theories to increase the level of fear. Each time Tasha or Octavia, or anyone else, hears about the murders on television—and especially as the number of missing children and faces splashed on the screen moves from nine to fourteen during the course of the new semester in fifth grade—the media inadvertently contributes to the increasing levels of fear. For a child alone watching late night television news, the fear and grief are compounded.

Octavia is disappointed in the way her teachers respond to Rodney's disappearance. When her favorite teacher, Mrs. Grier, tells her to "calm down," Octavia comments that "she wouldn't be calm if she was the one people was trying to kill" (169). When Mr. Harrell, the fifth-grade teacher, removes Rodney's chair from the row in which Octavia sits, Octavia is upset that "he just went on like our class was a creek and Rodney was just a cup of water that somebody dipped out" (173). Since Octavia's school is the only one "where two people got snatched from" (175), it is most appropriate that some more-significant memorial be paid to the missing children.

When Rodney's body is recovered, the impact upon Octavia is devastating, but the impact of the wake—to which her mother Yvonne will not allow her to go—is even more apparent on Yvonne. "My mama laid on my bed and cried like kids with their heads busted open. She cried like she was the one who knew Rodney Green and I laid stone still like I was the mama. . . .

Once you seen your mama cry, everything is different" (248). As a measure of her maturity during the course of the months of the Atlanta child murders, Octavia rises to support others emotionally on more than one occasion. Her comment that she is more like the mama echoes in other scenes, especially the one in which her mother, frightened for Octavia's safety when she is late coming home from school, slaps her and then breaks down crying.[11]

Rodney's death also occasions more astute analysis from Octavia. When Yvonne comments about Rodney's mother "losing" her "baby," Octavia's anger spills over: "'Why everybody always say you lost somebody? Rodney not lost. They make it sound like you mislaid your lunch box or something.' Now I was the one irritated. People need to say the words they mean. Rodney not *lost*, he *dead*" (251). Octavia's desire for accuracy and truth in speech is a recurring theme in the section since she notes that her mother always tells lies (Octavia lies as well). She wants her mother to be truthful about Rodney's death just as she desires truth in understanding why her mother is sending her away to South Carolina.

The fact that Rodney's body is recovered and buried brings a closure to at least one episode in *Leaving Atlanta*. That closure is a contrast to James Baldwin's notions of portraying circumstances in which black male bodies disappear on southern soil. Baldwin allows no closure when Peanut disappears in *Just Above My Head*. The holes in the hearts of people who loved him will remain. Rodney's funeral can allow the people to express their grief, which Octavia records in detail, with "a whole room full of people" crying (252). Rodney's body becomes symbolic of the recovered as well as the unrecovered bodies, for Miss Viola, Shante's mother, can grieve just as intensely as Rodney's parents, though there is a class factor that emerges at the funeral as well. Poorer people, such as Octavia, her mother, and Miss Viola, are in the balcony, while Rodney's parents are on the main floor of the church. Yvonne has observed of the wake that Rodney's mother "was too busy trying to be Jackie Kennedy" (250) to cry, but at the funeral the grief seems to be universal in spite of the "money people" being downstairs and the "projects" and "near projects" people upstairs.

As a participant as well as an observer of her community's responses to the missing and murdered children, Octavia shares the rumors with her community and recounts other tales provided to her. "Everybody been saying the child killer probably going around dressed up like the police or a fireman or somebody. I shouldn't believe that nobody is what they say they is" (179), she observes when she refuses to open the door for the mailman to deliver a package. She also notes one of the conspiracy theories that circulated. Mostly young black men were being killed, her friend Delvis tells her, "[b]ecause we going to get to be black men pretty soon and if it's one thing the white man scared of it's a black man" (196). Delvis also believes in Tasha's theory that missing fathers are a primary cause of the disappearances: "[T]hem boys— Jashante and them—not one of them had a daddy to run the white man off. And you see what happened" (197).

Octavia's vulnerability in the community might be multiplied with this logic because she not only has an absent father, but she lives near the projects. Also, she actually has two encounters with potential child molesters or child snatchers, and the threat of drug use is ever around her. Emotional assaults upon her begin with her mother telling her that discarded drug needles really belong to doctors and that they will be returning to claim them. Her mother's lies, which Octavia identifies as the most consistent trait with her, therefore make her initially unsuspecting of her Uncle Kenny's drug use when Kenny comes from Macon to live with Octavia and her mother. Kenny, who is Yvonne's younger brother, acts inappropriately with Octavia in her mother's absence. As in classic child abuse—or potential child abuse—cases, Octavia blames herself for getting Kenny thrown out of their house.

When Kenny calls while Yvonne is at work, Octavia observes: "He didn't sound mad at me. And I was grateful about that since I'm the one that got him put out in the first place" (184–85). She had discovered Kenny's heroin needles and mentioned to her mother that a doctor was probably going to be mad at Kenny for using his needles, which leads to Yvonne putting Kenny out of the house. While there is no explicit statement from Octavia that Kenny abused her sexually, at least in the sense of actually having sex with her, she certainly makes clear that he took inappropriate actions with her. He bounced her "on his lap hard and kissed the back" of her neck (154). His intentions were apparently not honorable, as he says to Octavia, "I'm not going to hurt you over the phone, Octavia" (185). Of Kenny being put out, Octavia comments: "I didn't tell her [Yvonne] that he was looking at me in the bathtub that time because it was an accident, like it was an accident that I told her about the dope needles" (217). Later, Octavia observes that Kenny put "his hands everywhere when he tickled" (229) her. And she finally tells her grandmother, Kenny's mother, that Kenny "used to kiss" her "too hard" (247) when she was little. Octavia's refusal to blame Kenny and her silence about what he has done prior to her comment to her grandmother are indications of her isolation from other kids and the general outcast status she holds in her school. Kenny was a fun companion for Octavia, someone with whom she could laugh, play games, and forget about how her peers treat her. "When Mama put him out," she asserts, "I was the one that suffered the most. When he was around, everything was fun like a day at Six Flags. . . . Uncle Kenny was more fun than television" (186). Unfortunately, Uncle Kenny is a child molester, one whose reputation remains hidden as long as it does because of the single-parent home in which Octavia lives. Her mother inadvertently creates a situation in which Kenny could just as easily harm Octavia as any child snatcher could.

In the second instance of Octavia's vulnerability in relation to men who could potentially do her harm, she creates the situation herself and seals her fate for the move to Orangeburg, South Carolina. She is suspicious when her father, Ray, keeps calling her mother and needs time to think things through. She goes to a park after school, swings, and pays less attention than she should to the approaching darkness. In the distance she sees a man who reminds her of her Uncle Kenny. She calls out to him, is uncertain when he takes a step in her direction, and then dashes toward home after she falls from the swing and busts open her lip. Arriving at home late and bloody, Octavia leads her mother to "pimp-slap" her "twice" (222) because of the anxiety she has caused Yvonne, who is getting ready to send out a search party. Yvonne's imagination, appropriately given the circumstances, has taken over. She says, "I didn't know if you were kidnapped, somewhere raped, laying dead in a ditch" (218). Deliberately—but innocently—placing herself in danger by going to the park, Octavia leads Yvonne from wavering to concluding that Octavia *must* move to Orangeburg. Yvonne realizes that she cannot keep Octavia safe and that she cannot provide the "things" that Octavia needs to prepare herself for college and adulthood. She therefore sacrifices Octavia—at least according to Octavia—in order to save her and to improve her class and educational opportunities.

By "leaving Atlanta," however, Octavia does not move from the South and the cultured hell that many writers define it as being. The move to South Carolina is the last resort of a desperate mother, one that she believes will save her child, for the distance Octavia will travel will not even change the weather, let alone the landscape. South Carolina is no more immune to young black bodies disappearing than is Atlanta. This means, again, that totally escaping the cultured hell of the South is not the issue for characters that African American women writers create; the issue is trying to find a way to live in it in spite of the insanity and the constant threats to life and limb. In South Carolina, Octavia will meet those threats with weapons that her father and stepmother will instill in her. While that outcome remains open, it nonetheless enables the novel to end on a more-hopeful note than contemplation of the Atlanta Child Murders initially portends.

THE WORST FEAR IMAGINABLE

Black Slave Owners in Edward P. Jones's
The Known World

Fears within African American communities in Randall Kenan's *A Visitation of Spirits* and Tayari Jones's *Leaving Atlanta* may be different in immediate manifestations, but neither is ultimately less devastating. Fear within the community in Edward P. Jones's *The Known World* (2003) returns to the originary site of fears for African Americans, that of slavery. The novel represents, however, slavery with a twist. It is no secret that some African Americans during the era of slavery actually enslaved other blacks. Large numbers of free blacks in various parts of the country made that practice viable. It is not, however, the subject of much African American literary creation, for that would make black people, like those Alice Walker depicts in *The Color Purple* (1982), responsible for their own victimization. Depicting black people who enslaved other blacks thus became one of the implicit taboos in African American literary creation. Certain subjects, at least until the mid-twentieth century, were simply not portrayed—or portrayed very briefly—in African American literature. They include the untouchables of homosexuality and lesbianism, as well as incest, unchurched black women, black women who had abortions or abandoned their children, insane black people, prostitution, and blacks who worked against the community. Notable early exceptions are Fenton Johnson's "The Scarlet Woman," a couple of Charles W. Chesnutt's short stories, the selections on homosexuality and prostitution included in *Fire!!* (1926), and some of the bawdy life that Claude McKay depicts in *Home to Harlem* (1928).[1]

Early African American literature was considered so close to black life that many characters were thought capable of jumping off the pages of literary creation and becoming representative of historical black communities, a misperception that stretched from the Harlem Renaissance to *The Color Purple*. The assumed documentary quality of African American literature led to self-censorship by African American writers from the beginnings of their creativity. One need only review articles in African American journals from the mid-nineteenth century to the beginning of the twentieth century to see the level of consciousness about collective African American behavior. From focus on hair, patterns of dress, and behavior to the call for education, black people were conscious that they were being judged as a group. A close look at the writings of Chesnutt, who wrote contemporarily with these concerns in the late nineteenth century, will make the tightrope-walking clear. Chesnutt walked the fine line of trying to incorporate black people into the American body politic through the social agenda of his literary creations without distracting from his purpose by showing too many of their blemishes. Writers had to be especially careful about their creations lest their characters give a struggling people even greater obstacles to overcome.

In the second half of the twentieth century, many of those self-imposed taboos were lifted, perhaps as a result of the questionable belief that African Americans were finally absorbed into the body politic and could be perceived individually instead of collectively. Thus Ralph Ellison portrayed his famous incest scene in *Invisible Man* (1952), James Baldwin included homosexuality in several of his works, Ann Allen Shockley presented lesbianism in *Loving Her* (1974), Toni Morrison depicted characters abandoning their children, and Alice Walker and others depicted incest and lesbianism. With the backward look that Morrison and other writers who created neo-slave (freedom) narratives made prominent in the 1980s and 1990s, the gloves came off the handling of slavery in fiction. From the vantage point of the late twentieth century and early twenty-first century, writers could re-create and/ or embellish the period however they wished. This made possible revelations of unrecorded history and the mythology surrounding it, of instances in which enslaved persons bested their masters, or in which they were impressively successful in running away.

As one of the latest renditions of those transformations, Jones's *The Known World,* winner of the 2004 Pulitzer Prize, goes a few steps beyond black people running away, heaping violence upon their so-called masters, or transcending race, culture, and history to become friends with the persons who previously enslaved them. Jones pulls the cover off ownership and reveals black people who not only enslaved other black people but also were kindred spirits to the whites who enslaved blacks. Issues of morality, commonality of color, and a need to bond with other blacks disappear in the face of the financial and lifestyle gains that owning human beings could engender. Most of Jones's elite black characters feel no compunction about owning other blacks. The lives they choose for themselves thus make them just as responsible for the history of slavery as their white counterparts. Even though there was no social equality for them with whites, they still elected to model their behavior upon that of those who enslaved their fellow blacks.

In creating *The Known World,* Jones embraced one fear and portrayed another. The fear he embraced is that of overcoming the belief that black writers should not portray certain kinds of subjects, because if they do then they are implicitly supporting the taboos being presented. By breaking ranks with his fellow African American writers on the subject of black people enslaving blacks, Jones joined hands with Zora Neale Hurston in her creation of white characters in *Seraph on the Suwanee* (1948), a move that reaped extensive and continuing criticism from black writers, scholars, and readers. By daring to break ranks, Jones was able to explore the world of slavery in a new way and to confront the fear of those blacks historically who might have been terrified of having people who looked like them enslave them. That fear is implicit among the fictional characters Jones creates, even when they manage to keep it contained.

The Known World is set between the 1830s and the 1880s in Manchester, Virginia, and other settings in which several of the characters sojourn.[2] The novel begins with the death of Henry Townsend, a black man who owns thirty-three other blacks. His death is the unifying event that provides the basis for meditation upon the county and its formation, the myriad histories of an abundance of characters (including an overzealous sheriff and a group of patrollers), and glimpses into the lives of those black persons who are enslaved on the Townsend plantation as well as into the lives of Henry's formerly enslaved parents, Augustus and Mildred Townsend. Henry's widow, Caldonia; her twin brother, Calvin; their teacher, Fern Elston; Henry's former owner, William Robbins; and Robbins's two children by a black woman—Louis and Dora—make up the primary cast of free characters. Moses, Henry's black overseer; Rita, Henry's "second mother" while he is waiting for his father to purchase him and whom Augustus mails to New York in a box of his walking sticks; Alice, a wandering, seemingly insane enslaved black woman; Elias, his wife (Celeste), and their children; Priscilla and Jamie, Moses's wife and child; and a few other members of the quarters also figure prominently in the text. Their lives are interjected into a scenario of accounting and explanation as the text revisits Henry and his parents' lives when Robbins owned them all, Augustus's work to purchase their freedom, and the general concerns of slaveholders during the period.[3] Chronology in the text is flexible and fluid, as Henry's death precedes episodes of his life and relationships. Henry is the centerpiece around which Jones creates a vast canvas of slavery and slaveholders. This "known world" is more limited for some than for others. Moses, for example, is described as "world-stupid," while Alice (the ultimate trickster), Priscilla, and Jamie escape to Washington, DC, where Alice becomes a well-known artist.

The novel ponders a troubling question: why would a black human being stoop to owning another black human being? That question, however, contains an implicit morality—and humanity—that does not hold sway in the novel. That becomes clear shortly after we meet the young Henry Townsend, who must remain on the Robbins plantation after his father purchases his own freedom from Robbins and then his mother's. Henry soon discovers a way to advance his situation on the plantation and to ingratiate himself to Robbins. With the food his parents bring him when Robbins allows them to visit on Sundays, Henry bribes Robbins's groom and gets the position for himself. Henry's behavior may be due to the absence of his parents, but that argument would not hold much sway during slavery, when many family members were separated and when it was perhaps the *unusual* thing to have a nuclear family intact. Rather, Henry develops character based upon his desire to better his situation, to please Robbins. Pleasing Robbins necessarily means that he will make the lives of some of the other blacks miserable. His move in this direction begins to take Henry away from identification with those enslaved and toward identification with those who enslave.

Consider his actions toward his parents, for example. They must journey far, often in miserable weather, to visit Henry on Sundays. They stop their wagon across from Robbins's plantation and wait for Henry to show up. "Sometimes Henry did not show up, even if the cold was bearable for a visit of a few minutes. Mildred and Augustus would wait hour after hour, huddled in the wagon under quilts and blankets, or walking hopefully up and down the road, for Robbins had forbidden them to come onto his land except when Augustus was making a payment on the second and fourth Tuesdays of the month."[4] At this time, Mildred and Augustus are in their late twenties, and Henry is nine years old. Yet he is still capable of telling his parents, "I just forgot," when they next see him after he does not/refuses to come out to meet them. On one wintry February day when the parents wait for more than two hours for Henry, and when he comes casually up to them, Augustus responds in a way that will cause him and Mildred great trouble with Robbins: "Augustus grabbed the boy when he shuffled up and shook him, then he pushed him to the ground. Henry covered his face and began to cry" (19). Although Augustus immediately regrets this act of frustration, Henry is not forgiving. He reports the incident to Robbins, and Robbins punishes Augustus and Mildred accordingly. When they next appear, ". . . Robbins was waiting. 'I heard you did something to my boy, to my property,' he said before Augustus and Mildred were down from the wagon. . . . 'I won't have you touching my boy, my property. . . . No more visits for a month'" (19). And the devastated parents have no redress to this power that Robbins has over them through their child.[5]

In the absence of his parents, Henry is envisioning and becoming acclimated to a life on the Robbins plantation beyond what his parents could have imagined. He knows that Robbins has the power to chastise/punish his parents, and he—perhaps through childish whim at this point—takes advantage of that power. Readers are left to imagine the scene between Robbins and Henry, but it was clearly one in which Robbins was sympathetic to Henry. Another factor of importance here is that Henry is fast making himself so essential to Robbins's existence and Robbins is developing such an attachment to him that he is reluctant for Augustus to buy him. Thus Robbins keeps raising the price on the boy. Henry's value to Robbins is work related and emotional. Henry succeeds in grooming horses better than anyone else, and since Robbins prefers riding his horse Sir Guilderham to using buggies, he appreciates Henry's skills. Also, Robbins suffers from memory lapses, which he calls "storms," perhaps symptoms of hypertension or early stages of Alzheimer's. These often occur when he has been to visit Philomena, his black mistress, where he spends evenings, and their children Dora and Louis. Unfailingly, Henry waits for Robbins to return, which often means hours of early morning lingering near the gate for Robbins to arrive so he can take care of his horse. "Henry would, in those early days when he was trying to prove himself to Robbins, stand in front of the mansion and watch as Robbins and Sir Guilderham emerged from the winter fog of the road, the boy's heart beating faster and faster as the man and the horse became larger and larger" (20). This faithful fixture in Robbins's life, especially given the fact that his marriage has dissolved due to his infidelity (though his wife and daughter still live in the mansion), provides one of the few stable and unqualified relationships that Robbins has. Seeing Henry waiting for him every morning, Robbins "came to develop a kind of love for the boy, and that love, built up morning after morning, was another reason to up the selling price Mildred and Augustus Townsend would have to pay for their boy" (28). Henry thus grows from perhaps seeming like a doted-upon pet to becoming as indispensable as any enslaved person could become in the life of his or her master. Over the years that it takes for his parents to purchase his freedom, therefore, Henry and Robbins form a bond that is perhaps stronger than the one he has with his parents, for, in these crucial formative years, Robbins is more parent to him than Mildred and Augustus are with their once-a-week, one-to-two-hour visits.

Henry's parents never evoke from him the great anticipation that Robbins's arrivals from Philomena's do. Henry's gut-level identity formation is therefore being shaped outside his parents and mostly outside the experiences of black people. Still, there are some things that he can learn from his parents if he allows himself to do so. When Augustus and Mildred make their final payment and come to take Henry home with them, Rita, his "second mother," refuses to return to the Robbins plantation. She clutches at the wagon and begs Augustus to take her with them. They do so reluctantly but soon become committed to the task of helping her to freedom. Augustus loads her into one of his boxes of walking sticks and mails her to one of his customers in New York.[6] Henry witnesses the scene, indeed questions how Rita will "do her business" (49), but ultimately fails to absorb the lesson to which he has been made privy. Augustus and Mildred, fearing for their own lives and possible reenslavement, nonetheless risk everything to help Rita escape. They value freedom, but Augustus is not certain that Henry values it equally: "Augustus remembered now [after the train with Rita aboard has departed] that Henry had told on him to Robbins about pushing him some years ago, and it occurred to him that if Robbins were ever to learn about Rita, Henry would be the one to tell him" (49). Recognition that the biological bond with parents is not as strong as the social/financial bond with a slaveholder is difficult for Henry's parents, but it is a fact that they must face with their son increasingly in the coming years.

Henry can also learn the value of freedom from the fact that his father purchased his own freedom and his wife's, then worked to buy Henry. When Augustus questions Henry about feeling different now that he is free, Henry cannot muster a distinction between being owned by Robbins and now being free with—as well as owned by—his parents, though the latter ownership is a mere perfunctory condition of purchasing a relative out of slavery. Henry does wonder, however, "who was waiting now for Robbins to come riding up on Sir Guilderham" (49). What Henry misses in the equation is that his parents have put their lives on hold for years to purchase family members, including him. If his parents value freedom enough to suffer Robbins's insults and misdealings, then they would certainly expect their son to do so as well. The problem is that their expectations are too late. Even in the face of their sacrifices, Henry has already turned toward the lifestyle that he has witnessed with Robbins.

In the world in which Henry lives, social status and lifestyle trump morality. While there is no evidence that he ever shares with Robbins what has happened to Rita, he clearly still sees Rita as property. When he sees his parents, seemingly older than in their thirties when they finally purchase him, he cannot/does not identify with them. Instead, he returns to Robbins to learn shoe and boot making. He also spends a surprising amount of time on the road with Robbins, serving as his companion and using his newly learned skills as Robbins directs him. Augustus and Mildred move to the farthest end of the county to escape everyday encounters with slavery, and a traveler must have their place as a destination in order to come upon them. By contrast, Robbins takes Henry everywhere he goes, including two trips into Richmond. Robbins's world serves the function that books serve in other situations; it takes Henry into places and experiences that open his eyes, lead him to imagine himself in ways that he could not if he had remained with Augustus and Mildred. It also taints him with slaveholding possibilities. As he embraces those possibilities, he pushes his parents and their practices into the background. He emerges as a man for whom morality can be elided easily.[7]

The elision of morality in this instance comes with an added dimension. Henry elides morality so that he can enslave persons who look like him for the sake of achieving a status comparable to that of Robbins. Indeed, Robbins plays a big role in Henry's ascent. Not only does Robbins allow Henry to purchase the first black person he will enslave from his own stock, but he makes other purchases for Henry.

> Being black, Henry could not in those days purchase a slave outright in Manchester County. He got his second slave through Robbins. . . . Henry stood at the very back of the market, and a stranger seeing him might have thought he was someone's servant waiting for the market to close and have his master take him back home. Using Henry's money, Robbins did all Henry's purchases of slaves before 1850 when a delegate from Manchester had the law changed. Most white men knew that when they sold a slave to Robbins, they were really selling to Henry Townsend. Some refused to do it. Henry was, after all, only a nigger who got big by making boots and shoes. Who knew what kind of ideas he had in his head? Who knew what a nigger *really* planned to do with other niggers? (50)

The hint of insurrection or some kind of plot against whites that might result with groups of blacks living and working together is the furthest thing from Henry's mind. He just wants to be one of the slaveholders. With this purchase of Zeddie, a cook, Henry feels a small bit of compunction, because "he knew by then what Augustus and Mildred felt about what he was doing" (50). That small amount of hesitation, however, is not sufficient to forestall the pattern that leads to thirty-three black people enslaved on Henry Townsend's plantation at the moment of his death.

Henry's parents offer stringent objection when Henry finally gets around to telling them about Moses, the man he purchased from Robbins. Although "part of him had been afraid to tell them about Moses" (135), he nonetheless does so.

> Mildred and Augustus looked at each other and Mildred lowered her head.
>
> Augustus stood up so quickly his chair tilted back and he reached around to catch it without taking his eyes from Henry. "You mean tell me you bought a man and he yours now? You done bought him and you didn't free that man? You *own* a man, Henry?"

> "Yes. Well, yes, Papa," Henry looked from his father to his mother.
>
> Mildred stood up, too. "Henry, why?" she said. "Why would you do that?"...
>
> "Don't you know the wrong of that, Henry?" Augustus said.
>
> "Nobody never told me the wrong of that."
>
> "Why should anybody haveta teach you the wrong, son?" Augustus said. "Ain't you got eyes to see it without me telling you?" (137)

Apparently Henry has eyes only for what the labor of enslaved persons will allow him to do and to be in the world. His capitalistic intentions may be alien to his parents, but they are commensurate with the life he has shared with Robbins.

The disappointment his parents register, especially his father, is evident in the following passage: "Augustus said quietly, 'I promised myself when I got this little bit of land that I would never suffer a slaveowner to set foot on it. Never. . . . Of all the human beins on God's earth I never once thought the first slaveowner I would tell to leave my place would be my own child. I never thought it would be you. Why did we ever buy you offa Robbins if you gon do this? Why trouble ourselves with you bein free, Henry? You could not have hurt me more if you had cut off my arms and my legs'" (138). Whatever initial hesitation Henry may have felt in telling his parents about Moses fades in the face of their anger and disappointment, and he reasserts what he perceives to be his rights. "Papa, I ain't done nothing I ain't a right to. I ain't done nothin no white man wouldn't do" (138). To Augustus's directive, "You best leave, and you best leave now," Henry reiterates that he has broken no law and has done no more than a white man would do. That, of course, is the rub. Henry Townsend is *not* a white man, a small distinction that he never fully registers, but which is abundantly clear as he stands at the back of the market watching the white Robbins purchase blacks for him. However, he has been transformed into a veritable imitation white man. Augustus and Mildred, having known slavery under a white man and having wished fervently for that condition to end, can only see a little monster standing in front of them, a monster who shares kinship to them. Though they visit Henry in later years, and though they attend his funeral, they never become reconciled to Henry's transformation. Even when they visit his mansion, they stay in the quarters with those enslaved rather than in Henry's Big House. There is no indication in the text that Henry ever again attempts to visit his parents' home.

This one troublesome visit ends with Augustus "slamming" one of his walking sticks across Henry's shoulder, thus breaking the shoulder. When Augustus explains, "Thas how a slave feel!" Henry takes the stick from his father, breaks it over his knee, and exclaims, "Thas how a master feels" (138) before he exits his parents' house. The rift is complete, for the parents will never understand their son, and the son will not deviate from the very profitable path he has chosen. That path means a huge house, the leisure of being waited upon and catered to, giving orders and having them carried out, existing in a comfortable circle of other free blacks who own blacks, and being called Master or Massa, which probably takes on more weight when the person so referenced is black. Henry can experience a superiority in his own specially carved-out world, a superiority whites deny him when they interact with him. Indeed, Henry can mediate his ownership of other blacks with the notion that he will be a better master than the whites among whom he lives. The irony in such a desire is inherent in a comment following Caldonia's address to blacks after Henry's death. "Henry had always said that he wanted to be a better master than any white man he had ever known. He did not understand that the kind of world he wanted to create was doomed before he had even spoken the first syllable of the word *master*" (64). It is not clear if these are Caldonia's thoughts or textual editorializing, but they nonetheless make clear the problematic path on which Henry based his life and wealth. Later, however, Caldonia provides clearer commentary on Henry's plan to be a better master. She recalls him "talking about how he would be a master different from any other, the kind of shepherd master God had intended. He had been vague, talking of good food for his slaves, no whippings, short and happy days in the field. A master looking down on them all like God on his throne looked down on him" (180).

Not having owned other people from birth, Henry must learn the art of slaveholding, just as Dana Franklin must learn how to be enslaved. That is also something that Robbins teaches him. From the moment he purchases Moses, Henry sees him as more of a companion than a person owned. They share the same cabin while Henry is building his house, they work side by side, and they play together. When Robbins witnesses such a scene of "tussling," he schools Henry on the proper behavior toward "property." Just as little white children learned early to distinguish their privileged lives from the lives of those enslaved around them, so too must Henry learn the status difference between him and Moses. Robbins lectures him:

... the law expects you to know what is master and what is slave. And it does not matter if you are not much more darker than your slave.... But if you roll around and be a playmate to your property, and your property turns round and bites you, the law will come to you still, but it will not come with the full heart and all the deliberate speed that you will need. You will have failed in your part of the bargain. You will have pointed to the line that separates you from your property and told your property that the line does not matter.... You are rollin round now, today, with property you have a slip of paper on. How will you act when you have ten slips of paper, fifty slips of paper? How will you act, Henry, when you have a hundred slips of paper? Will you still be rollin in the dirt with them? (123)

Fern Elston, the free black teacher—and slaveholder—that Robbins sought out for Henry, maintains that Henry Townsend was the best student she ever had. His ability to learn is evident immediately following Robbins's lecture. He orders Moses to halt work for the day, and when Moses questions why, he "slapped him once, and when the pain begin [*sic*] to set in on Moses's face, he slapped him again" (124), and asks why Moses will not simply do what Henry tells him to do. He also calls him "nigger." Since the novel began with Moses in the role of overseer on the Townsend plantation, he has obviously learned his place and his role as enslaved person just as successfully as Henry learned his role as master.

The tussling incident Robbins witnesses leads him to take over Henry's education in other matters related to mastery. That literally means that Robbins arranges for Henry to go to school, to acquire the manners and behavior of the well-to-do. "I have someone who needs to be educated," Robbins tells Fern Elston, "starting with writing and whatnot. He can't even write his own name. He should know how to do that and much else besides. He should know how to conduct himself in Virginia" (126–127). Although Henry is almost twenty when he begins his lessons, he learns well, and that education adds to the separation between him and his parents. Neither Augustus nor Mildred ever learns to read. In fact, Augustus pays someone to read his free papers to him over and over until he memorizes the contents. That does not help when one of the patrollers who know him eats Augustus's free papers one night and sells him back into slavery. Reading and ciphering, then, measure the final distance between Henry and his parents.

Henry learns to become master, but what kind of master is he, and what kinds of enslaved persons does he make? The text gives snippets of his interactions with those enslaved as it meanders its way through the lives of many characters, both central and extraneous. His primary relationship is with Moses, his overseer. Robbins leads Henry to place Moses in a position comparable to those in which whites at a certain age realized that they must place those enslaved; social distance mattered more than early friendships. Though Henry pledges to be a better master than the whites around him, he nonetheless slaps Moses into submission when he questions him. (Of course, it could be argued that Henry is "better" because he does not lash Moses; however, he is successful in establishing dominance with the slaps, so lashing is unnecessary.) The lesson is immediately clear to Moses, who follows Henry's directive to get his horse and to work in his absence. After working well into the night, Moses "went out to the cabin he and Henry had shared, and he knew that now the cabin would be his alone" (125). In place as a person of lesser status, Moses will remain in his role as overseer until after Henry's death.

Henry gets Moses to act as he wants him to, and he apparently succeeds with other enslaved persons as well. The glimpse we get of the house servants suggests that they are content, and the field workers do not complain. Only Elias attempted to escape, which leads Henry to address him when he is captured: "What in the hell I'm gonna do with you? If you want a hard life, I will oblige" (84). He slaps Elias and has him chained in the barn while he meditates on suitable punishment; "watching Moses tell him that Elias was gone, he had decided that a whipping would not be enough, that only an ear would do this time" (89) and, against Caldonia's wishes, Henry has one of Elias's ears cropped. While punishments might not be abundant on the Townsend plantation, it is clear that Henry does not balk when he deems harsh punishment necessary. We must thus mediate Caldonia's meditations, following Henry's death, on Henry's interactions with blacks on his plantation.

> Henry had been a good master, his widow decided, as good as they come. Yes, he sometimes had to ration the food he gave them. But that was not his fault—had God sent down more food, Henry would certainly have given it to them. Henry was only the middleman in that particular transaction. Yes, he had to have some slaves beaten, but those were the ones who would not do what was right and proper. Spare the rod . . . , the Bible warned. Her husband had done the best he could, and on Judgment Day his slaves would stand before God and testify to that fact. (181)

Implicit in Caldonia's reflections is a divinely sanctioned sense of place. If only the people who are supposed to be enslaved would consent to their condition and act accordingly, then all would be right with the world. Caldonia attempts to excuse Henry morally and socially for his slaveholding, which, in spite of the dressing up, has been in the same mold and acted out with the same attempts at justification as that of his white counterparts. While there are no escapes from the Townsend plantation while Henry is alive, once he dies, Priscilla, Alice, Jamie, Gloria, Clement, and Moses all attempt to escape (all succeed except Moses), which suggests that Henry's brand of slaveholding has not in the least bit been the godly version Caldonia suggested that he intended. He is at best a "good" slaveholder and at worse a trampler on the very humanity of his fellow blacks.

In terms of the kinds of enslaved persons Henry creates, a close look at Moses is instructive. Initially, Moses is shocked that Henry buys him:

> It took Moses more than two weeks to come to understand that someone wasn't fiddling with him and that indeed a black man, two shades darker than himself, owned him and any shadow he made. Sleeping in a cabin beside Henry in the first weeks after the sale, Moses had thought that it was already a strange world that made him a slave to a white man, but God had indeed set it twirling and twisting every which way when he put black people to owning their own kind. Was God even up there attending to business anymore?[8] (8–9)

Surprise finally leads to acceptance, for, in the world as Moses knows it, he has no more redress to his situation than Augustus and Mildred had when Robbins forbade them to see Henry. As a "world-stupid" person, Moses does not have the directional sense to escape to the North and create a different world. Even when he sends Alice, Priscilla, and Jamie away, he is doing so with the hope that that will free him to become Caldonia's husband, not because he has any real expectation of following after them. Just as he grants Henry the power to slap him and does not retaliate, so he settles into life as an enslaved person.

In Moses, it appears that Henry succeeds in creating an obedient, acquiescent enslaved person who has learned implicitly to fear his master. That surface, however, bears a bit of scratching. Moses certainly does not give Henry any trouble once Henry establishes himself as the master and Moses as the "nigger." How Moses, as overseer, treats other blacks on the Townsend plantation reveals a different side of his personality. Before the text moves into the scene where Caldonia and others are holding the death watch for Henry, it gives an extended look at Moses in his world. He pinches a bit of dirt and eats it as a way of determining when the earth might be ready to be planted and seeded. He then goes out into the woods in a rainstorm, strips, lies down, masturbates, and allows the rain to pour over him. A novel beginning this way might suggest that the character is one with nature, someone with whom readers might identity and sympathize with against his master. Those early scenes, rather warmly presented, are more a distraction from Moses's true personality than who he actually is. Certainly he appreciates nature and the land over which he has watched ten years as overseer for Henry, but he has also embraced the more abusive sides of power and enslavement. He uses his position to intimidate other blacks and to remind them constantly that he is a step above them. In the hierarchical chain of slavery, therefore, he willingly fits into the slot just below the masters.

Immediately following his sojourn in the woods, Moses returns to the quarters, to encounter Elias, up beyond what Moses considers an appropriate hour. Moses's reaction is direct and aggressive.

> Moses, a few feet before passing Elias, said, "You gotta meet that mule in the mornin."
>
> "I know," Elias said. Moses had not stopped walking. "I ain' hurtin a soul here," Elias said. "Just fixin on some wood." Now Moses stopped and said, "I ain't caring if you fixin God's throne. I said you gotta meet that mule in the mornin. That mule sleepin right now, so maybe you should follow after him." Elias said nothing and he did not move. Moses said, "I ain't but two minutes off you, fella, and you seem to wanna keep forgettin that.". . .
>
> Now Moses said to Elias, "If you ain't waitin for me here when the sun come up, not even Massa Henry will save you." (8)

Perhaps Moses's animosity toward Elias is linked to Elias's having run away from the plantation. That would certainly appear as a poor reflection upon Moses, whose job it is to keep all the other blacks in line. More to the point, perhaps, is the implicit pleasure that Moses gets out of playing mini-master. Like Henry adopting the patterns and behaviors of white slaveholders, Moses has adopted the ruling attitude of his black owner. His reference to Henry as "Massa Henry" yields no memory of the time when Moses and Henry tussled together. By easily elevating Henry to "Massa," the counterpart to whites, then Moses can become second to "Massa," the one who lords his status over other enslaved blacks.

The little monster that Henry has created is also apparent in Moses's treatment of his wife, Priscilla, and his son, Jamie. He has taken to Priscilla because she was available, not because he loves her. He mistreats her emotionally and shows no warmth toward her or Jamie. Indeed, he finds them a burden, especially after Henry dies and he can imagine himself moving into the Big House with Caldonia. He comes to think "that his wife and child could not live in the same world with him and Caldonia. . . . Where did a slave wife and a slave son fit in with a man who was on his way to being freed and then marrying a free woman? On his way to becoming Mr. Townsend?" (292, 293). Priscilla recognizes that Moses is "not a good husband but he was all she had" (297), and she is reluctant to leave when he directs her to run away with Alice. That directive makes clear that Moses treats Priscilla and Jamie as if they are secondhand shoes, on par with his threatening Elias. Moses threatens Elias because he is the big voice in the quarters, and no one there can challenge him.

The historical basis for what Moses does is connected to sociological patterns. A black person who has no status in the world external to his environment, in this case, Moses, with his interactions with Henry and other slaveholders, finds status within his own community (the quarters for Moses) and elevates himself psychologically and physically over those around him. Through threat and promises of violence, as well as through actual violence, such a person becomes a bully to those who are at or below his status. And since no one in the quarters is equal to Moses as overseer, that territory becomes his domain to act as he wishes.

Perhaps there is some veracity in Caldonia's suggestion that Henry tried to be a little god of a master, for, as soon as he dies, things begin to fall apart. That is no less the case with Moses. Having had his identity stabilized as second in command to Henry, Moses has to find a new status. Unfortunately, he aspires to take Henry's place, to marry Caldonia, for he imagines that he could be an even better master than Henry. This aspiration leads to a brief affair with Caldonia, but it leads more directly to frustration and mistreatment of other blacks. That is especially vivid after an occasion on which Caldonia refuses to have sex with Moses. The next day, he insists that everyone go to the fields to work, including Celeste, Elias's wife, who is six months pregnant. Celeste has a miscarriage, which leads everyone to blame Moses. This mistake in judgment occurs because Moses has been having sex with Caldonia and is expecting her to free him. He handles that expectation with as much tact as he handles the situation with Celeste. What Henry has created in

Moses is an acquiescent human being and that acquiescence does not carry with it an instinct for mastery.

Moses's lack of mastery is obvious in his so-called courting of Caldonia. Reporting to her each evening after Henry's death, Moses finally gets into her arms and into her pants. He begins to envision marrying Caldonia and taking over the plantation. His high hopes lead him to encourage Alice, Priscilla, and Jamie to escape. With them gone, there will be no obstacle, he believes, to marrying Caldonia. His gruffness and lack of persuasive powers with Caldonia doom him to failure in his quest for freedom. Consider the context of his initial request:

> That evening Caldonia allowed Moses to make love to her for the first time since the three slaves [Alice, Priscilla, Jamie] went missing. He had wanted a night with her in her bed and he told her that, but she just lay in his arms on the floor afterward and said nothing. Then he asked, "When you gonna free me?"
>
> "What?"
>
> "I say when you gonna free me?" She withdrew from him and stood up. "I thought you was supposed to free me." He could not be her husband without first being free, not a proper husband anyway with authority over everyone and everything. (324)

Having played his presumed sexual trump card without knowing the hand that Caldonia is holding, Moses is left to her mercy. Although she had considered freeing him, she does not respond, and Moses leaves "in a quiet rage" (325). A master would have planned a better strategy, would perhaps have considered that a woman of such a higher class might use him for sexual release after her husband's death but might not be willing to consent to the plan he has in mind.

The quiet rage in which Moses leaves leads to anger and desperation as Caldonia becomes more interested in the affairs of the plantation than in her sexual relationship with him; indeed, she chastises him for what has happened with Celeste and dismisses him after labeling his action a "disappointment." Angrily entering the house the next evening and demanding to speak with Caldonia, Moses creates a scene that makes it impossible for him ever to be any more than he is currently. "'Why you got me waitin round like this, like I'm somebody's child?'" he asks Caldonia, "'Why ain't you done freed me?' He raised his fist into the air between them. 'Why you doin this?'" (330). A step closer to Caldonia reaps her maid's arm around his neck with a knife pressed to his throat. Moses leaves, abandons his overseer duties, and runs away from the plantation a few days later. What the scene makes clear is Moses's lack of mastery combined with a clash of class, status, and color to which he has apparently not been privy.

First of all, Moses is no master of the English language. As a former student of Fern Elston's, Caldonia is acutely sensitive to the language. Second, Moses has failed to realize the impact of class and status upon his aspirations. Caldonia may have sex with him "on the floor," but she never invites him to her bed. Like white slaveholders who found sexual pleasure in the quarters, Caldonia is like Flo Hatfield in Charles Johnson's *Oxherding Tale*; she brings virile black men into her quarters for such pleasure. Instead of being trained to seduce, as Nathan was in Williams's *Dessa Rose*, Moses depends on pure animal attraction and the lies he tells about Henry to bed Caldonia. Third, while Moses understands that he must close the gap between the free and the enslaved in his relationship with Caldonia, he refuses to take into consideration—or perhaps does not even have awareness of—what she would be giving up to marry him (not to mention the fact that Henry is only very recently buried). She could not take him into her circle of friends without running the risk of embarrassment, and he is probably too old at thirty-five to be schooled in the way that Henry was—even if Caldonia were committed to such improvement in Moses. Caldonia can assert in the quiet of her bedroom that she loves Moses, but that assertion has no practical application in the real world. Her mother alone would destroy the possibility of any such connection.[9] Caldonia, then, is having a time out with Moses, a sexual excursion into how the other side lives, a little happy time across the tracks. When duty calls, she reverts to her status of slaveholder, marries a man of her class (Louis), and moves on with her life. She may, like Jadine in Toni Morrison's *Tar Baby*, regret briefly the lack of a relationship with Moses, especially after the patrollers catch and hobble him, but she soothes her conscience just as easily as Jadine files away a troublesome fingernail.

Caldonia's ability to walk away from Moses, to see the larger vision in this known world, is characteristic of the members of the class of free blacks Jones portrays in the novel. Conscience may intervene at times, but they ultimately do nothing to change their status as black slaveholders—or they do terrible things to retain that status. Early in the novel, Caldonia thinks of "the times that made her want to rethink the road they were all going down. Such a long road for such a legacy, for slaves. 'My legacy,' her mother Maude often said.

'We must protect the legacy'" (96). Such thoughts, however, do not make Caldonia free blacks on her plantation and send them to the North or elsewhere. Caldonia's twin brother, Calvin, would very much like to escape from the slaveholding tradition, especially from the thirteen enslaved persons that his mother owns (66), but he does nothing except learn the names of all the blacks in the quarters at the Townsend plantation and feel sympathy toward them.[10] Fern Elston keeps a man enslaved even as she knows that he is telling the truth about her husband owing him money, and she has him flogged when he consistently mentions that debt to her and makes innuendos about her too-often absent husband. Yet she is one of the most upstanding and well-respected citizens in this community, the one to whom a pamphleteer, Anderson Frazier, comes many years later to get her opinion on free blacks who enslaved other blacks.[11] On the other hand, and in a complete dissolution of any sense of morality, Caldonia's mother, Maude, kills her husband when she learns that he is considering freeing the blacks they own. Retaining what she calls her "legacy," that is, the enslaved people on her farm, is more important to her than her husband's life, so she uses poison to take it.

This class of free black slaveholders is held together not only by their refusal to see moral inconsistency in owning members of their own race but also by what I refer to as *skin affinity,* that is, pigmentocracy or other names that might be applied to those who are so mixed race that it is difficult to distinguish them easily from whites. This skin affinity enables Henry, Fern, and Caldonia and Calvin to socialize with Louis and Dora, the offspring of Robbins and Philomena, his black mistress.[12] Robbins is exceptional in interacting publicly with his children, and they quickly learn that their place is among the class with which Fern Elston, who is also their teacher, socializes, and not among those of their mother's class. (Robbins does free Philomena and set her up in a house, which echoes the nineteenth-century *placage* traditions in Louisiana as well as Molly Walden's position in Chesnutt's *The House Behind the Cedars.*) Skin affinity also gives these characters access to education that their enslaved counterparts could never envision, thus an additional level of elitism gets established.

In this community of color, some of the free blacks could easily pass for white. Fern is among that number; when she deals with one slaveholder, he "thought he was dealing with a white woman and he was never to know any different" (255). In electing not to pass for whites, they create a mulatto world that earns the fear and envy of those blacks who are darker than they are and, at times, the grudging respect of whites. Robbins, as noted earlier, respects Fern enough to ask her to teach not only Henry but his own children, Louis and Dora. While there are restrictions on interactions between blacks and whites, such as Robbins not getting down from his horse when he speaks with Fern, these high mulattos are still many times better off than other blacks. Fern and Caldonia, for example, can go to Skiffington's office and request help to retrieve Augustus after he is resold into slavery. Skiffington's cousin Counsel might not respect the women, but Skiffington acts immediately upon learning that Augustus has been sold. He goes to Augustus's wife, Mildred, and assures her that he will try to find Augustus.[13] Fern and Caldonia's request fuels Skiffington's desire to assist, which reflects a status for them that Mildred alone does not have. And an enslaved black such as Moses would have absolutely no sway with whites; after all, Moses was sold to Robbins in Skiffington's office.

One way of assuaging their superiority is for Fern and her friends to create a linguistic aura around slavery that will make it more tolerable. Like so many white slaveholders, they refer to black people they have purchased as "servants" as often as they refer to them as "slaves." "Servants" has benign connotations, including ideas of volunteerism and reciprocity. A servant ideally would work for a reasonable wage, and the employer of that servant would value the labor. There would then be no dissatisfaction, as instanced when Caldonia finds it "difficult to believe that two women and a boy [Alice, Priscilla, Jamie] would leave what she and Henry had made" (317). If an enslaved person can be labeled a servant, then the master or mistress, especially if either is black, does not have to confront the moral issue of enslavement. Whites such as Skiffington and Robbins also use the word to cover up the reality of black people's existence during slavery (126, 153).

Gender politics also hold sway in the novel, for perhaps at the heart of Skiffington's responding to the women is some sense of Southern courtesy, of some expanded notion of the gentleman. That might be true as well with how Robbins treats Fern and Caldonia. Such politics are also apparent in different ways in the patrollers' response to Caldonia's questionable ability to run the Townsend plantation, as well as in Moses's expectations of romantic success with Caldonia. The Townsend plantation earns a bad reputation when so many enslaved persons escape following Henry's death. It suggests a lack of control, and it creates more work for the patrollers, who are not sympathetic to a woman being in charge. "Somebody," one of them asserts about Caldonia, "should close the gate at her place, or teach her how to own a slave. A man dies and a woman runs his place into the ground" (348). We can read the assessment even more negatively given the fact that Caldonia is not a white woman. It also continues to locate "rightful" ownership with males, for it is "his [Henry's] place," not her own, that Caldonia is running into the ground.

In the political move he attempts to make, Moses relies upon the only weapon he has: his body. Once he starts meeting with Caldonia every evening, he demands that Bennett, who works in the house, give him new pants and a new shirt. He will spruce up his appearance, as much as is possible given the sweaty nature of his work in the fields, when he visits Caldonia. That improvement, he hopes, will potentially lead to sexual conquest. He succeeds in having sex with Caldonia, but he miscalculates in expecting that she will so easily succumb and immediately grant him freedom. She is a woman, and he assumes that she will want him and will do what he wants in return. His masculinity, however, gets sacrificed easily on the altar of Caldonia's need to stay within her class and color. When her brother Calvin invites Caldonia to leave and go with him to New York, her response is: "Calvin, you have only yourself and whatever is on your back. I have the responsibility of so many people. Adults and children. I cannot choose not to have that. My husband has built something here, and now it is mine and I can't abandon that for a foreign land" (291). Or for a "foreign" lover and potential husband such as Moses.

Caldonia's commitment to slaveholding, in spite of her earlier moments of wavering, is the final position of most of her class. Her husband Henry bought into a slaveholding model, and she casts her future with that model. Marrying Louis ensures that continuation. Moses might have imagined that he could be a better slaveholder than Henry Townsend, but Louis has the breeding to make it so. Like Henry, Louis has adapted the model from Robbins and, despite its horrific moral lapses, the slaveholding path is what they are committed to following. It is a flaw of all the free black characters limned in the text that they see no connection between themselves and the blacks they own. That separation leaves Moses and Elias to ponder the aberration, but it reaps no sleepless nights for the owners. Henry's death means for those enslaved on his plantation that "their world had changed but they could not yet understand how. A black man had owned them, a strange thing for many in that world, and now that he was dead, maybe a white man would buy them, which was not as strange. No matter what, though, the sun would come up on them tomorrow, followed by the moon, and dogs would chase their own tails and the sky would remain just out of reach" (60–61).

Perhaps the stoicism contained in that quotation, even in the recognition of "strangeness," is the only comfort with which we are left. At some point, black people owning black people during slavery becomes as natural as other occurrences in the world. The fear an enslaved person may have of that possibility might give him or her pause for a while, but not throughout a lifetime. Just as those enslaved on the Townsend plantation learned to refer to Henry as "Massa Henry," they became accustomed to someone of their own color having the power of sale over them; familiarity thus teaches status and acquiescence. Being owned by a white man might not be as strange, but it is still ownership; thus the fears of slavery ultimately equalize around black and white masters. Though those masters might recognize differences among themselves in terms of race, class, and economics, for those enslaved, a black face dishing out inadequate rations is no more aggravating than a white face dishing out inadequate rations. At some point to those enslaved, color gets set aside in the wake of a condition that divides on the basis of race, economics, education, class, *and* color, not just on the basis of the color implicit in race.

NO FEAR; OR, AUTOEROTIC CREATIVITY

How Raymond Andrews Pleasures Himself in *Baby Sweet's*

In the course of working and lecturing on this project, I have constantly encountered a series of questions. Is there no African American writer, in the South or elsewhere, the curious want to know, who is not at war with or made uncomfortable by the southern United States? Certainly the history in blood and slavery is understandable, they continue, but is there no black writer who has managed to transcend that history and is at peace with herself or himself? Does Octavia Butler leave us with a Dana Franklin who is more optimistic about the future than she is fearful about the past? Does Sherley Anne Williams suggest with Dessa Rose that southern black history is changeable, even if it means moving west? Does Phyllis Alesia Perry's Lizzie DuBose presage something hopeful about the soil we traditionally identify as southern territory? In other words, is there no black writer who, having tunneled her or his way through the pain of history, the muck and mire of psychological, physical, or other violations, comes out with a healthy response to the South? My answer to those questions has always been to cite

After contemplating and selecting a title for this chapter, I discovered that Andrews actually uses the word "autoeroticism" in the novel (30) in reference to John Junior's masturbatory practices when he gets horny watching Baby Sweet in their teenage years. Perhaps this is the power of suggestion?

Raymond Andrews. Born in a small town in Georgia in 1934, Andrews lived through the racism of segregation, escaped it by moving north and joining the military, and ultimately returned to embrace it in humorous renditions across three novels and a memoir. For Andrews, humor is the balm against a history of racism and repression in the South. He does not balk at depicting black women being raped by white men, black men being wrongly jailed, or the strictures placed on black life in general. Andrews handles all these uncomfortable subjects with honesty, but he also handles them with humor. As perhaps a lone representative of an African American writer who can be just as humorous in claiming the South as he can be critical in his indictments of it, Andrews gives us voices and characters whose slightly altered notes of oppression provide us with fresh looks at much-worn southern territory. To illustrate this distinctive black southern voice, therefore, I offer the following.

I can probably say with certainty that George Moses Horton was not giggling to himself or cracking jokes when he wrote poems and letters directed to possible northern benefactors in the 1830s in the hope that they would purchase his freedom from slavery. It would similarly be difficult to imagine Claude McKay finding anything remotely humorous in his construction of "If We Must Die" or in the riot circumstances in East St. Louis, Illinois, that inspired him to create that poem. And goodness knows Richard Wright was probably one of the most humorless writers ever to put pen to paper. I remember once when I was teaching a graduate seminar at the University of North Carolina at Chapel Hill and included Wright's *Uncle Tom's Children* (1938) as a part of the readings. The seminar participants arrived in class one day uniformly depressed. Since I was kind of dragging as well, we took a survey to see what the heck was causing us such misery. It was Wright's vision of the world, we all agreed. Those bleak, humorless characters and their bleak, humorless circumstances with the bleak, humorless weather always surrounding them were just taking away our joy, as the church folks would say.

Horton, McKay, and Wright all created their works out of a sense of mission, a sense of purpose-oriented writing that had guided most black writers from their beginnings in America. The implicit message was: "Use your craft to get yourself out of slavery, to help other black people get out of slavery, or to help them reap the benefits of democracy." African American writers should not, as Nikki Giovanni avowed decades after *Uncle Tom's Children*, waste their time contemplating the beauty of trees or sky. They had work to do, like loading their guns and learning how to make Molotov cocktails—and inspiring the masses to follow their lead. Mission was more important than pleasure.[1]

Raymond Andrews is also on a mission, but his mission *is* pleasure. Unlike other writers I cover in this text, Andrews exhibits an unmasked love of the South, of the small-town kinds of communities in which he grew up and the storytelling traditions that are so central to them. Whether he is poking fun at white ladies in Appalachee who hate football, or applauding the sheer bodily pleasure of watching a young black woman dance in a peach orchard, or appreciating the black nipples that a young white man paints so obsessively, Andrews is in the writing game for the sheer fun of it. As creator, spectator, and shadow character, Andrews exhibits a love of language for the sake of language. He does not allow a single one of his characters to have more fun than he has, and he gets his fun by laughing *at* his characters and the circumstances in which they find themselves just as much as he laughs *with* them.

Now, unless an author is really of a morose temperament, he or she gets something positive out of the creative venture. Even mission-oriented writing can be positive and can bring the satisfaction of knowing that one has done one's best work for a cause. There can be the quiet reflection upon a job well done. By contrast, there is nothing quiet about the pleasure Andrews creates for himself and gives to others in most of his writing, though I am going to concentrate on *Baby Sweet's,* his 1983 novel and the third in his Appalachee trilogy.

Baby Sweet's takes up two years after *Appalachee Red* (1978). Baby Sweet, who was Red's love interest in the first novel in the trilogy, hides out in the upstairs portion of the old Red's Café and gains fifty pounds before John Morgan Jr. convinces her to allow him to transform the place into a whorehouse primarily for white men of the town. The novel fleshes out background on John Junior as the bohemian artist and lost older son of John Morgan Sr. (father of Appalachee Red) and on several of the characters who appear in the first novel, such as Snake, Darling, Big Apple, and Mary Mae Mapp. New characters are the three whores who come to work in Baby Sweet's, especially Lea, the mixed-race daughter of Rosiebelle Lee Wildcat Tennessee's oldest son and a poor white girl who lived near the family. *Baby Sweet's* also ties up loose ends about Red and his first trip to Appalachee, but it does not illuminate Morgan's daughter Roxanne's return to Appalachee or her marriage to a Yankee who befriended John Junior when they were both in college. This brief accounting of the narrative does not in any way reveal the narrative methods Andrews uses, nor does it focus on the many tentacles that branch out from the larger story in their own slightly connected ways. It is in the unveiling of all mysteries and the tying up of loose ends from the previous two novels—but especially the first—that Andrews finds such pleasure. He knows the paths down which he leads readers, and he takes great pleasure in exhibiting those paths to his followers, listeners, readers.

Andrews's satisfactions are loud, unapologetic, self-conscious, and almost bordering on the obnoxious. If we could imagine the writer as flasher, that description might fit Andrews. And he enjoys every minute of the flashing. Of course we readers can find enjoyment in his texts as well, but I contend that Andrews is having such a good time that he could give a flying flip about whether or not we come along for the ride. I voluntarily come along for the ride because it is such fun watching him having fun.

And how does Andrews manage to have such fun? He uses several methods, from language to structure to what I call cultural contextual familiarity. Anyone familiar with Andrews's work knows that he loves storytelling and is a masterful storyteller. He meanders his way through whatever threaded balls of history, race, and culture capture his imagination and ties up loose ends—or not—as he sees fit. But lots of writers are good storytellers. With Andrews, the distinction is in the dual roles he plays as creator and spectator, or as writer and voyeur. There is always duality if not multiple layers in his narrations as one side of his mind gives and the other side applaudingly receives. In other words, he creates, and he applauds his creations. He is preacher and congregation, storyteller and audience. This pattern is revealed in the linguistic punctuations he provides to the tales he tells as well as in his structuring of those tales. No matter how many little narratives he introduces to bring into focus the large canvas of the novel, he never misses an opportunity to applaud his own genius.

The linguistic duality of creating and applauding creation is visible in numerous places in *Baby Sweet's*. Several examples from the many will suffice to make the point. When Andrews indicates that Baby Sweet has gained weight since Red's departure, his final declaration is: "Honey, Black Peach was now a fat peach!"[2] When he is stage setting and explaining how integration has reduced business at Red's Café because black folks can now go into the city for their food and entertainment, he punctuates that pronouncement with "Yes, Lord, the big cities done gone and stolen the little towns' Saturday night. Have mercy!" (10). When John Junior violates family tradition and becomes an artist instead of cultivating an officer's assignment in the military, Andrews's benediction is, "Lord help him!" (19). Other such punctuations are "'Nuf said, honey!" (29), "Honey, hush!" (49, 116), "Lord, ain't it the truth!" (53), "No way, honey babe!" (64), "Lord, what is this world coming to?" (66—when Christopher Robin rejects his mother's horse for his grandmother's car), "Lord, have mercy!" (80), and, most common, "Amen!" (77, 134, 181, 190). The most screamed of such punctuations is the one that occurs after John Junior loses his virginity to T Cake, a black prostitute. After describing John Junior's orgasm, the text screams in all capital letters: "LORD-HAVEMERCYHONEYHUSHSWEETGODDAMNAMEN!" (42).

T Cake is one of the sites on which Andrews uses cultural contextual familiarity to engage readers. Most Southerners know what tea cakes are, and most readers of African American literature have encountered prior to Andrews's text the wonderful portrait of Tea Cake, Janie's soul mate, who graces the pages of *Their Eyes Were Watching God* (1937). By locating such sweetness in a black woman named T Cake, Andrews evokes the folkloristic notion of "the blacker the berry, the sweeter the juice," which John Junior has obviously discovered by his venture into darktown. The exclamation of his success, then, indicates his move from the front yard to the backyard, his immersion into blackness, so to speak, even as that exclamation serves the structural reiterative pattern that Andrews develops.

Andrews uses his punctuating comments to ridicule the presumed sensibilities of southern white women in at least three instances in the text. Stereotypically portrayed as unable to deal with anything out of the ordinary, Andrews's imaginary white woman is the handkerchief-sniffling, flutteringly fainting type. In describing Bonnie B, the horseback riding, unladylike young white woman who refuses to follow the rules of southern gentility and craves the smell of rodeos as she imagines becoming a jockey, Andrews observes: "Lord, Lord, Bonnie B was just too much for a white lady!" (62), especially white ladies of the variety the staid Mrs. Morgan, mother of John Junior, represents. When the returned Roxanne announces that she is going to marry a Yankee, the exclamation is again, "Lord, just too much for a white lady!" (129). That imaginary southern white lady, kin to the Mrs. Morgan variety again, would have great difficulty condoning such a union. When John Junior learns from Big Apple that the stranger to whom he has given a ride into Appalachee back in 1944 is Red, which means that he has given his own blood brother a lift, the text announces: "Lord, Lord, just too much for a white lady" (190), again perhaps referring to Mrs. Morgan, who would be the white lady perhaps most shocked by this revelation.

As these quotations illustrate, throughout *Baby Sweet's* Andrews does not leave it solely to the text—and to his audience's possible denseness—to make his jokes and satire clear. He punctuates his own cleverness with his own chorus of amens. Usually placed at the ends of paragraphs and almost one hundred percent punctuated with exclamation points, the unnecessary but funny addenda serve to highlight Andrews's appreciation of his own creation and the loudness with which he suggests that we readers enjoy the text. They also serve the function of explaining the jokes, or at least letting readers know that laughter is expected in response to irony, humor, or striking coincidences.

Structurally, the punctuating exclamations operate on the call-and-response pattern that informs much of African American culture. Andrews the writer creates a portion of the text, and Andrews the implied member of his own audience responds. Indeed, the text relies upon a symbiotic relationship between an implied audience with whom the shadow character of Raymond Andrews the author identifies. Together, they operate as a church congregation would or as a blues performer and his audience would. In any given call-and-response exchange, one section of the narrative might be comparable to B. B. King singing or to a preacher preaching, and the extra comments are comparable to B. B. King simply playing his guitar Lucille without mouthing words or to a congregation shouting its amens to something the preacher has said that resonates in a particular way with them. As a master storyteller, Andrews is familiar with these cultural patterns and replicates them in the visual structure of the text as well as in the invited exchanges that his own satisfied responses to the text evoke in his audience.

Structurally, the punctuating exclamations also serve as orgasmic relief in the autoerotic analogy. The beginning of the paragraphs and the sentences building up whatever Andrews is describing serve as an elaborate form of foreplay. Then the crescendo of exclamation provides the relief to that build-up of pressure and excitement from the foreplay. During the course of the narrative, therefore, Andrews pleasures himself again and again. And since writing is a handy route to creation, the linguistic pleasure multiplies. Remember, though, that pleasure is to be shared, and Andrews always wants his audience to share whatever pleasure he experiences.

Andrews's pleasure in having his audience share the same space with him is particularly observable in one scene in the text. When the locals learn that Red's Café is going to become Baby Sweet's whorehouse (while there is much discussion about the use of the word "whorehouse," Darling forcefully asserts that that name is most appropriate and simply cannot be dressed up in any way), they gather on the porch of Blackshear's funeral home directly across the street to watch for the procession of white males into their neighborhood on Independence Day in 1966 when the whorehouse is scheduled to open at noon (recall the iconic use of the Fourth of July in previous works). When they learn that Lea, one of the whores, will service the black men, Andrews's comment is: ". . . Appalachee's first official whorehouse was now officially open to niggers! Amen for Civil Rights!" (116). Many of the watchers fast become customers. More important, from their initial gathering, they are voyeurs, and the shadow character Raymond Andrews places himself on Blackshear's porch with them.

From that vantage point, he has the pleasure of gawking with the black men as well as recording their transformation from rejects to customers. Through language, his location on the porch is clear. Of the Blackshear's crowd, Andrews remarks, "[M]ost of the folks *over here*[,] having gotten peeved at the sun for refusing to stay up with them any longer to see the faces of those who were now entering Baby Sweet's . . . went on home themselves" (182; my emphasis). He comments that the now aged T Cake, having been re-fused work at the whorehouse, is "standing by *over here* on the funeral home's porch determinedly awaiting an SOS from a fast-filling-up Baby Sweet's" and "Also included *over here* were most of those males who had 'been to the top of the stairs' to keep company with the Motorcycle Momma [Lea] and who were now standing around swapping experiences among themselves and at the same time lording it over those who hadn't risen to the heights" (185; my emphasis), an obvious jab at sexual arousal as well as the top of the stairs where Lea plies her trade.

Linguistically and spatially, Andrews is able to continue his voyeuristic pleasure. The front porch of Blackshear's echoes the many porches of the South as well as the general mythology of porch sitting and porch telling. There is certainly irony in the gathering of the watchers on the porch of a funeral home, but there is also tradition in it. It allows for constant gazing across the street as well as for the internal gazing of those who measure a man by his ability to produce an erection at the appropriate time. That ability, captured in the storytelling of the adventurers themselves and challenged or confirmed by those who share the experience, brings the text into a substantive realm of historical replication just as Andrews brings it into a linguistic realm of historical replication. The watchers are having a good time, and Andrews is having one with them.

The porch enables the watchers to use segregation to their voyeuristic advantage. They cannot go into the parlor of the whorehouse, because that is for white males and the black whores only. However, they can witness, judge, and make the subject of gossip any white male who enters the front door at Baby Sweet's. They can do the same for the black males who rush to line up at the back stairs for sexual visits to Lea, but it is the white men who hold their curiosity most intensely. Who of the many white males who hold power over them—even in 1966—is willing to walk the gauntlet of black eyes and stride up to the door of a whorehouse in a black neighborhood in broad daylight? As they watch the white men enter Baby Sweet's, the black men gain linguistic power over them and take as much pleasure from that gain as white men might take in their economic and social control of blacks. The white men who enter will become the subject of gossip and perhaps as much the source of legend as the unorthodox John Junior.

The porch, therefore, becomes a voyeuristic leveling space in that it equates the black men with John Junior—at least at the level of watching. In his youth, John Junior was fascinated with the colored section of Appalachee, an attractive but forbidden space such as the one Gwendolyn Brooks depicts in "A Song in the Front Yard," which serves as the epigraph for the first part of the novel. From his front yard of southern white riches, John Junior was always curious about black folks. He spied on them as often as he could, and he lost his virginity by entering the black vagina representative of the blackness that he has mythologized. Just as he gazed with John Junior upon the black side of town, so Andrews gazes with the black men upon John Junior, who has, by the time of the opening of the whorehouse, morphed into a user of black slang that is conspicuous by its self-consciousness. The language of gossip and legend—at which they are experts—that the black men use to discuss the white men is unavailable to John Junior and, just as he is inferior as an artist, so is he inferior as a storyteller. He thus becomes as much a spectator in the events of the novel as some of the men are; indeed, on Independence Day when the whorehouse opens, he is as much a watcher as are the men on the porch (he had initiated two of the whores the night before).

Ever the watcher himself, Andrews also has the pleasure of taking readers on a trip through the whorehouse. "What caught your eye," he writes, "as soon as you walked in the front door of the 'new' Baby Sweet's was the long black leather couch that lined the room's right wall" (82), and he proceeds to take "you" on a trip through the space. Pleasure for Andrews, then, is both external to the whorehouse and within it. He combines that pleasure with a focus on audience when he allows two of the women in the whorehouse to tell how they became whores. Fig, a naive young woman who believes that she is relieving men's sinful natures by allowing them to use her body instead of lusting, relates her narrative in three pages. Lea, whom Andrews avows the novel is about, does a "Max-in-the-Courtroom-*Native-Son*" kind of speech from which Andrews as omniscient narrator disappears for almost forty pages from the text. In the Fig narrative, Andrews succeeds, like Toni Morrison, in leaving holes and spaces for his audience to enter in and engage with the text. With the much-longer Lea narrative, Andrews answers questions that were left hanging in the earlier novels and reveals his inability to leave out details of what he considers a good story. He finds Lea's account of her mother's encounter with John Junior and her ensuing years of singing, waitressing, and whoring totally irresistible, and he expects his audience members/readers to do so as well. How did the white mother of a mixed-race daughter, whose family rejects her, survive in Atlanta in the 1940s and 1950s? Talent alone did not do it, so she was forced into giving sex in exchange for being allowed to sing in various restaurants, bars, and juke joints, then prostituting herself to give her daughter an education. The combination of interracial sex, then sex for food, then sex for money carries its own voyeuristic engagement. Andrews places his readers in the position of absorbing that tale as voyeurs even as he appreciates delivery of the voyeurism.

Andrews's ultimate pleasure, though, is in creating, witnessing, applauding, and commenting on a sexual encounter in the whorehouse. After all, what else is a whorehouse for if not the pleasure of sexual encounter? After John Junior asks him about fathering Appalachee Red, John Morgan Sr. ventures off the hill where his mansion is located and into the whorehouse on opening day, which is also the day on which he and his wife are celebrating an anniversary that has been recorded lavishly in the local newspaper, portions of which Andrews deposits at strategic points in the text. Coupling with Lea in an intense sexual encounter, John Morgan Sr. dies—without his boots on.

First, Lea is willing to accommodate the old man, although she has just announced an end to her whoring. Second, there is the time she takes to get him aroused—in contrast to her treatment of several guys earlier. Then the old man gets an erection in spite of his years and has an explosive sexual encounter. More than watching the old dude's sexual success, however, is what Andrews does to him in that context. By his having John Sr. come down from the Morgan mansion to chase black gold, the mighty is brought low. Also, by having John Sr. desire Lea, the mixed-raced woman with her kinky blond hair (to which he surprises his son by being attracted), Andrews echoes the sexual relationship between John Sr. and Little Bit Thompson that occurred in *Appalachee Red,* the first novel in the trilogy. His socially unacceptable desire, at least publicly, reiterated in the space of the whorehouse makes John Sr. seem less powerful and ultimately destroys him. Blackness kills the oppressor of blackness, the text seems to posit, and what better way to kill him than by having him undone by the child of a racially illicit sexual encounter. As Appalachee Red's spiritual sister by her mixture of black and white blood, Lea inadvertently becomes the avenger that Red could never become with John Sr., and thus the past lives in the present. The sins the old man has committed earlier come back to haunt him in the form of his own lust, for it is lust that kills him. If he had been content to stay home with his staid, respectable wife instead of following his son from the front yard to the backyard, then he would not have suffered such an ignominious demise.

That demise, however, is poetic justice and the ultimate voyeurism for Andrews. How else to bring the mighty low than to hoist them on their own interracial sexual petard? The desire inherent in voyeurism, the desire that led John Sr. to seduce Little Bit in spite of the fact that she was married to Big Man Thompson, also leads him down off the hill to Baby Sweet's. Like his son, who has a fascination with the nipples of black women, John Sr. can never forget black pussy. To reduce him to being killed by it encourages readers to join Andrews in believing that it could not have happened to a better candidate.

The image of a rich white man, the number-one citizen of his town, dying atop a black whore in a small country southern town is enough to bring giggles from a variety of quarters. Certainly, death is not funny. What *is* funny is the placement of bodies in the positions and location in which we find them. The ensuing potential embarrassment will be worth many legends. Even if John Sr.'s family is powerful enough to cover up the *real* story, they cannot control the power of gossip and the pathway to legend. Just as Andrews meanders his way through the narrative with generations of little stories about the people who make up Appalachee, so too will John Sr.'s demise become a part of that lore—from the subject of immediate voyeurism to the subject of imaginative and speculative voyeurism in the future. Nothing in Muskhogean County or Appalachian city history will top this Independence Day when the emperor was not only caught without his clothes but also died from the exposure. For all of John Sr.'s sins, the way in which he dies is the ultimate in textual and linguistic revenge.

To the father Andrews assigns death through the sexual act, but the pleasure derived from contemplation of an engagement in sex with black women lives on in his son John Junior. From his early fascination with the black side of town, John Junior is painted as desiring the socially and racially forbidden. He is tremendously attracted to Baby Sweet while, as a teenager, she is working at the Morgan House Hotel from which Appalachee Red rescues her. John Junior goes into the hotel again and again as a horny teenager to watch "*every* move" (30) of Baby Sweet (and the narrator punctuates that "baby, this child had *some* moves"). John Junior is too timid to approach Baby Sweet, but he is totally absorbed in watching her move through her duties as a kitchen helper, and his voyeurism gives rise to sexual expression: "These undulations of female flesh exuding uncut sex into the atmosphere were enough to keep John Junior in a constant state of rut . . . thus driving him for the first time deep into the realm of autoeroticism—the finger art whose grasping clutches kept him in a thumb-to-pinkie death grip throughout most of his solitary moments that torrid summer of '45. Shame!" (30). But . . . while Andrews pronounces shame on John Junior, he clearly relishes in that finger art and everything else in the text that might be labeled shameful. He is the voyeur who creates the voyeurs, and he is the final master of autoeroticism who can recognize a kindred spirit when he conjures him up. John Junior's pleasures are Raymond Andrews's pleasures, and the text suggests that Andrews enjoys them just as much—if not more.

After contemplating *Baby Sweet's* and what Andrews does with character and audience there, another question arises: is Raymond Andrews sufficient evidence to change the overall thesis about African American writers and the South? My answer to that question is a very strong "No." While I love what Andrews does, the overall tone of his work at time belies the seriousness of the issues he covers. His comical presentations and his healthy attitude toward southern cultures and peoples serve to make him an exception to the rule of fear and serious indictment of the South. The lightheartedness he provides offers relief from the prevailing tragic modes in which so many African American writers encounter the South. While we can appreciate that pause from the usual and applaud the success with which it is executed, it goes but a small way in alleviating the almost-unrelenting discomfort that African American writers hold toward the South. Andrews's works were mostly written about thirty years ago, and no younger African American writers have followed in his path. Indeed, the most recent work I treat in this text, Edward P. Jones's *The Known World* (2003), sends readers back into the world of slavery and black repression. Jones certainly offers a twist on the topic, but the basic mode is still the same.

From the vantage point of the twenty-first century, therefore, African American writers are still wrestling with the attraction and repulsion of the South. It consistently provides the historical background as well as the contemporary landscape on which to locate the drama of African American lives. While Daniel Black in *The Sacred Place* (2007) is the only twenty-first-century African American writer who has presented a form of summary justice on southern territory (an engaging twist on the Emmett Till case), and while no writer in this century has depicted a lynching, there is still the quest for identity and some sense of reconciliation with the part of the country that served as the central shaping force in African American life and culture. A superb example of this is Natasha Trethewey's *Native Guard* (2007), which won the 2007 Pulitzer Prize for poetry. In such poems as "Pastoral," "Miscegenation," "Blond," "Southern Gothic," "Incident," and especially "South," Trethewey uncovers a plethora of emotions in relation to her native Mississippi, especially the pain of her family history. In spite of that pain, she claims the land that has shaped her into the person she is, and I reiterate her claiming: "I return/ to Mississippi, state that made a crime/ of me—mulatto, half-breed—native/in my native land, this place they'll bury me."[3] Like her predecessors, the South dominates her imagination just as it continues to dominate the imaginations of African American writers throughout the United States.

Notes

INTRODUCTION

1. James Baldwin, *No Name in the Street* (New York: Dial, 1972), 68.

2. Richard Wright, *Black Boy* (1945; repr. New York: Perennial, 1966), 284–85.

3. Claude McKay, "America," in *Selected Poems of Claude McKay* (New York: Harcourt, Brace & World, 1953), 59. In *No Name in the Street,* Baldwin specifically refers to the South as hell. "I felt as though I had wandered into hell," he says of a trip to the South (*No Name,* 55), and when a white man directs him to the back door, colored entrance of a restaurant in Montgomery, he comments: "I realized that this man thought that he was being kind; and he was, indeed, being as kind as can be expected from a guide in hell" (*No Name,* 72–73).

4. See Daryl Cumber Dance, ed., *Shuckin' and Jivin': Folklore from Contemporary Black Americans* (Bloomington: Indiana University Press, 1978), 174. Dance also includes the tale in her *From My People: 400 Years of African American Folklore* (New York: Norton, 2002), 55, where she notes that this was one of her mother's favorite folktales.

5. Langston Hughes and Arna Bontemps, *The Book of Negro Folklore* (New York: Dodd, Mead, 1958), 507.

6. James Baldwin, *Nobody Knows My Name* (New York: Dial, 1961), 100. I will place other references to this source in parentheses in the text.

7. Alice Walker, *The Third Life of Grange Copeland* (1970; repr. New York: Harvest, 1988), 8, 9. I will place other references to this source in parentheses in the text.

8. See Trudier Harris, *Exorcising Blackness: Historical and Literary Lynching and Burning Rituals* (Bloomington: Indiana University Press, 1984).

9. For my discussion of Kelley's attempt to depict the South and southern characters, both black and white, see "William Melvin Kelley's Real Live, Invisible South," *South Central Review* 22, no. 1 (Spring 2005): 26–47. An aura of mythology surrounds Kelley's portrayals as he depicts a larger-than-life African, a wheelchair-bound raconteur who purports to understand the African and his descendants, a southern white liberal who truly has gut-level good intentions, a sexualized white southern woman, and a diminutive black chauffeur who manages to transform the lives of his employers and lead a revolution without knowing it.

10. When Beck spends some time at Tuskegee Institute, he is chastised for having sex with a number of coeds and local women. He recounts that the president calls him into his office and complains: "Boy, yu ah a disgrace to oauh fine institushun. Ahm'm shocked thet sech has occurred. Yo mothah has bin infaumed of yo bad conduck. Oauh bord is considurin yo dismissul." Beck labels the president's speech a "sneaky Southern drawl." For a discussion of his adventures in the South, see Candice Love Jackson, "The Literate Pimp: Robert Beck, Iceberg Slim, and Pimping the African American Novel," in *New Essays on the African American Novel: From Hurston and Ellison to Morrison and Whitehead,* ed. Lovalerie King and Linda F. Selzer, 167–83 (New York: Palgrave, 2008).

11. See Bebe Moore Campbell, *Your Blues Ain't Like Mine* (New York: Putnam's, 1992); Toni Morrison, *Song of Solomon* (New York: Knopf, 1977); Nagueyalti Warren, "Winter/Spring/Summer," in the *African American Review* 36, no. 2 (2002): 325; and Marilyn Nelson, *A Wreath for Emmett Till* (Boston: Houghton Mifflin, 2005), n.p. I will place other references to this last source in parentheses in the text.

12. Gloria Naylor, *The Women of Brewster Place* (New York: Penguin, 1983), 154; the backstory appears in "The Two," 129–73, in explanation for Ben's being especially considerate of Lorraine, one of the lesbian women, who reminds him of his daughter.

13. Alice Walker, *In Love and Trouble: Stories of Black Women* (New York: Harcourt Brace Jovanovich, 1973), 120.

14. Kansas-born and Illinois-bred Gwendolyn Brooks also treats lynching in one of her poems. See "The Ballad of Pearl May Lee," in *Blacks,* 60–63 (Chicago: David, 1987). In reference to Sammy being lynched, Brooks simply observes: "They wrapped you around a cottonwood tree," instead of portraying any gruesome detail. The bulk of the poem focuses on the rejected lover, the black woman over whom Sammy preferred the white woman who has accused him of rape. The distinctive feature of Brooks's poem is that the cross-racial relationship was a voluntary one. As early as the 1880s, Ida B. Wells-Barnett asserted that white women involved in such relationships sometimes cried rape, as Brooks's character does, and that cry became an excuse for the lynching of black men.

15. Paul Laurence Dunbar, "The Haunted Oak," in James Weldon Johnson, ed., *The Book of American Negro Poetry,* 58–61 (New York: Harcourt Brace Jovanovich, 1922). One of the sonnets in Nelson's *A Wreath for Emmett Till* also personifies a tree on which a black man has been lynched; indeed, Nelson's notes to the volume make clear that she is echoing Dunbar. The tree is so shocked that a part of it dies.

16. Toni Morrison, *Beloved* (New York: Knopf, 1987), 6.

17. See "Ole Sis Goose" in Hughes and Bontemps, *Negro Folklore,* 13.

18. Of course, this pattern held true during slavery, but since this study is focused primarily on twentieth-century works, I take my examples from those.

19. I should note that black males were also subjected to sexual violation, a pattern that the literature depicts as well. Consider the positions into which the black boys in Ellison's *Invisible*

Man are placed when they are forced to watch the nude white woman dancing; at least one of the boys cannot hide his involuntary erection. Consider as well the case of Cholly Breedlove, in Morrison's *The Bluest Eye,* who is forced to continue having sex with Darlene by a couple of flashlight-wielding white hunters; it could be argued that this disruption of his first sexual encounter warps him for life. And think of Flo Hatfield in Charles Johnson's *Oxherding Tale* and Nathan's owner in Sherley Anne Williams's *Dessa Rose;* both white women trained enslaved young black men to make love to them. No matter the pleasure, there is also exploitation.

20. Margaret Mead and James Baldwin, *A Rap on Race* (New York: Laurel, 1971), 32. Baldwin's use of the electrified rug image obviously brings to mind the Battle Royal scene in *Invisible Man,* where young black men in the South are forced to pick up gold coins, which they later discover are fake, from an electrified rug. It teaches the narrator, he says, to "contain electricity."

21. In 2005, there were conversations about reopening the Atlanta Child Murder cases. Tayari Jones commented on that new development in her blog. See www.tayarijones.com/blog/archives/2005. She likened the cases to a broken bone. "But as we know, the only way to repair a bone badly set is to break it again, and then set it right" (May 22, 2005). For a recent scholarly study of the Atlanta Child Murders, see Eric Gary Anderson, "Black Atlanta: An Ecosocial Approach to Narratives of the Atlanta Child Murders," *PMLA* 122, no. 1 (January 2007): 194–209. Anderson treats the cases from an ecocritical perspective.

22. Tina McElroy Ansa, for example, is vocal in claiming her status as a Southerner and her love of the South ("What's the Confederate Flag Got to Do with It?" *Callaloo* 24, no. 1 [2001]: 5–7). In spite of the difficulties it has caused her in familial and racial history, Natasha Trethewey, the 2007 winner of the Pulitzer Prize for poetry, also warmly embraces the South. She ends her prize-winning volume with this declaration: "Where the roads, buildings, and monuments / are named to honor the Confederacy, / where that old flag still hangs, I return/to Mississippi, state that made a crime/of me—mulatto, half-breed—native / in my native land, this place they'll bury me" (*Native Guard* [New York: Houghton Mifflin, 2007], 46).

23. Langston Hughes, "The Negro Artist and the Racial Mountain" (1926); reprinted in Angelyn Mitchell, *Within the Circle: An Anthology of African American Literary Criticism from the Harlem Renaissance to the Present* (Durham, NC: Duke University Press, 1994), 59.

CHAPTER 1

1. James Baldwin, *Just Above My Head* (New York: Dell, 1979), 399. I will place other references to this source in parentheses in the text.

2. James Baldwin, *No Name in the Street* (New York: Dial, 1972), 57. I will place other references to this source in parentheses in the text.

3. See Trudier Harris, "The South as Woman: Chimeric Images of Emasculation in *Just Above My Head,*" in *Studies in Black American Literature,* vol. 1, *Black American Prose Theory,* ed. Joe Weixlmann and Chester J. Fontenot, 89–109 (Greenwood, FL: Penkevill, 1984).

4. For my treatment of this story, see *Exorcising Blackness: Historical and Literary Lynching and Burning Rituals* (Bloomington: Indiana University Press, 1984), 86–94.

5. Meredith M. Malburne argues that Richard is much more important in death than in life, though she does not subscribe to the suicide theory ("No Blues for Mister Henry: Locating Richard's Revolution," in *Reading Contemporary African American Drama: Fragments of History, Fragments of Self,* ed. Trudier Harris , 39–57 [New York: Lang, 2007]).

6. James Baldwin, *Blues for Mister Charlie* (New York: Dial, 1964), 27. I will place other references to this source in parentheses in the text.

7. Richard's derogatory use of the word "nigger" anticipates Procter Lewis's equally derogatory use in Ernest J. Gaines's "Three Men," which I treat in chap. 2. Richard and Procter evince a superiority to other black males that they do not match in their actions.

8. I also discuss the failure of Christianity in chap. 6 in considering various kinds of fears in Randall Kenan's *A Visitation of Spirits* (1989). Notably as well, female characters after Mama Lena and Mother Henry are far less willing to take their burdens to the Lord and leave them there. Christianity is not a factor with Dana in Butler's *Kindred* (1988) or with Elizabeth "Lizzie" DuBose in Phyllis Alesia Perry's *Stigmata* (1998). For my discussion of the diminishing significance of Christianity to black female characters after 1970, see "Failed, Forgotten, Forsaken: Christianity in Contemporary African American Literature," E. Maynard Adams Lecture (Program in the Humanities and Human Values, University of North Carolina at Chapel Hill, October 7, 2007).

9. James Baldwin, *The Fire Next Time* (New York: Dial, 1963), 67.

10. Of course, since this is a *staged* production, nuances of tone could convey emotion that a flat reading of lines in the text would not convey. The lines could therefore be delivered in a straightforward manner, or they might be sarcastically or antagonistically delivered.

11. Lyle comments to Parnell about the sequence of events at the store and the gossip that resulted from it: "Everybody heard about it, it was all over this town quicker'n a jack-rabbit gets his nuts off" (70). Lyle is thus forced to live up to his legendary status, for no white man can allow himself to become the butt of jokes by black people. The sexual reference again centers the conflict as an assertion of manhood.

12. Lyle calls Richard by the derogatory appellation "boy" on several occasions—as do Jo and Parnell. There is the southern custom of disrespecting black males that is inherent in this designation, but there is also the implied sexual connection. Lyle is a man, and Richard is a boy, still too immature in any realm in which he confronts Lyle. Papa D. also uses the word "boy" in a chastising way to Richard; however, the connotations are decidedly different.

13. Langston Hughes, *The Collected Poems,* ed. Arnold Rampersad (New York: Knopf, 1995), 50.

14. For especially poignant commentary on Baldwin's travels to various Southern cities, see *Nobody Knows My Name* (New York: Dial, 1961) and *No Name in the Street* (New York: Dial, 1972).

15. Countee Cullen, "Heritage," in *Black Writers of America: A Comprehensive Anthology,* ed. Richard Barksdale and Keneth Kinnamon, 531–33 (New York: Macmillan, 1974).

16. Alice Walker, *You Can't Keep A Good Woman Down* (New York: Harcourt Brace Jovanovich, 1981), 3–20.

17. Horace Porter agrees that Baldwin adheres to a certain mythology about the South. Porter comments that Baldwin "was victimized partly by the mythology of the South. He viewed the South rather reductively as a slow, backward, and brutal land, trapped perpetually in the nightmare of its racial history." Porter further concludes, from Baldwin's description of his first trip to the South in 1957, that Baldwin was "preoccupied . . . with a sense of the South's emasculating, murderous, and bloody past, a picture of the region paradoxically as mythological as it was real." Finally, Porter posits that Baldwin displays an "outsider's contempt" for the South. See "The South in *Go Tell It on the Mountain:* Baldwin's Personal Confrontation," in *New Essays*

on "Go Tell It on the Mountain," ed. Trudier Harris, 61, 62, 63 (New York: Cambridge University Press, 1996).

CHAPTER 2

1. A couple of years ago, Ernest Gaines and his wife Dianne built a house in Louisiana and returned permanently to the territory that Gaines made famous in his fiction.

2. Ernest J. Gaines, "Three Men," in *Bloodline* (New York: Dial, 1968), 121. I will place other references to this source in parentheses in the text. "Three Men" was composed prior to the publication of *Of Love and Dust* in 1967. Gaines lifted the Procter character from the story into the Marcus character of that novel. See n. 5 below.

3. As noted earlier, Procter, like Richard, uses the word "nigger" freely in describing other blacks. Such usage is a reflection of the times, though it might bang against our twenty-first-century ears.

4. Mary Ellen Doyle refers to Munford as a preacher delivering a sermon, the importance of which becomes apparent to the recipient only much later. See Doyle, *Voices from the Quarters: The Fiction of Ernest J. Gaines* (Baton Rouge: Louisiana State University Press, 2002), 61. In following a pattern in Gaines criticism of characters searching for fathers, a pattern that Gaines has verified, Valerie Melissa Babb argues that Munford acts as a father figure to Procter just as Procter will later act as a father figure to the young boy (*Ernest Gaines* [New York: Twayne, 1991], 29–31).

5. In interviews, Gaines has commented that Procter and the decision he attempts to make to stay in jail offer a contrast to Marcus's decision about jail in *Of Love and Dust* (1967). "I should point out," said Gaines to John O'Brien in 1972, "that Procter Lewis and Marcus Payne are the same character; I wanted to show what would have happened to Procter Lewis had he gotten out of prison, the chances he would have taken to attain his freedom." See John Lowe, *Conversations with Ernest Gaines* (Jackson: University of Mississippi Press, 1995), 27. Gaines makes the same point in speaking with Dan Tooker and Roger Hofheins in 1976 (Lowe, 107), in 1986 in an interview with William Parrill (Lowe, 182), and in a 1994 interview with John Lowe (Lowe, 319).

6. Keith Clark argues that same-sex desires underlie most of the actions of the three men in the story, with Procter and Munford working hard to tone down that possibility. See "Que(e)rying the Prison-House of Black Male Desire: Homosociality in Ernest Gaines's 'Three Men,'" *African American Review* 40, no. 2 (Summer 2006): 239–55.

7. For a discussion of how the names in the text function to suggest same-sex desire, see Keith Clark.

8. Gaines speaks of Procter's action in several interviews. It is striking in one, however, that he refers to Procter's killing Bayou as "murder," which casts a different light on the events. See Lowe, *Conversations*, 36: "In 'Three Men' the boy is nineteen and has committed murder."

9. For commentary on how narrative voice unfolds in the text, especially in terms of its creation of a certain kind of immediacy, see Doyle's discussion of "Three Men" in *Voices from the Quarters.*

10. Sheila Smith McKoy notes that, in the story, "Gaines actually negates the socially transformative power of homoerotic desire by validating heterosexual desire and heterosexist moral authority" ("Rescuing the Black Homosexual Lambs: Randall Kenan and the Reconstruction

of Southern Gay Masculinity," in *Contemporary Black Men's Fiction and Drama,* ed. Keith Clark, 15–36 [Urbana: University of Illinois Press, 2001], 24). She also comments that "Procter washes the boy, symbolically and physically cleansing him of any residue of his association with Hattie. And, as is true of his black gay characters in *Of Love and Dust,* Hattie remains silent in the narrative from the moment Procter becomes the masculine and moral authority in the narrative. Procter's manhood, then, becomes visible only when Hattie's is denied" (McKoy, "Rescuing the Black Homosexual Lambs," 26).

11. It is noteworthy that Procter's so-called transformation has been accompanied by wrenching tears. He tries as hard as he can to muffle his crying, but cry he does. Since he has noted Hattie's crying on several occasions, this is another one of the less-than-manly actions that could be applied to him. However, Procter, once again, couches the crying in a "manly" light so that the label of womanliness cannot be applied to him. He cries as he comes to a difficult decision; Hattie cries at the drop of a hat, which is a fault. Procter has also viewed Grinning Boy's crying as a sign of weakness after Procter killed Bayou. Grinning Boy cries and clings to the steering wheel when Procter tries to put him out of the car and otherwise acts in a most unmanly fashion from Procter's perspective. On another note, smoking is also one of the habits Procter shares with Hattie that he does not view as equalizing them in any way.

12. Procter comments that he feels a certain amount of "love" for the boy, which enhances the idea of the father/son relationship. Doyle posits that, for Procter, the boy "is what he once was" (*Voices from the Quarters,* 59), which might suggest a progression to self-love, which has not been apparent in Procter's previous actions.

13. In making his decision, Procter recounts the tale of Jack, a black man respected in his community. He landed in jail and was hired out to a Cajun who deliberately broke him down. Procter sees political motive in that process—taking away from black males the one conspicuous role model they had (147). In the author's assertion of what Jack meant to the community, there are echoes of Etheridge Knight's "Hard Rock Returns to Prison from the Hospital for the Criminal Insane" in the narrative. Hard Rock, like Jack, is destroyed physically and mentally because he serves as a political role model, a model of resistance, for the black prisoners incarcerated with him.

14. Both Doyle and Karen Carmean find this an acceptable ending to the story. Doyle comments in *Voices from the Quarters* that the story "needs to end where and how it does, in the immediacy of his [Procter's] struggle to decide" (58). She adds that Procter's focus on the stars and not cheating in locating one he has identified signals that he will indeed remain in jail, because at his "moment of breakthrough" (59) a "million little white, cool stars" appear through his cell window. In *Ernest J. Gaines: A Critical Companion* (Westport, CT: Greenwood, 1998), Carmean asserts "Procter's uncertainty is far more realistic than his earlier, confident claims" (148). For other commentary on the story, see Herman Beavers, *Wrestling Angels into Song: The Fictions of Ernest J. Gaines and James Alan McPherson* (Philadelphia: University of Pennsylvania Press, 1995), 27–31; and Keith Byerman, *Fingering the Jagged Grain: Tradition and Form in Recent Black Fiction* (Athens: University of Georgia Press, 1985), 79–83. Beavers notes that Procter's decision to remain in jail ties him to the resistance of the civil rights movement.

15. Jasmine Rippy, a student in one of my classes in the fall semester of 2007, suggests that "three men" might also refer to the three stages of development in Procter's life—his violent, irresponsible stage that led to the death of Bayou, his jail cell reflections, and the implications of his futuristic resolve to be a better man. In an interview with Marcia Gaudet and Carl Wooten, Gaines comments on the various rebellious options for black males responding to oppression.

Some use religion or drugs, others gamble, some remain hopeful, and others believe they will never have a chance. "And then you have the others who say I'm a defeatist. Now that's what 'Three Men' is all about. You have the defeatist . . . like Hattie—the effeminate, the homosexual type thing, you know, just given up: I'll be whatever the world wants me to be. I will not try to be a man. Munford has gone just the opposite way: if anything gets in my way, I'm going to knock it over with a gun, or with an axe, or with anything. And then you have this other guy, Proctor [sic] who says, 'I just want to exist, and I don't give a damn how I exist'—until he realizes the only thing is, when you give up [indifference to] life, then you become something"—in *Porch Talk with Ernest Gaines: Conversations on the Writer's Craft* (Baton Rouge: Louisiana State University Press, 1990), 52; ellipsis in original.

CHAPTER 3

1. Deborah E. McDowell notes that "it is significant that the majority of contemporary novels about slavery have been written by black women" and that those novels dramatize "not what was *done* to slave women, but what they *did* with what was done to them." McDowell also comments that "Afro-American writers who tell a story of slavery are increasingly aiming for the same thing: to reposition the stress points of that story with a heavy accent on particular acts of agency within an oppressive and degrading system." See "Negotiating between Tenses: Witnessing Slavery after Freedom—Dessa Rose," in *Slavery and the Literary Imagination,* ed. Deborah E. McDowell and Arnold Rampersad, 146, 160 (Baltimore: Johns Hopkins University Press, 1989). For other commentary on neo-slave (freedom) narratives, see Bernard Bell's *The African American Novel: Its Folk Roots and Modern Literary Branches* (Amherst: University of Massachusetts Press, 2004). Bell originated the phrase "neo-slave narrative."

2. Octavia E. Butler, *Kindred* (1979; repr. 25th Anniversary Edition, Boston: Beacon Press, 2003). I will indicate references to the novel in parentheses in the text. The bicentennial year in which the novel is set makes the name of "Franklin" keenly resonant in its connection to American history, independence, and possibility. Dana, in the tradition of Franklin, tries to shape a more hopeful past than recorded history suggests.

3. Butler scholar Sandra Y. Govan identifies the "What if . . .?" question as the essence of the speculative mode, what distinguishes it from pure science fiction. There is less science in *Kindred* than a focus on alternative possibilities for existence, a kind of laboratory of slavery created to see how twentieth-century characters will fare in that environment.

4. Several scholars have commented on Butler's setting her novel in 1976, the bicentennial year. The implication is that the heritage of slavery applies to *all* Americans, no matter their skin color.

5. Dana remarks on other occasions on her role in Rufus's and Alice's lives. "I wouldn't dare act as though they weren't my ancestors. I wouldn't let anything happen to them, the boy or girl, if I could possibly prevent it" (47). Then, "The boy was literally growing up as I watched—growing up because I watched and because I helped to keep him safe. I was the worst possible guardian for him—a black to watch over him in a society that considered blacks subhuman, a woman to watch over him in a society that considered women perennial children" (68).

6. Dana also comments on the things that Sarah and Carrie inadvertently teach her: "I liked to listen to them talk sometimes and fight my way through their accents to find out more about how they survived lives of slavery. Without knowing it, they prepared me to survive" (94).

7. Brian K. Reed describes the relationship as Dana becoming "wife" to Rufus. In response

to the comments that Dana and Alice look alike, Reed offers: "These two halves become Rufus's perfect whole. By pretending that Alice and Dana are one woman, a woman he makes love to at night and chats with pleasantly over breakfast the next morning, he tricks himself into believing that this woman is his wife" (Reed, "Behold the Woman: The Imaginary Wife in Octavia Butler's *Kindred*," *CLA Journal* 47, no. 1 [September 2003]: 70). In an earlier article, Sandra Y. Govan, without referring to Dana as Rufus's "wife," also commented on the inextricable link between the two women: "Dana and Alice are virtual doubles of each other. Physically, they look alike; intellectually and emotionally, they function as two halves of the same woman, flawed duplicates separated by the dictates of their respective historical time and the resultant sexual-political consciousness each maintains by virtue of their particular social circumstances" (Govan, "Homage to Tradition: Octavia Butler Renovates the Historical Novel," *MELUS* 13 [1986]: 93).

8. Marc Steinberg is one of the critics who put forth the argument that Dana suffers a kind of slavery in her marriage to Kevin: "When he is transported back in time with Dana, Kevin must confront the direct query of a slaveholder: 'Does Dana belong to you now?' (60) His response equates matrimony with possession: 'In a way.... She's my wife' (60). Thus, Butler uses Kevin to extend into the present a classic type of human ownership in western civilization—the marital exchange. Even Kevin's proposal to Dana smacks of a kind of servitude when he remarks, 'I'd let you type all of my manuscripts' (109). Whether spoken in jest or seriousness, Kevin essentially assures Dana that in marriage she could work for him, that he might even expect that she would work for him. Kevin is not, however, a villainous character. Butler implies, nonetheless, that Kevin, along with many men, is quietly guilty of a kind of contemporary enslavement that mirrors the notions of servitude apparent in the antebellum South. The line between slavery and marriage is further blurred in the present when Dana's friends and family, oblivious to her time travel, confuse the markings from her beating by Rufus, her white slave owner with marks she suffers from spousal abuse in her marriage to Kevin" (Steinberg, "Inverting History in Octavia Butler's Postmodern Slave Narrative," *African American Review* 38, no. 3 [Fall 2004]: 469). For an impressively detailed discussion of the historical and contemporary racial implications of Kevin and Dana's marriage, see Guy Mark Foster, "'Do I look like someone you can come home to from where you may be going?': Re-Mapping Interracial Anxiety in Octavia Butler's *Kindred*," *African American Review* 41, no. 1 (Spring 2007): 143–64.

9. Dana is surprised on a couple of other occasions when she refers to the Weylin house as home. See pp. 190, 191, 192. She discovers that Kevin experiences the same feelings; even though he may have wandered throughout the North during the five years he was stranded in the nineteenth century without Dana, he viewed the Weylin plantation as the stationary foot of the compass around which he revolved. Ashraf H. A. Rushdy discusses the idea of home in the novel in "Families of Orphans: Relation and Disrelation in Octavia Butler's *Kindred*," *College English* 55, no. 2 (February 1993): 140–41.

CHAPTER 4

1. Sherley Anne Williams, *Dessa Rose* (New York: Morrow, 1986; I use the 1987 Berkley edition [William Morrow] for quotations here). I will place references to the novel in parentheses in the text. The novel is an elaborate expansion of a long short story that Williams published. Mae G. Henderson briefly compares the two in "The Stories of O(Dessa): Stories of Complic-

ity and Resistance," in *Female Subjects in Black and White: Race, Psychoanalysis, Feminism,* ed. Elizabeth Abel, Barbara Christian, and Helene Moglen, 285–304 (Berkeley: University of California Press, 1997).

2. Joanne V. Gabbin captures Dessa's situation succinctly when she comments that Dessa "worries about having her name, identity, humanity stolen by Nehemiah." Note to author, June 3, 2007.

3. Of course, since *Adam* Nehemiah undertakes this naming process, it evokes a perverse, yet strangely appropriate comparison to the biblical Adam, who had responsibility for naming all the animals God created.

4. See Nehemiah, chaps. 2–4.

5. As Deborah McDowell comments ("Negotiating between Tenses: Witnessing Slavery after Freedom—Dessa Rose," in *Slavery and the Literary Imagination,* ed. Deborah E. McDowell and Arnold Rampersad (Baltimore: Johns Hopkins University Press, 1989), Nehemiah wants to fit Dessa "into a recognizable proslavery text" (148). Writing also becomes an issue and is occasionally used against Dana in *Kindred;* for example, Rufus refuses to send her letters to Kevin when he has left Maryland for the North during one of Dana's absences from the Weylin plantation. Rufus may be jealous of the writing skill that Dana has, or he may simply be determined to keep her on the plantation. On the other hand, he manipulates her into writing letters to some of his creditors after his father's death; thus he attempts to contain her literacy, to have it at his beck and call.

6. Mary Kemp Davis comments on the connection between Kaine and the biblical Cain in "Everybody Knows Her Name: The Recovery of the Past in Sherley Anne Williams's *Dessa Rose,*" *Callaloo* 12 (40), no. 3 (Summer 1989): 549–50.

7. Lawrence W. Levine, *Black Culture and Black Consciousness: Afro-American Folk Thought from Slavery to Freedom* (New York: Oxford University Press, 1977), 122. Levine draws his information from a variety of sources that he cites in the text. In *Kindred,* Dana tries to use her intelligence to get Rufus to change his slaveholding ways.

8. As Gabbin points out, in many ways Nehemiah is like the biblical Adam in this context. "This is his universe to do as he pleases." Note to author, June 3, 2007. Several scholars make this point. See, for example, Mary Kemp Davis in "Everybody Knows Her Name" and Adam McKible, "'These Are the Facts of the Darky's History': Thinking History and Reading Names in Four African American Texts," *African American Review* 28, no. 2 (Summer 1994): 223–35. McKible also comments on naming in Octavia E. Butler's *Kindred* (1979).

9. Brent Wade has his character, Billy Covington, discuss "thingafication" in his novel *Company Man* (Chapel Hill, NC: Algonquin, 1992).

10. Ruth also scripts Ada (the runaway cook at Sutton Glen) and her daughter Annabelle in a narrative other than the one that has caused them to be at Sutton Glen—that the white master slept with Ada and fathered Annabelle and is about to sleep with Annabelle. True to her cultural breeding, Ruth remarks: "(White man, indeed! Both of them probably run off by the mistress for making up to the master)" (95). Sexuality seems to provide the constant in Ruth's evaluation of black female/white male interactions, with the black female always being to blame.

11. McDowell ("Negotiating between Tenses") makes a distinction between Rufel as a "visual" person and Dessa as a "verbal" one. Rufel's changes can be measured, therefore, in accordance with her willingness to give up her desire to *see* everything in order to believe it. This is especially relevant to her denial of Dessa's having scars because she has not seen them.

12. For a detailed discussion of Dessa's reclaiming of her body as a form of "textual healing," see Farah Jasmine Griffin, "Textual Healing: Claiming Black Women's Bodies, the Erotic and Resistance in Contemporary Novels of Slavery," *Callaloo* 19, no. 2 (Spring 1996): 519–36. Ann E. Trapasso also discusses healing in the novel in "Returning to the Site of Violence: The Restructuring of Slavery's Legacy in Sherley Anne Williams's *Dessa Rose*," in *Violence, Silence, and Anger: Women's Writing as Transgression,* ed. Deirdre Lashgari, 219–30 (Charlottesville: University Press of Virginia, 1995).

13. For a detailed discussion of the Mammy role in the novel, see Ashraf H. Rushdy, "Reading Mammy: The Subject of Relation in Sherley Anne Williams' *Dessa Rose*," *African American Review* 27, no. 3 (Fall 1993): 365–89. Mary Kemp Davis also discusses the Mammy figure in *Dessa Rose* in "Everybody Knows Her Name."

14. As Langston Hughes asserts, black people must learn to tell their own stories and write against the voyeurs who "have taken their songs" and turned them into various unrecognizable forms. See "You've Taken My Blues and Gone," in *The Collected Poems of Langston Hughes,* ed. Arnold Rampersad, 215–16 (New York: Knopf, 1995).

15. For other commentary on Dessa's subverting Nehemiah's power over her and controlling her own narrative, see Mae G. Henderson, "(W)riting The Work and Working the Rites," *Black American Literature Forum* 23, no. 4 (Winter 1989): 631–60; and Mae Gwendolyn Henderson, "Speaking in Tongues: Dialogics, Dialectics, and the Black Woman Writer's Literary Tradition," in *African American Literary Theory: A Reader,* ed. Winston Napier, 348–68 (New York: New York University Press, 2000). In the second article, Henderson comments that "the latter part of the novel, recounted from Dessa's perspective and in her own voice, establishes her as the successful author of her own narrative" (359); she adds that "as the author of her own story, Dessa writes herself into the dominant discourse and, in the process, transforms it" (362). McDowell ("Negotiating between Tenses") maintains that Dessa "is the final authority on her story, controlling her own text" (160).

16. McDowell ("Negotiating between Tenses") asserts that when Dessa tells her story, "she tells it first and mainly to an audience of black women" (155). However, McDowell does not share how she arrived at that conclusion.

17. Dessa also says, "I wasn't no Christian then" (208), which may be a passing attempt on her part to excuse some of the activities in which she and the others engaged. She makes this statement specifically in reference to having sex with Harker before they are married. In terms of then and now, Dessa also remarks: "I don't think I ever forgive the ignorance they kept us in" (227). It would be easier to forgive "the beatings, the selling, the killings."

CHAPTER 5

1. As Komunyakaa scholar Angela M. Salas so eloquently points out in *Flashback through the Heart: The Poetry of Yusef Komunyakaa* (Selinsgrove, PA: Susquehanna University Press, 2004), reading Komunyakaa's poetry through the lens of race is but one of the potentially fruitful approaches to his poetry. She does admit, however, that "race is crucial in *Dien Cai Dau*, and Komunyakaa attempts to build a bridge for his readers, showing how racial inequalities *underscore* our common humanity" (69). Given the context of my study, the racial lens enhances the points I make about southern American territory and its attraction for African American writers.

2. In "Slim in Hell," poet Sterling A. Brown identifies restrictive racial attitudes and practices in the South with conditions in hell. See *The Collected Poems of Sterling A. Brown,* ed. Michael S. Harper (Chicago: TriQuarterly, 1989), 89–92.

3. Myra MacPherson in *Long Time Passing: Vietnam and the Haunted Generation* (New York: Anchor, 1984) points out that white American soldiers in Vietnam actually burned crosses and raised Confederate flags in celebration of King's death (562). One black soldier recalled the reaction of one of his fellow black soldiers when King was murdered: "'Brother man,' he bellowed, 'these rednecks have got to be *stopped;* they have murdered Dr. King and declared war on our people . . .'" The narrator then concluded: "Some of us perceived that there *was* an attack on blacks. It's kinda hard not to feel that when you're in a company that's got a lot of blacks, and you go back into the rear and it's a different story altogether" (555). Komunyakaa refers to King's assassination in several of his poems about Vietnam.

4. For a discussion of Komunyakaa's incorporation of American issues into his poetry, see Michael C. Dowdy, "Working in the Space of Disaster: Yusef Komunyakaa's Dialogues with America," *Callaloo* 28, no. 3 (Summer 2005): 812–23.

5. Yusef Komunyakaa, *Dien Cai Dau* (Middletown, CT: Wesleyan University Press, 1988), 29. I will place additional references to this source in parentheses in the text.

6. Salas also notes the transference of Jim Crow practices from the American South to Vietnam. She comments that Komunyakaa's archetypal soldier finds "that race rules in effect in the Jim Crow South have been transplanted to this place so far from home," and she observes that "Jim Crow meets Vietnam and brings along all its ugliness and inherent absurdity." See *Flashback through the Heart,* 83, 84.

7. Komunyakaa offers the following about this mingling of kisses and semen on the bodies of Vietnamese women: "Well, in a certain sense, that is a moment of humanization because there's conflict not only out in the field, there's also conflict back in the rear areas where the soldiers should be getting along together as fellow citizens who have put their lives on the line. But they are divided by race and the culture of social apartheid in America. They brought it across the sea with them. And, yes, they are divided within their collective psyche, but brought together, without them being conscious of it, through this nameless person, this lady of the night. They relied on her to keep them human" (C. F. Mitrano, "A Conversation with Yusef Komunyakaa," *Callaloo* 28, no. 3 [Summer 2005]: 524).

8. Angela Salas asserts that the soldiers murder the woman. See "Race, Human Empathy, and Negative Capability: The Poetry of Yusef Komunyakaa," *College English* 30, no. 4 (Fall 2003): 38. In *Flashback through the Heart,* Salas is less certain, however, that the woman is murdered and refers to her fate as a "[probable] murder" (82).

9. The narrator of "One More Loss to Count" is in many ways like the writers I cover in this study. He is unable to conceive "authentic" blackness without routing it through the South.

10. Salas devotes a section of *Flashback through the Heart* to Komunyakaa's poems in which the death of Martin Luther King Jr. serves a central purpose (see 70–77).

11. Salas notes of the soldiers in "Hanoi Hannah" that "Komunyakaa portrays the well-armed and battle-weary soldiers as emasculated victims of psychological assault" (*Flashback through the Heart,* 72). The helplessness that the soldiers feel as they lay down fire in an effort to hit the ever-elusive Hannah intensifies the helplessness that Thomas J. Washington, who has no kind of weapon with which to fight back against his equally manipulative foe, must feel.

12. Vince Gotera identifies the real Hanoi Hannah in his discussion of Komunyakaa's poetry

("Yusef Komunyakaa," in *Radical Visions: Poetry by Vietnam Veterans* [Athens: University of Georgia Press, 1994], 335, n. 1 for chap. 8).

13. African Americans commonly believe that only black people in America have the last name of Washington. Whether folklore or fact, the belief holds sway, and Komunyakaa seems to be privy to it.

14. See Langston Hughes, *The Ways of White Folks: Stories by Langston Hughes* (1934; repr. New York: Vintage, 1962), 33–49.

15. For a sampling of Etheridge Knight's works, see *Poems from Prison* (Detroit: Broadside, 1968), *Born of a Woman: New and Selected Poems* (Boston: Houghton Mifflin, 1980), and *The Essential Etheridge Knight* (Pittsburgh: University of Pittsburgh Press, 1986). Also, as I noted in the Introduction, Marilyn Nelson is a poet who believes that form controls chaos. Nelson maintains that she used the "heroic crown of sonnets" to write about Emmett Till in order to distance herself from the torrent of emotions that could have overwhelmed her.

CHAPTER 6

1. Randall Kenan, *A Visitation of Spirits* (New York: Grove, 1989), 13. Further references to this source will be indicated in parentheses in the text.

2. Lorraine Hansberry, *A Raisin in the Sun* (1959; repr. New York: Signet, 1988), 51.

3. The pattern that Edward P. Jones's major character, Henry Townsend, follows in *The Known World* is similarly flawed in his modeling of success; he, too, looks to whites for examples of land ownership and financial security.

4. Richard Wright explores the same phenomenon in his presentation of the character Silas in "Long Black Song." Silas acquires acres of land and tries desperately to emulate white success, but it all ends tragically when he is caught in a web of racism that undermines completely any hope he had for success. See *Uncle Tom's Children*.

5. There are echoes of Walter Younger's "five generations of sharecroppers" speech in Zeke's speech. If a black family that was not generally expected to achieve very much has nonetheless beaten the odds and arrived at a kind of success, then how can one of its own members forget his pride and do something stupid? See *Raisin*, 147–48.

6. It is striking in one instance when Jimmy forgets his "calling" and begins to eat before he has blessed the food. To Zeke and Ruth, that borders on the criminal. See p. 194. The scene makes clear that Jimmy's inspiration to preach is more other-inspired than internally inspired. He is also "unrepentant" about refusing to forgive his mother Rose for having left him with his grandparents (121). Such resistance to forgiveness is certainly not the high road of Christianity.

7. Sheila Smith McKoy observes: "The legacy of sexual debauchery seems to touch even the minor characters in the novel. In short, there is no moral authority in Tims Creek, with its numerous and 'fleshy affairs' (221). In delineating the fact that everyone in Tims Creek has committed secret sexual sins, Kenan refuses to characterize Horace's death as a necessary sacrifice for the moral integrity of the community." See "Rescuing the Black Homosexual Lambs: Randall Kenan and the Reconstruction of Southern Gay Masculinity," in *Contemporary Black Men's Fiction and Drama*, ed. Keith Clark, 20 (Urbana: University of Illinois Press, 2001).

8. For a discussion of how biblical language informs the text and how the variously named sections have their bases in the Bible, see James W. Coleman, *Faithful Vision: Treatments of the*

Sacred, Spiritual, and Supernatural in Twentieth-Century African American Fiction (Baton Rouge: Louisiana State University Press, 2006), 61–76.

9. The Bible, King James Version, Ecclesiastes 12:13.

10. For my discussion of this Kenan story, see *South of Tradition: Essays on African American Literature* (Athens: University of Georgia Press, 2003), 160–74.

11. See one version of the song in *Call and Response: The Riverside Anthology of the African American Literary Tradition,* ed. Patricia L. Hill et al. (Boston: Houghton Mifflin, 1998), 238.

12. Toni Morrison's *Sula* comes to a similar conclusion—that she can depend upon no one but her self—but she, like Horace, finds that the self cannot ultimately be counted on either. See Morrison, *Sula* (New York: Knopf, 1974), 118–19.

CHAPTER 7

1. Gladys-Marie Fry, *Night Riders in Black Folk History* (Knoxville: University of Tennessee Press, 1975), 63. I will place additional references to this source in parentheses in the text.

2. Lawrence Levine, *Black Culture and Black Consciousness: Afro-American Folk Thought from Slavery to Freedom* (New York: Oxford University Press, 1977), 119. I will place other references to this source in parentheses in the text.

3. Equiano makes this observation about white men when he is captured in the interior of African and trekked to the coast for transport to the New World. See *Equiano's Travels: The Interesting Narrative of the Life of Olaudah Equiano or Gustavus Vassa, the African* (1789; repr. Long Grove, IL: Waveland, 2006).

4. Phyllis Alesia Perry, *Stigmata* (New York: Anchor, 1998), 172. I will place additional references to this source in parentheses in the text.

5. The text obviously invites readers to a willing suspension of disbelief, for the fantastic occurs alongside the "real," and there is frequently little distinction between them.

6. Lisa A. Long describes what happens to the women in this family as a "rape" by history. In her discussion of Butler's *Kindred* and Perry's *Stigmata,* Long comments that "[t]he episodes of history that Dana's and Lizzie's living bodies enact come unbidden. They are invasive, disorienting, and excruciatingly painful, both physically and psychologically. 'Rape' might seem an unnecessarily provocative word to use to characterize the trauma associated with remembering in these novels. Yet the sexual vulnerability of African American women, both pre- and post-emancipation, permeates American fiction and history." She adds that "[t]heir histories hunt them down, disfigure their bodies, terrorize their minds." See "A Relative Pain: The Rape of History in Octavia Butler's *Kindred* and Phyllis Alesia Perry's *Stigmata,*" *College English* 64, no. 4 (March 2002): 464, 463.

7. Perhaps it is only through pain, Long offers, that Lizzie can hear and respond, for "Perry and Butler offer up bodily pain as a universal, ahistorical signifier of authenticity" ("A Relative Pain," 461).

8. As Stefanie Sievers points out, Lizzie does learn from her institutionalizations. "In retrospect, however, Lizzie comes to understand the time spent in clinics as a time she needed to focus on what was happening to her. So despite the overall negative connotations of this long period of external stasis and lack of genuine communication, the novel also suggests that a necessary development is happening within Lizzie during that time" ("Embodied Memories—

Sharable Stories? The Legacies of Slavery as a Problem of Representation in Phyllis Alesia Perry's *Stigmata*," in *Monuments of the Black Atlantic: Slavery and Memory,* ed. Joanne M. Braxton and Maria I. Diedrich, 135 [Munster: LIT, 2004]).

CHAPTER 8

1. There are several internet sources that feature information about the disappearances and murders of the children and adults in Atlanta. A simple Google search for "Atlanta Child Murders" will yield police reports, lists and photographs of the victims, crime journal analyses, and a plethora of other materials. Tayari Jones's blog also refers to the cases; see www.tayarijones .com/blog/archives/2005. Strikingly, these Web-based sources are not matched in quantity by scholarly focus on the cases. A recent exception is Eric Gary Anderson's "Black Atlanta: An Ecosocial Approach to Narratives of the Atlanta Child Murders," *PMLA* 122, no. 1 (January 2007): 194–209. Indeed, we could argue, reasonably and easily, that the Atlanta Child Murders are the best-known ignored and unsolved murder cases in American history. Though Wayne Bertram Williams was convicted of killing two of the victims, the majority of the remaining cases have not been solved. Folklore scholar Patricia A. Turner treats the cases from the perspective of the impact of rumor upon African American communities ("The Atlanta Child Murders: A Case Study of Folklore in the Black Community," in *Contemporary Legend: A Reader,* ed. Gillian Bennett and Paul Smith, 299–310 [New York: Garland, 1996]). I will indicate references to this source in parentheses in the text. James Baldwin completed a long meditative reflection upon the cases that he published as *The Evidence of Things Not Seen* (New York: Holt, Rinehart & Winston, 1985). There is also a docudrama about the murders as well as a fictional film version of them.

2. See Tayari Jones's blog. The item was posted on May 22, 2005. Hanging back and listening when she is not supposed to be doing so is also the way in which LaTasha Baxter, on whom the first section of *Leaving Atlanta* focuses, manages to get as much information as she does about the murders.

3. That assessment appears in Turner's "The Atlanta Child Murders," 304.

4. Patricia A. Turner also discusses how the KKK enters into rumors in black communities in other ways (*I Heard It through the Grapevine: Rumor in African-American Culture* [Berkeley: University of California Press, 1993]). General conspiracy theories among blacks easily led them to expect that the KKK could be involved in the Atlanta Child Murders.

5. Jones was responding to the possibility that the cases would be reopened in 2005. They were—but they were closed again in 2006. The cases had been reopened once before—in 1987—but they had also been closed then without any conclusive new findings.

6. Tayari Jones, *Leaving Atlanta* (New York: Warner, 2002), 25. I will place other references to this source in parentheses in the text.

7. Sarah Anne Beane, who was a student in my contemporary African American literature course during the summer of 2007, offered this evaluation of Rodney's situation.

8. Rodney also recognizes his running inadequacy. "Some even say that you run like a girl" (107). Remember that Horace Cross's great-aunt Jonnie Mae in *A Visitation of Spirits* considers it "girlish" for Horace to wear an earring and joins the family in condemning him for it, a rejection that is partly responsible for his suicide.

9. My students generally remarked that they were inclined to reach into the text and pull Rodney back from getting into the car, or they wanted to scream, "Don't get in that car!" The

comparison to horror movies is again appropriate. Picture the damsel innocently going about her business in her house or apartment, and the audience has seen the monster lurking in the shadows. We desire to yell out warnings, but we are locked into our positions as viewers just as the damsel is locked into her role as victim. The extent to which we identify with the damsel and the extent to which we identify with Rodney are measures of how successful filmmaker and novelist have been in creating points of view that advance identification with their characters.

10. As in this image of a dirty napkin, Octavia is particularly astute at providing figurative language to describe the various situations around her. It is another mark of her success as a first person narrator.

11. Significantly, Octavia's maturity is also measured by the fact that she begins menstruation during the course of the fall semester when the children are being snatched. Instead of freaking out, as readers might imagine Tasha doing, Octavia calmly seeks out Mrs. Grier and asks for supplies to take care of herself. She knows from the book Mrs. Grier or her mother has supplied her with what is happening, and she is not the least bit frightened. (Compare her response to Pecola's in *The Bluest Eye.*) In recognition of her newfound maturity, Octavia gets taken out to dinner at Red Lobster, which she says is her favorite restaurant. Octavia dons a special dress, and Yvonne lies to the waiters and tells them it is Octavia's birthday so that Octavia will get special recognition from the wait staff and free cake.

CHAPTER 9

1. Fenton Johnson, "The Scarlet Woman," in *Black Writers of America: A Comprehensive Anthology,* ed. Richard Barksdale and Keneth Kinnamon, 456 (New York: Macmillan, 1974). See *The Short Fiction of Charles W. Chesnutt* ed. Sylvia Lyons Render (Washington: Howard University Press, 1974), esp. "Dave's Neckliss," which treats insanity. See also Claude McKay, *Home to Harlem* (New York: Harper, 1928). *Fire!!* is the little magazine that Langston Hughes and Wallace Thurman edited; see "Smoke, Lilies and Jade, A Novel. Part I" for a treatment of drug use and "Cordelia the Crude" for a representation of prostitution. Facsimile edition issued in 1982 by Thomas H. Wirth.

2. Jones joins Randall Kenan, Gloria Naylor, and Raymond Andrews in creating mythical fictional territories to which they return again and again. Naylor created Willow Springs, an island off the coasts of South Carolina and Georgia, in *Mama Day* (1988), and Andrews created Muskhogean Country with a county seat of Appalachee, located in northeast Georgia, for fictional settings in three of his novels.

3. While the novel focuses on blacks owning blacks during slavery, usually through purchase for lifetime enslavement, another dimension of that ownership occurs when blacks who buy their relatives out of slavery, as Augustus does, become the owners of the persons whom they have purchased. Mildred, Augustus's wife, is thus his property until he frees her, just as his son Henry is his property until he frees him. Clearly, there are bold distinctions between buying blacks to keep them in slavery and buying blacks *out* of slavery, but the notion of ownership is relevant to both.

4. Edward P. Jones, *The Known World* (New York: HarperCollins, 2003; Amistad 2004), 18. I will place additional references to this source in parentheses in the text.

5. This clash over who has claim to enslaved black children evokes Harriet Jacobs's *Incidents in the Life of a Slave Girl.* She recounts an incident in which her master and her father call her

brother at the same time. When the boy hesitates, the father lectures him on the person to whom his loyalty should lie, no matter that that person is enslaved. Fatherhood bests slavery, and the boy should respond to his father first. Henry feels no sense of divided loyalty.

6. Of course, this evokes the historical tale of Henry "Box" Brown, who mailed himself out of slavery near Richmond, Virginia, into the free territory of Philadelphia, Pennsylvania.

7. The role that Christianity plays in the text is an intriguing one. Although Henry has a preacher come in to offer sermons to those enslaved on his plantation, there is no indication of serious commitment to religion on his part or the part of his wife, Caldonia. On the other hand, John Skiffington, the sheriff, believes that he is earnestly living by God's word, even when he has to pray fervently not to have sex with the young black girl Minerva, who has been gifted as a servant to his wife by his cousins from North Carolina. God is considered responsible for Louis's "traveling eye," and some of the enslaved persons believe that God supports slavery, as does Skiffington. Elias "had never believed in a sane God and so had never questioned a world where colored people could be the owners of slaves . . ." (9). Nowhere in the text is there a Christianity consistently representative of that usually presented in African American texts prior to the middle of the twentieth century.

8. The paradox evokes that of poet Countee Cullen, who "marvels" that God could "make a poet black and bid him sing" ("Yet Do I Marvel," in Barksdale and Kinnamon, *Black Writers of America*, 531).

9. Maude, Caldonia's mother, is so intent upon protecting her "legacy," that is, those enslaved to her, that she poisons her husband when he makes statements to the effect that he wants to free the blacks he has purchased. Maude is also formidable enough to convince Caldonia, who has been insistently opposed to doing so, to buy insurance on the enslaved blacks on her plantation once Alice, Priscilla, and Jamie run away.

10. In later years, when Calvin encounters Alice, Priscilla, and Jamie in Washington, DC, he at least has the decency to be ashamed of his past and to fear that they—and others—could judge him harshly for it. See his long letter to Caldonia (383–86).

11. Fern's encounters with Anderson Frazier occur at several places in the text, but esp. on 106–9 and 134–35. Fern also mimics white slaveholders when she renames a twelve-year-old black boy that her husband brings home as part of a gambling debt. She names him "Zeus" because "he had come with a name that she did not like and so she, then a new wife, had renamed him. Named him for a god she would have worshiped had she been the worshiping kind" (129). I should point out that several names in the text are noteworthy, either for their stereotypical historical connections or for their following of a pattern of naming that slaveholders used historically. Naming blacks from the Greek and Roman traditions, as Fern does with Zeus, was a common pattern among slaveholders, as was giving blacks biblical names. A little farther along the historical continuum, names such as Caldonia and Philomena fit into the stereotypical names given to black women in musical comedies and films of the first half of the twentieth century.

12. Henry, darker than Caldonia, has overcome his lack of skin affinity by being reasonably wealthy. Fern tells the pamphleteer that Henry was able to court Caldonia only because her father was alive at the time. What she does not reveal to him is that Maude, Caldonia's mother, would not have approved the relationship initially because she would not have thought that Henry's skin was "worthy" (143) enough to marry Caldonia. After Henry's death, it is clear that Maude very much appreciates the "legacy" of enslaved persons that Henry has left Caldonia.

13. The speculator to whom Augustus is sold takes him to Georgia, where he sells him for fifty-three dollars to keep from having to take him into Florida. Augustus refuses to become property again, and, when he walks away from the poor white man who bought him, the man shoots Augustus; he dies a couple of days later. His death introduces another feature into the novel, that of magical realism, for Augustus immediately leaves his body and travels back to Virginia (346). Mildred will have a similar out-of-body experience following her accidental shooting death at the hands of Sheriff Skiffington (365–66).

CHAPTER 10

1. See, for example, Nikki Giovanni's "For Saundra," in *Black Feeling Black Talk Black Judgement* (New York: Morrow, 1970), 88–89.

2. Raymond Andrews, *Baby Sweet's* (1983; repr. Athens: University of Georgia Press, 1988), 9. I will place additional references to this source in parentheses in the text.

3. See Natasha Trethewey, *Native Guard* (New York: Houghton Mifflin, 2007), 46.

Works Cited/Consulted

African American Review, Black South Issue, Part 1 of 2, 27, no. 1 (Spring 1993).

————, Part 2 of 2, 27, no. 2 (Summer 1993).

Anderson, Eric Gary. "Black Atlanta: An Ecosocial Approach to Narratives of the Atlanta Child Murders." *PMLA* 122, no. 1 (January 2007): 194–209.

Andrews, Raymond. *Appalachee Red.* New York: Dial, 1978.

————. *Baby Sweet's.* 1983. Reprint, Athens: University of Georgia Press, 1988.

————. "The Necessity of Blacks' Writing Fiction about the South." *African American Review* 27, no. 2 (1993): 297–99.

Ansa, Tina McElroy. "What's the Confederate Flag Got to Do with It?" *Callaloo* 24, no. 1 (2001): 5–7.

Babb, Valerie Melissa. *Ernest Gaines.* New York: Twayne, 1991.

Baldwin, James. *Go Tell It on the Mountain.* New York: Grosset & Dunlap, 1953.

————. *Nobody Knows My Name.* New York: Dial, 1961.

————. *Another Country.* New York: Dial, 1962.

————. *Notes of a Native Son.* New York: Dial, 1963.

————. *The Fire Next Time.* New York: Dial, 1963.

————. *Blues for Mister Charlie.* New York: Dial, 1964.

————. "Going to Meet the Man." In his *Going to Meet the Man.* New York: Dial, 1965.

————. "Sonny's Blues." In his *Going to Meet the Man.* New York: Dial, 1965.

————. *No Name in the Street.* New York: Dial, 1972.

———. *Just Above My Head.* New York: Dial, 1979.

———. *The Evidence of Things Not Seen.* New York: Holt, Rinehart & Winston, 1985.

Bambara, Toni Cade. *The Salt Eaters.* New York: Random House, 1980.

———. *Those Bones Are Not My Child.* New York: Pantheon, 1999.

Beaulieu, Elizabeth Ann. "'Cause I Can': Race, Gender, and Power in Sherley Anne Williams' *Dessa Rose.*" In her *Black Women Writers and the American Neo-Slave Narrative: Femininity Unfettered,* 29–55. Westport, CT: Greenwood, 1999.

Beavers, Herman. *Wrestling Angels into Song: The Fictions of Ernest J. Gaines and James Alan McPherson.* Philadelphia: University of Pennsylvania Press, 1995.

Bell, Bernard W. *The Contemporary African American Novel: Its Folk Roots and Modern Literary Branches.* Amherst: University of Massachusetts Press, 2004.

Betts, Doris. "Randall Garrett Kenan." In *Southern Writers at Century's End,* ed. Jeffrey J. Folks and James A. Perkins, 9–20. Lexington: University Press of Kentucky, 1997.

Black, Daniel. *The Sacred Place.* New York: St. Martin's, 2007.

Bradley, David. *The Chaneysville Incident.* New York: Harper & Row, 1981.

Brooks, Gwendolyn. *Blacks.* Chicago: David, 1987.

Brown, Sterling. *The Collected Poems.* Ed. Michael S. Harper. Chicago: TriQuarterly, 1989.

Burke, William. "*Bloodline:* A Black Man's South." *CLA Journal* 19, no. 4 (June 1976): 545–58.

Butler, Octavia E. *Kindred.* 1979. Reprint, 25th Anniversary Edition, Boston: Beacon, 2003.

Butler, Robert James. "Alice Walker's Vision of the South in *The Third Life of Grange Copeland.*" *African American Review* 27, no. 2 (Summer 1993): 195–204.

Byerman, Keith. *Fingering the Jagged Grain: Tradition and Form in Recent Black Fiction.* Athens: University of Georgia Press, 1985.

Callaloo 1, no. 3 (May 1978). "Ernest J. Gaines: A Special Issue."

——— 28, no. 3 (Summer 2005). "Yusef Komunyakaa: Special Issue."

Campbell, Bebe Moore. *Your Blues Ain't Like Mine.* New York: Putnam's, 1992.

Carmean, Karen. *Ernest J. Gaines: A Critical Companion.* Westport, CT: Greenwood, 1998.

Chesnutt, Charles W. *The Conjure Woman.* Boston: Houghton Mifflin, 1899.

———. *The House Behind the Cedars.* Boston: Houghton Mifflin, 1901.

———. *The Marrow of Tradition.* Boston: Houghton Mifflin, 1901.

———. *The Short Fiction.* Ed. Sylvia Lyons Render. Washington: Howard University Press, 1974.

Clark, Keith. "Que(e)rying the Prison-House of Black Male Desire: Homosociality in Ernest Gaines's *Three Men.*" *African American Review* 40, no. 2 (Summer 2006): 239–55.

Cleage, Pearl. *Flyin' West.* New York: Dramatists Play Service, 1995.

Coleman, James W. *Faithful Vision: Treatments of the Sacred, Spiritual, and Supernatural in Twentieth-Century African American Fiction* (Baton Rouge: Louisiana State University Press, 2006), 61–76.

Cooper, J. California. *Family.* New York: Doubleday, 1991.

Cullen, Countee. "Heritage." In *Black Writers of America: A Comprehensive Anthology,* ed. Richard Barksdale and Keneth Kinnamon, 531–33. New York: Macmillan, 1974.

Daileader, Celia R., Rhoda E. Johnson, and Amilcar Shabazz, eds. *Women and Others: Perspectives on Race, Gender, and Empire.* New York: Palgrave Macmillan, 2007.

Dance, Daryl Cumber. *Shuckin' and Jivin': Folklore from Contemporary Black Americans.* Bloomington: Indiana University Press, 1978.

———. *From My People: 400 Years of African American Folklore.* New York: Norton, 2002.

Davis, Mary Kemp. "Everybody Knows Her Name: The Recovery of the Past in Sherley Anne Williams's *Dessa Rose.*" *Callaloo* 12 (40), no. 3 (Summer 1989): 544–58.

Dawson, Emma Waters. "Psychic Rage and Response: The Enslaved and the Enslaver in Sherley Anne Williams' *Dessa Rose.*" In *Arms Akimbo: Africana Women in Contemporary Literature,* ed. Janice Lee Liddell and Yakini Belinda Kemp, 17–31. Gainesville: University of Florida Press, 1999.

Douglass, Frederick. *Narrative of the Life of Frederick Douglass.* 1845. Reprint, Cambridge, MA: Belknap, 1960.

Dowdy, Michael C. "Working in the Space of Disaster: Yusef Komunyakaa's Dialogues with America." *Callaloo* 28, no. 3 (Summer 2005): 812–23.

Doyle, Mary Ellen. *Voices from the Quarters: The Fiction of Ernest J. Gaines.* Baton Rouge: Louisiana State University Press, 2002.

Du Bois, W. E. B. *The Souls of Black Folk.* 1903. Reprint, New York: Borzoi/Knopf, 1993.

Ellison, Ralph. *Invisible Man.* New York: Random House, 1952.

Equiano, Olaudah. *The Interesting Narrative of the Life of Olaudah Equiano or Gustavus Vassa, the African.* 1789. Reprint, Long Grove, IL; Waveland, 2006.

Fire!! Ed. Wallace Thurman, Langston Hughes, et al. New York: The *Fire!!* Press, 1926.

Foster, Guy Mark. "'Do I look like someone you can come home to from where you may be going?': Re-Mapping Interracial Anxiety in Octavia Butler's *Kindred.*" *African American Review* 41, no. 1 (Spring 2007): 143–64.

Fry, Gladys-Marie. *Night Riders in Black Folk History.* Knoxville: University of Tennessee Press, 1975.

Gabbin, Joanne V. Personal correspondence with the author.

Gaines, Ernest. *Of Love and Dust.* New York: Dial, 1967.

———. *Bloodline*. New York: Dial, 1968.

———. *The Autobiography of Miss Jane Pittman*. New York: Dial, 1971.

———. *A Gathering of Old Men*. New York: Knopf, 1983.

———. *A Lesson Before Dying*. New York: Random House, 1993.

Gaudet, Marcia, and Carl Wooten, eds. *Porch Talk with Ernest Gaines: Conversations on the Writer's Craft*. Baton Rouge: Louisiana State University Press, 1990.

Gayle, Addison. *The Way of the New World: The Black Novel in America*. Garden City, NY: Anchor Press/Doubleday, 1976, 367–76.

Giovanni, Nikki. "For Saundra." In *Black Feeling Black Talk Black Judgement*, 88–89. New York: Morrow, 1970.

Gotera, Vince. "Yusef Komunyakaa: 'Depending on the Light.'" In his *Radical Visions: The Poetry of Vietnam Veterans*, 302–16. Athens: University of Georgia Press, 1994.

Govan, Sandra Y. "Connections, Links, and Extended Networks: Patterns in Octavia Butler's Science Fiction." *Black American Literature Forum* 18 (1984): 82–87.

———. "Homage to Tradition: Octavia Butler Renovates the Historical Novel." *MELUS* 13 (1986): 79–96.

Grandt, Jurgen E. "(Un-)Telling Truth: An Interview with Tayari Jones." *Langston Hughes Review* 19 (Spring 2005): 71–81.

Griffin, Farah Jasmine. *"Who Set You Flowin'?": The African-American Migration Narrative*. New York: Oxford University Press, 1995.

———. "Textual Healing: Claiming Black Women's Bodies, the Erotic and Resistance in Contemporary Novels of Slavery." *Callaloo* 19, no. 2 (Spring 1996): 519–36.

Guy-Sheftall, Beverly. "Black and White Womanhood in Sherley Anne Williams' *Dessa Rose*: Mammies, Ladies, Rebels (1986)." In *Women in Literature: Reading through the Lens of Gender*, ed. Jerilyn Fisher and Ellen S. Silber, 91–94. Westport, CT: Greenwood, 2003.

Hansberry, Lorraine. *A Raisin in the Sun*. 1959. Reprint, New York: Signet, 1988.

Harris, Trudier. *Exorcising Blackness: Historical and Literary Lynching and Burning Rituals*. Bloomington: Indiana University Press, 1984.

———. "The South as Woman: Chimeric Images of Emasculation in *Just Above My Head.*" *Studies in American Literature I: Black American Prose Theory*, ed. Joe Weixlmann and Chester J. Fontenot, 89–109. Greenwood, FL: Penkevill, 1984.

———. "Porch-Sitting as a Creative Southern Tradition." *Southern Cultures* 2, nos. 3–4 (1996): 441–60.

———. *The Power of the Porch: The Storyteller's Craft in Zora Neale Hurston, Gloria Naylor, and Randall Kenan*. Athens: University of Georgia Press, 1996.

———. Review of Edward P. Jones's *The Known World*. *The New Crisis* 110, no. 5 (September/October, 2003): 53.

———. *South of Tradition: Essays on African American Literature*. Athens: University of Georgia Press, 2003.

———. "William Melvin Kelley's Real Live, Invisible South." *South Central Review* 22, no. 1 (Spring 2005): 26–47.

———. "Failed, Forgotten, Forsaken: Christianity in Contemporary African American Literature." E. Maynard Adams Lecture. Program in the Humanities and Human Values, University of North Carolina at Chapel Hill, 2007.

Hayden, Robert Earl. *Collected Poems.* New York: Liveright, 1985.

Henderson, Mae G. "(W)riting The Work and Working the Rites." *Black American Literature Forum* 23, no. 4 (Winter 1989): 631–60.

———. "The Stories of O(Dessa): Stories of Complicity and Resistance." In *Female Subjects in Black and White: Race, Psychoanalysis, Feminism,* ed. Elizabeth Abel, Barbara Christian, and Helene Moglen, 285–304. Berkeley: University of California Press, 1997.

Henderson, Mae Gwendolyn. "In Memory of Sherley Anne Williams: 'Some One Sweet Angel Chile' 1944–1999." *Callaloo* 22, no. 4 (Fall 1999): 763–67.

———. "Speaking in Tongues: Dialogics, Dialectics, and the Black Woman Writer's Literary Tradition." In *African American Literary Theory: A Reader,* ed. Winston Napier, 348–68. New York: New York University Press, 2000.

Hill, Patricia L., et al. *Call and Response: The Riverside Anthology of the African American Literary Tradition.* Boston: Houghton Mifflin, 1998.

Horton, George Moses. *The Hope of Liberty.* 1829. Reprint, Nendeln/Liechtenstein: Kraus, 1973.

Hughes, Langston. "The Negro Artist and the Racial Mountain." 1926. Reprinted in *Within the Circle: An Anthology of African American Literary Criticism from the Harlem Renaissance to the Present,* ed. Angelyn Mitchell, 55–59. Durham, NC: Duke University Press, 1994.

———. *The Weary Blues.* New York: Knopf, 1926.

———. *The Ways of White Folks.* New York: Knopf, 1934.

———. *The Collected Poems.* Ed. Arnold Rampersad. New York, Knopf, 1995, 50.

Hughes, Langston, and Arna Bontemps. *The Book of Negro Folklore.* New York: Dodd, Mead, 1958.

Hunt, V. "A Conversation with Randall Kenan." *African American Review* 29, no. 3 (Fall 1995): 411–20.

Hurston, Zora Neale. *Their Eyes Were Watching God.* 1937. Reprint, New York: HarperCollins, 1991.

———. *Seraph on the Suwanee.* New York: Scribner's, 1948.

———. "Spunk." In *Spunk: The Selected Short Stories of Zora Neale Hurston,* 1–8. Berkeley, CA: Turtle Island Foundation, 1985.

Jackson, Candice Love. "The Literate Pimp: Robert Beck, Iceberg Slim, and Pimping the African American Novel." In *New Essays on the African American Novel: From Hurston and Ellison to Morrison and Whitehead,* ed. Lovalerie King and Linda F. Selzer, 167–83. New York: Palgrave, 2008.

Jackson, Lawrence P. "An Interview with Edward P. Jones." *African American Review* 34, no. 1 (Spring 2000): 95–103.

Jacobs, Harriet. *Incidents in the Life of a Slave Girl.* 1860. Reprint, New York: Washington Square Press, 2003.

Johnson, Charles. *Oxherding Tale.* Bloomington: Indiana University Press, 1982.

———. *Middle Passage.* New York: Atheneum, 1990.

Johnson, Fenton. "The Scarlet Woman." In *Black Writers of America: A Comprehensive Anthology,* ed. Richard Barksdale and Keneth Kinnamon, 456. New York: Macmillan, 1974.

Johnson, James Weldon. *The Autobiography of an Ex-Colored Man.* 1912. Reprint, New York: Knopf, 1927.

———, ed. *The Book of American Negro Poetry.* New York: Harcourt Brace Jovanovich, 1922.

Jones, Edward P. *The Known World.* New York: Amistad, 2003.

Jones, Gayl. *Corregidora.* Boston: Beacon, 1975.

Jones, Leroi. *Blues People: Negro Music in White America.* London: MacGibbon & Key, 1965.

Jones, Tayari. *Leaving Atlanta.* New York: Warner, 2002.

———. www.tayarijones.com/blog/archives/2005.

Kelley, William Melvin. *A Different Drummer.* 1962. Reprint, New York: Anchor, 1969.

Kenan, Randall. *A Visitation of Spirits.* New York: Grove, 1989.

———. *Let the Dead Bury Their Dead.* New York: Harcourt Brace Jovanovich, 1992.

Knight, Etheridge. *Poems from Prison.* Detroit: Broadside, 1968.

———. *Born of a Woman: New and Selected Poems.* Boston: Houghton Mifflin, 1980.

———. *The Essential Etheridge Knight.* Pittsburgh, PA: University of Pittsburgh Press, 1986.

Komunyakaa, Yusef. *Dien Cai Dau.* Middletown, CT: Wesleyan University Press, 1988.

Levine, Lawrence W. *Black Culture and Black Consciousness: Afro-American Folk Thought from Slavery to Freedom.* New York: Oxford University Press, 1977.

Long, Lisa. "A Relative Pain: The Rape of History in Octavia Butler's *Kindred* and Phyllis Alesia Perry's *Stigmata.*" *College English* 64, no. 4 (March 2002): 459–83.

Lowe, John, ed. *Conversations with Ernest Gaines.* Jackson: University of Mississippi Press, 1995.

———. Review: "Fingering the Jagged Grain: Edward P. Jones and *The Known World*" (personal copy to the author, November 2007).

Lydon, Meghan. "'The American Dream—and the Black Man's Nightmare': Remaking America in Raymond Andrews's Fiction." *South Atlantic Review* 71, no. 3 (Summer 2006): 57–75.

MacPherson, Myra. *Long Time Passing: Vietnam and the Haunted Generation.* New York: Anchor, 1984.

Malburne, Meredith. "No Blues for Mister Henry: Locating Richard's Revolution." In *Reading Contemporary African American Drama: Fragments of History, Fragments of Self,* ed. Trudier Harris, 39–57. New York: Lang, 2007.

McDowell, Deborah E. "Negotiating between Tenses: Witnessing Slavery after Freedom—Dessa Rose." In *Slavery and the Literary Imagination,* ed. Deborah E. McDowell and Arnold Rampersad, 144–63. Baltimore: Johns Hopkins University Press, 1989.

McKay, Claude. *Home to Harlem.* New York: Harper, 1928.

———. *Selected Poems of Claude McKay.* New York: Harcourt, Brace & World, 1953.

McKible, Adam. "'These Are the Facts of the Darky's History': Thinking History and Reading Names in Four African American Texts." *African American Review* 28, no. 2 (Summer 1994): 223–35.

McKoy, Sheila Smith. "Rescuing the Black Homosexual Lambs: Randall Kenan and the Reconstruction of Southern Gay Masculinity." In *Contemporary Black Men's Fiction and Drama,* ed. Keith Clark, 15–36. Urbana: University of Illinois Press, 2001.

Mead, Margaret, and James Baldwin. *A Rap on Race.* New York: Laurel, 1971.

Mitchell, Angelyn. *Within the Circle: An Anthology of African American Literary Criticism from the Harlem Renaissance to the Present.* Durham, NC: Duke University Press, 1994.

Mitrano, C. F. "A Conversation with Yusef Komunyakaa." *Callaloo* 28, no. 3 (Summer 2005): 521–30.

Moody, Joycelyn K. "Ripping Away the Veil of Slavery: Literacy, Communal Love, and Self-Esteem in Three Slave Women's Narratives." *Black American Literature Forum* 24, no. 4 (Winter 1990): 633–48.

Morrison, Toni. *The Bluest Eye.* New York: Holt, Rinehart & Winston, 1970.

———. *Sula.* New York: Knopf, 1974.

———. *Song of Solomon.* New York: Knopf, 1977.

———. *Tar Baby.* New York: Knopf, 1981.

———. *Beloved.* New York: Knopf, 1987.

———. *Paradise.* New York: Knopf, 1998.

Naylor, Gloria. *The Women of Brewster Place.* New York: Viking, 1982.

———. *Mama Day.* New York: Ticknor & Fields, 1988.

Nelson, Marilyn. *A Wreath for Emmett Till.* Boston: Houghton Mifflin, 2005.

Packer, Z. Z. "Z. Z. Packer Talks with Edward P. Jones." In *The Believer Book of Writers Talking to Writers,* ed. Vendela Vida, 133–57. San Francisco: Believer, 2005.

Perry, Phyllis Alesia. *Stigmata.* New York: Anchor, 1998.

Porter, Horace. "The South in *Go Tell It on the Mountain:* Baldwin's Personal Confrontation." In *New Essays on "Go Tell It on the Mountain,"* ed. Trudier Harris, 59–75. New York: Cambridge University Press, 1996.

Reed, Brian K. "Behold the Woman: The Imaginary Wife in Octavia Butler's *Kindred.*" *CLA Journal* 47, no. 1 (September 2003): 66–74.

Reed, Ishmael. *Flight to Canada.* New York: Random House, 1976.

Rowell, Charles. "An Interview with Randall Kenan." *Callaloo* 21, no. 1 (Winter 1998): 133–48.

Rushdy, Ashraf H. A. "Families of Orphans: Relation and Disrelation in Octavia Butler's *Kindred.*" *College English* 55, no. 2 (February 1993): 135–57.

———. "Reading Mammy: The Subject of Relation in Sherley Anne Williams' *Dessa Rose.*" *African American Review* 27, no. 3 (Fall 1993): 365–89.

Salas, Angela M. "'Flashbacks through the Heart': Yusef Komunyakaa and the Poetry of Self-Assertion." In *The Furious Flowering of African American Poetry,* ed. Joanne V. Gabbin, 298–309. Charlottesville: University of Virginia Press, 1999.

———. "Race, Human Empathy, and Negative Capability: The Poetry of Yusef Komunyakaa." *College Literature* 30, no. 4 (Fall 2003): 32–53.

———. *Flashback through the Heart: The Poetry of Yusef Komunyakaa.* Selinsgrove, PA: Susquehanna University Press, 2004.

Salvaggio, Ruth. "Octavia Butler." In *Suzy McKee Charnas, Octavia Butler, and Joan D. Vinge,* ed. Marleen S. Barr, Ruth Salvaggio, and Richard Law, 1–44. Mercer Island, WA: Starmont House, 1986.

Shelton, Frank W. "Ambiguous Manhood in Gaines's *Bloodline.*" *CLA Journal* 19, no. 2 (December 1975): 200–209.

Shockley, Ann Allen. *Loving Her.* 1974. Reprint, Boston: Northeastern University Press, 1997.

Sievers, Stefanie. "Embodied Memories—Sharable Stories? The Legacies of Slavery as a Problem of Representation in Phyllis Alesia Perry's *Stigmata.*" In *Monuments of the Black Atlantic: Slavery and Memory,* ed. Joanne M. Braxton and Maria I. Diedrich, 131–39. Munster: LIT, 2004.

Stein, Kevin. "Vietnam and the 'Voice Within': Public and Private History in Yusef Komunyakaa's *Dien Cai Dau.*" *Massachusetts Review* 36, no. 4 (Winter 1995–96): 541–61.

Steinberg, Marc. "Inverting History in Octavia Butler's Postmodern Slave Narrative." *African American Review* 38, no. 3 (Fall 2004): 467–76.

Thurman, Wallace. *The Blacker the Berry.* New York: Macaulay, 1929.

Toomer, Jean. *Cane.* New York: Liveright, 1923.

Trapasso, Ann E. "Returning to the Site of Violence: The Restructuring of Slavery's Legacy in Sherley Anne Williams's *Dessa Rose.*" In *Violence, Silence, and Anger: Women's Writing as Transgression,* ed. Deirdre Lashgari, 219–30. Charlottesville: University Press of Virginia, 1995.

Trethewey, Natasha. *Native Guard*. Boston: Houghton Mifflin, 2007.

Tucker, Lindsey. "Gay Identity, Conjure, and the Uses of Postmodern Ethnography in the Fictions of Randall Kenan." *Modern Fiction Studies* 49, no. 2 (Summer 2003): 306–31.

Turner, Patricia A. *I Heard It through the Grapevine: Rumor in African-American Culture*. Berkeley: University of California Press, 1993.

———. "The Atlanta Child Murders: A Case Study of Folklore in the Black Community." In *Contemporary Legend: A Reader*, ed. Gillian Bennett and Paul Smith, 299–310. New York: Garland, 1996.

Wade, Brent. *Company Man*. Chapel Hill, NC: Algonquin, 1992.

Walker, Alice. *The Third Life of Grange Copeland*. New York: Harcourt Brace Jovanovich, 1970.

———. *In Love and Trouble: Stories of Black Women*. New York: Harcourt Brace Jovanovich, 1973.

———. *You Can't Keep a Good Woman Down*. New York: Harcourt Brace Jovanovich, 1981.

———. *The Color Purple*. New York: Harcourt Brace Jovanovich: 1982.

———. *In Search of Our Mothers' Gardens: Womanist Prose*. New York: Harcourt Brace Jovanovich, 1983.

Walker, Margaret. *Jubilee*. New York: Houghton Mifflin, 1966.

Warren, Nagueyalti. "Winter/Spring/Summer." *African American Review* 36, no. 2 (2002): 325.

Williams, Sherley Anne. "Meditations on History." In *Midnight Birds: Stories of Contemporary Black Women Writers*, ed. Mary Helen Washington, 195–248. New York: Anchor, 1980.

———. *Dessa Rose*. New York: Morrow, 1986.

———. "Some Implications of Womanist Theory." In *Reading Black, Reading Feminist: A Critical Anthology*, ed. Henry Louis Gates Jr., 68–75. New York: Penguin, 1990.

Wilson, August. *Joe Turner's Come and Gone*. New York: New American Library, 1988.

Wirth, Thomas H. Facsimile edition of *Fire!!* 1982.

Wright, Richard. "The Ethics of Living Jim Crow," "Big Boy Leaves Home," and "Long Black Song." In *Uncle Tom's Children*. 1938. Reprint, New York: HarperPerennial, 1993.

———. *Black Boy*. 1945. Reprint, New York: Perennial, 1966.

———. *The Long Dream*. Circa 1958. Reprint, Boston: Northeastern University Press, 2000.

Young, Reggie. "Ernest J. Gaines: A Portfolio." *Callaloo: A Thirtieth Anniversary Issue, Prose Fiction and Non-Fiction Prose* 30, no. 3 (Summer 2007): 697–713.

Index

African American literature. *See also specific works*
  humor used to handle uncomfortable situations, 196–97, 205–6
  purpose of, 196–97
  subjects taboo in and exceptions to, 174–76
African American men
  personal experiences of the South, 20th century, 12
  stereotyped as animals, 12, 24, 47, 48, 52–53, 55–56, 87
  subjection to sexual violation, 208n19, 209n19
African American men, sexuality of. *See also* lynching of black men
  as animalistic, 24
  attempts by whites to transfer, 21, 22, 106
  created through notions of black manhood, 45–46
  embracing to their own destruction, 38
  imagined by whites, 24, 34

  lynching as justification for, 12, 106, 112, 208n14
  potency contained in genitals, 106
  sexual pollution threatened by, 23–26, 36
African Americans
  mask wearing as survival strategy, 4, 44–45, 67–69
  ownership of other blacks, 181, 221n3. See also *The Known World* (Jones)
  stereotyped as animals, 69
African American women
  enslaved, mythology surrounding, 84–85, 92–93
  exploitation of black men for sexual use, 188–90, 193
  fictionally enslaved, survival of, 7–8, 13, 15–16, 67–69
  religion and the church for coping, 28–29
  sexuality of, imagined, 27
  sexual vulnerability of, 7–8, 13, 24–28, 85, 87, 219n6

African American women writers. *See also*
    specific writers
    emergence of female-centered novels, 62
    fear of the South in writing of, 7–9
    on white southern experience, 9–10
African American writers. *See also specific*
    writers
    humor used by, 196
    nonsouthern, 16–18, 40
    at peace with the South, 195–96
    Pulitzer Prize winners, 113, 176
    race as element in success of, 16
    scariness, meaning for creativity, 10
    South in shaping the identity of, 1–2, 14–18,
        40, 62–64, 154, 206
"America" (McKay), 3, 207n3
Anderson, Gary, 220n1
Andrews, Raymond, writing of, 13, 25, 196–
    98, 201–6, 221n2. *See also specific works*
Another Country (Baldwin), 21, 40
Ansa, Tina McElroy, 15, 209n22
Appalachee Red (Andrews), 13, 197, 204
"A Song in the Front Yard" (Brooks), 202
Atlanta child murders. See also *Leaving At-*
    lanta (Jones)
    about, 152–53
    in fiction, 14, 22, 220n1
    Internet sources, 220n1
    reopening of, 154–55, 220n4
    rumors and conspiracy theories to explain,
        153–54, 220n4
audience
    impact on the narrative, 96, 98, 140, 142
    impact on the oral tradition, 140, 142
    role in "seeing," 98
    voyeuristic engagement of, 203
The Autobiography of an Ex-Colored Man
    (Johnson), 5
The Autobiography of Miss Jane Pittman
    (Gaines), 41, 125

Babb, Valerie Melissa, 211n4
Baby Sweet's (Andrews)
    Appalachee Red (Andrews) and, 197, 204
    "A Song in the Front Yard" (Brooks) com-
        pared, 202

audience in, 200, 203
    cultural contextual familiarity to engage
        readers, 199–202
    dates in, implications of, 201, 202, 205
    leveling space between races, 201–4
    linguistic duality in, 198–99
    sexuality in, 200, 203–5
    spaces of possibility in, 15
    stereotypes of white women, 199–200
    synopsis, 197–98
Baldwin, James, writing of. *See also specific*
    works
    authentic imagining of the South, 17–21,
        39–40
    black-white conflict as central to, 39
    on codes of the unwritten rules for action
        and interaction, 13–14
    compared
        Andrews, Raymond, 25
        Butler, Octavia E., 80
        Gaines, Ernest J., 40, 42
        Toomer, Jean, 25
    duality of attraction/repulsion to the
        South in, 2, 19–21, 40
    fearful spaces in
        of disappearance, possible and real,
            21–22, 153, 170
        of lynching and castration, 4, 11, 20,
            21–23
        sexual vulnerability of black women, 24
        of violence, real and imagined, 21
    giving the white man the blues as concept
        in, 38
    his nonsouthernness in shaping, 39–40
    Porter on, 210n17
    taboo subjects in, 175
"The Ballad of Pearl May Lee" (Brooks),
    208n14
Bambara, Toni Cade, 14, 150
Baxter, LaTasha, 220n1
Beane, Sarah Anne, 220n4
Beck, Robert (pseud. Iceberg Slim), 6,
    208n10
Beloved (Morrison)
    clarity of cultural saturation in characters
        in, 11–13, 15, 17, 92